ROWMAN & LITTLEFIELD STUDIES IN FOOD AND GASTRONOMY

General Editor: Ken Albala, Professor of History,
University of the Pacific (kalbala@pacific.edu)

Rowman & Littlefield Executive Editor:
Suzanne Staszak-Silva (sstaszak-silva@rowman.com)

Food studies is a vibrant and thriving field encompassing not only cooking and eating habits but also issues such as health, sustainability, food safety, and animal rights. Scholars in disciplines as diverse as history, anthropology, sociology, literature, and the arts focus on food. The mission of **Rowman & Littlefield Studies in Food and Gastronomy** is to publish the best in food scholarship, harnessing the energy, ideas, and creativity of a wide array of food writers today. This broad line of food-related titles will range from food history, interdisciplinary food studies monographs, general interest series, and popular trade titles to textbooks for students and budding chefs, scholarly cookbooks, and reference works.

Appetites and Aspirations in Vietnam: Food and Drink in the Long Nineteenth Century, by Erica J. Peters

Three World Cuisines: Italian, Mexican, Chinese, by Ken Albala

Food and Social Media: You Are What You Tweet, by Signe Rousseau

Food and the Novel in Nineteenth-Century America, by Mark McWilliams

Man Bites Dog: Hot Dog Culture in America, by Bruce Kraig and Patty Carroll

New Orleans: A Food Biography, by Elizabeth M. Williams (Big City Food Biographies series)

A Year in Food and Beer: Recipes and Beer Pairings for Every Season, by Emily Baime and Darin Michaels

Breakfast: A History, by Heather Arndt Anderson (The Meals series)

Celebraciones Mexicanas: History, Traditions, and Recipes, by Andrea Lawson Gray and Adriana Almazán Lahl

Food History Almanac: Over 1,300 Years of World Culinary History, Culture, and Social Influence, by Janet Clarkson

The Food Section: Newspaper Women and the Culinary Community, by Kimberly Wilmot Voss

Small Batch: Pickles, Cheese, Chocolate, Spirits, and the Return of Artisanal Foods, by Suzanne Cope

Nazi Hunger Politics: A History of Food in the Third Reich, by Gesine Gerhard

The Carrot Purple and Other Curious Stories of the Food We Eat, by Joel S. Denker

ALSO BY JOEL DENKER

The World on a Plate: A Tour through the History of America's Ethnic Cuisine
Capital Flavors: Exploring Washington's Ethnic Restaurants
Unions and Universities: The Rise of the New Labor Leader
No Particular Place to Go: The Making of a Free High School (with Steve Bhaerman)

the Carrot Purple

AND OTHER
CURIOUS STORIES
OF THE
FOOD WE EAT

JOEL S. DENKER

ROWMAN & LITTLEFIELD
Lanham • Boulder • New York • London

Published by Rowman & Littlefield
A wholly owned subsidiary of The Rowman & Littlefield Publishing Group, Inc.
4501 Forbes Boulevard, Suite 200, Lanham, Maryland 20706
www.rowman.com

Unit A, Whitacre Mews, 26-34 Stannary Street, London SE11 4AB

British Library Cataloguing in Publication Information Available

Library of Congress Cataloging-in-Publication Data

Denker, Joel.
  The carrot purple and other curious stories of the food we eat / Joel S. Denker.
    pages cm. — (Rowman & Littlefield studies in food and gastronomy)
  Includes bibliographical references and index.
  ISBN 978-1-4422-4885-4 (cloth : alk. paper) — ISBN 978-1-4422-4886-1 (electronic)
  1. Food—Anecdotes. 2. Food crops—Anecdotes. 3. Vegetables—Anecdotes. 4. Fruit—Anecdotes. 5. Cooking—Anecdotes. I. Title.
  TX353.D4329 2015
  641.3—dc23   2015015016

Printed in the United States of America

To Peggy, without whose belief in this work and dedication to the project, it would never have been.

CONTENTS

ACKNOWLEDGMENTS

First and foremost, this multiyear project would not have been accomplished without the unstinting support, encouragement, and tireless work of my wife, Peggy, on all phases of it. When I doubted at times whether it would ever be done, Peggy urged me to keep the faith.

I owe a good deal to my editors Ken Albala and Suzanne Staszak-Silva. Suzanne's assistant, Kathryn Knigge, was also very helpful.

This book grew out of the food writing I did for more than two decades for the Washington newspaper, *The InTowner*. Peter Wolff, the paper's editor and publisher, provided me with strong backing and encouragement throughout. He gave me a wide berth to develop my own voice, my own style of food journalism.

My good friend, Patrick McDonough, offered me invaluable assistance in carrying out the research.

My association with the Oxford Symposium on Food and Cookery, at which I first presented my early carrot discoveries, was invaluable. This annual gathering of culinary amateurs and professionals, of students, scholars, artists, writers, gardeners, and a host of other food enthusiasts, was a major influence. Reading its proceedings and attending its meetings convinced me that I was part of a larger community. Oxford is a model of serious writing about food in all its dimensions for the general reader. Its vast body of work is cultivated without being prissy or pedantic. Attending a meeting at St. Catherine's College in the company of luminaries like Elisabeth Luard, Claudia Roden, Barbara K. Wheaton, Madhur Jaffrey, Sami Zubaida, Gillian Riley, Bruce Kraig, Raymond Sokolov, and Jill

Norman, among many others, was inspirational. Oxford veterans Charles Perry and Ken Albala made me feel welcome and graciously shared their wealth of food knowledge with me.

There are many others to thank for their assistance. In my quest for a publisher, Sara Roahen, the late Steven Shaw, Andrew Smith, Matthew Goodman, John T. Edge, and Susan R. Friedland all offered advice, and Ken Albala brought me together with Rowman & Littlefield.

A wide range of experts offered me the benefits of their food learning. Philipp W. Simon, an authority on carrots, took time out for many conversations, and taught me that a seemingly ordinary vegetable could have a fascinating and intricate history. Larry Pierce, Carlos Quiros, David Gentilcore, Jim McCann, Susan Tax Freeman, Helen Saberi, and David Plotnikoff each lent a very helpful hand. Pat Hooper from the Artichoke Advisory Board schooled a novice about the history of her industry and helped me to locate indispensable materials. Hugo Tottino from Ocean Mist Farms, the artichoke grower, and Margaret D'Arrigo-Martin, a former executive at D'Arrigo Brothers, the purveyor of Andy Boy broccoli and other vegetables, provided useful information about the history of their businesses.

My visits to restaurants and cafés helped me to flesh out my stories. The late, beloved Fred Cooper and his wife Barbara accompanied Peggy and me on many of our early expeditions. Fred was always enthusiastic about any new ethnic food discovery. Charles S. Vizzini offered companionship and insights about Italian vegetables and the food lore of Sicily, the land of his forebears. Emebet ("Amy") Tsiga taught me a great deal about coffee and the spices of Ethiopia, her birthplace. In recent years, I have leaned on Luis Marroquin, the proprietor of Washington's Taqueria Distrito Federal, for help in understanding Mexican food, as well as Latin cooking in general.

Two Washington coffee shops gave me a haven in which to write and imagine during my many years in the city. Jolt 'N Bolt, where Amy worked, and Soho Tea and Coffee have been homes away from home.

INTRODUCTION

The familiar orange carrot was once an oddity. It is just a little more than four hundred years old. The purple carrot, originally domesticated in Afghanistan in AD 900, was dominant until the orange root was bred by Dutch gardeners in the 1600s. As surprising as this tale is, its discovery is equally intriguing. Scouring paintings in the Louvre and other museums during the 1950s, an unsung Dutch agronomist made a stunning discovery about the change in the carrot's color. By the seventeenth century, he observed, the orange carrot was becoming more prominent in the still-life paintings of his homeland.

The story of the carrot is just one of the hidden tales this book will recount. Like the carrot, most of the foods we eat have reached us only after traveling a long, intricate path, with many twists and turns along the way. I will explore how a wide range of ingredients, from artichokes to strawberries, were, in different locations and times, invested with new meaning. They acquired not only culinary significance but also ceremonial, medicinal, and economic importance. Foods were variously relished, revered, and reviled.

For as long as I can remember, food has fascinated me. My father, who had grown up in New York City, introduced me to garlicky hot dogs at Nathan's, sauerbraten at the Blue Ribbon, and roast beef sandwiches on a kaiser roll (a surprise to this youngster) at McGinnis's of Sheepshead Bay. He also introduced me to that fixture of the Jewish deli, Cel-Ray tonic.

I continued my food adventures as the decades went on. While teaching in Dar es Salaam, the Indian Ocean capital of Tanzania, southern Africa, I savored spicy cubes of beef and chapati (Indian bread) at an Arabic café. I washed the cheap meal down with fresh passion-fruit juice. And I tried out samosas at the Kozy Café, a popular snack bar in this African city, which has a large Indian population.

Later, when I lived in New York City, I sought out Ukrainian, Armenian, and Jewish-dairy restaurants that were just being discovered. In other cities, I roamed ethnic enclaves—San Francisco's Little Manila, Newark's Portuguese Ironbound neighborhood, and Boston's Chinatown.

In Washington, D.C., my present home, I have watched the explosion of immigrant cooking in a once white-bread city. This sleepy Southern town has evolved into a polyglot capital. I was intoxicated by visits to Trinidadian, West African, and Indonesian dining rooms.

Soon I began profiling these restaurants and their owners for a local community newspaper, *The InTowner*. After many years of writing about ethnic food, I shifted direction. For all my pleasure in tasty and exotic food, I knew little about the ingredients that made up my favorite dishes. I was excited by *baba ghanouj*, the Arabic dip, but unacquainted with the history of eggplant, its main constituent. Did eggplant always grow in the Middle East? If not, where did it come from?

I took many foods, common and unusual, for granted. Determined to overcome my complacency, I began the quest out of which this book was created. Along the way, I uncovered a vast number of materials—botanical, cultural, historical—that shed light on my interests. Specialists, I learned, had investigated scores of topics, but their findings were often unknown to a wider audience. Their detailed research needed to be synthesized.

The carrot was one of my early subjects. When my wife, Peggy, urged me to dig into its story, I first resisted, wondering how such an ordinary vegetable could be of any interest. As I delved into its history, however, I was surprised to learn of the carrot's beginnings as a purple root. When I shared my discovery with friends, they were also tantalized. I presented the results of my investigation to a meeting of the Oxford Symposium on Food and Cookery, held each year in England. The audience of historians, cooks, gardeners, and culinary amateurs reacted with enthusiasm. I was spurred to continue.

Like the carrot's, the other tales I was gathering were engrossing in their own right. How could one, for example, not marvel at the story of the strawberry, in which two varieties of the New World fruit mated in the Old World, producing the ancestor of the modern berry? But as I looked over my work, I also noticed wider themes.

The Carrot Purple reveals the curious journey of foods from obscurity to familiarity. Each portrait tells a unique history of the incorporation of specific ingredients in varied cultural settings. Read together, they illustrate patterns of their culinary assimilation and acceptance.

It is easy to forget that commonplace foods were once mystifying. Fernandez de Oviedo, the sixteenth-century Spanish traveler, groped for ways to describe the alien avocado. "In the center of a fruit is a seed like a peeled chestnut." Its paste, he observed, was "similar to butter." Since the avocado resembled a pear, the Spaniard recommended enjoying it with cheese.

Similarly, the tomato, a recent import to Italy from Spain, puzzled the Italian physician Pietro Andrea Mattioli. It is another "species of eggplant," he reported.

In the Middle East, the banana, which was probably carried there from India by Arab traders, piqued the curiosity of Crusaders in the Holy Land. "There is also another fruit called apples of Paradise," wrote Burchard of Mount Zion in 1282. "It grows like a bunch of grapes, having many grains [fruits]. . . . These grains are oblong in shape, sometimes six fingers and thick as a hen's egg."

Before strange foods became ordinary and commonplace, people had to overcome their visceral distaste for them. One of those reviled was the cucumber. As the sixteenth-century English adage ("Raw cucumber makes the churchyards prosperous") suggests, the cucumber once raised the specter of death. Scientific opinion and popular prejudice combined to give the gourd a fearsome quality. "It has been a common saying of physicians in England that a cucumber should be well sliced and dressed with pepper and vinegar, and then thrown out, as good for nothing," Samuel Johnson wrote. Culinary authorities could also be dismissive. Isabella Beeton, the Victorian food writer, wrote that a "cucumber is a cold food and difficult of digestion when eaten raw." She added that "delicate stomachs should avoid the plant, for it is cold and indigestible."

Some herbs and spices, now in fashion, only slowly came into vogue once distaste for them had faded. Coriander, whose leaves perk up Mexican, Indian, and Thai cooking, was once dubbed the "stinking herbe." Older commentators compared its scent to that of the stinkbug. Modern food opinion was also initially disdainful. Food anthropologist Margaret Visser suggests that the "green leaves of the plant are said to smell like squashed bed-bugs."

Other foods suffered from ethnic stigmas. The chickpea, so vital to our beloved hummus, was one such ingredient. First tilled in the Fertile Crescent, it was grown widely in Spain by the Moors, whose armies swept into Iberia in the early eighth century. Among wealthy Spaniards, the bean was scorned as Muslim grub, a staple suited only for "country people" and not for the Christian nobility.

Long after the original offense, stereotypes of foods persist. Intrigued by a chickpea and salt-cod salad offered at a Portuguese café in Newark, New Jersey's Ironbound neighborhood, I asked a customer about it. She said the salad was called *Meia-Desfeita*, or "half an insult." The chickpea was still branded as a hostile alien.

Foods were also surrounded by superstitions and taboos. The eggplant was viewed suspiciously from its earliest days. In Spain, it was viewed as not only a "Semitic" food but also a carrier of ills. Wherever the eggplant migrated, feelings of dread followed. The Moors in Spain, the story went, planted the poisonous vegetable in order to kill Christians. In Italy, where it was transported by Arab traders, the eggplant was called *melanzane*, from the Latin *mala insana*, or mad apple. A host of maladies were imputed to it. Castore Durante, the sixteenth-century physician, blamed melancholy, cancer, leprosy, and headaches on eating eggplant.

Because eggplant, like potatoes and chili peppers, was a member of the deadly nightshade family, some regarded it as toxic. John Gerard, the sixteenth-century English herbalist, worried that its leaves resembled those of henbane, a poisonous nightshade. "I rather wish English men to content themselves with the meat and sauces of our owne country, than with fruit and sauce eaten with such peril," he cautioned. "Doubtless these Apples have a mischievous qualitie . . . it is therefore better to esteem this plant and have it in the garden for your pleasure and the rarenesse thereof, than for any virtue or good qualities yet knowne."

Even in the Middle East, where it would be passionately embraced, it was originally disdained. In his book on poisons, Ibn Wahshiyya, an Arab toxicologist, declared the raw vegetable poisonous. "Its color is like the scorpion's belly and its taste is like the scorpion's sting," according to an eleventh-century Bedouin saying, cited by food scholar Charles Perry.

Conversely, foods, especially those invested with sacred symbolism, could also inspire wonder and awe. In ritual, ceremony, and primal rites, they gave a larger meaning to life. The crimson pomegranate was a symbol of holiness, fertility, and abundance. Both Jews and early Christians were devoted to the fruit. Renaissance painters who linked the pomegranate to the Christ child made it a religious motif.

Another fruit, the strawberry, captivated religious imagination. Artists who were trying to convey purity and righteousness were drawn to the plant. *Ma-*

donna of the Strawberries, a painting by Martin Schongauer, elevates the straw-berry, as the Virgin Mary is depicted sitting on a raised bed of the rosy fruit.

Certain plants were essential to daily religious practice. In India, where holy basil graces temple courtyards, the Hindu faithful pray and chant in the presence of the plant. Basil is said to be the embodiment of Tulsi, the goddess of creation.

Because of its aura of purity, basil was also a funereal herb. In India, the dead were cleansed with basil water. Cinnamon, another venerable spice, was burned at funerals in the ancient world. Its fragrance also permeated the atmosphere at joyful events. "Myrrh, cassia and frankincense rose in smoke . . . all the old women wailed, and the men raised a fine cry," the Greek poet Sappho wrote of a wedding in Troy.

Just as food plants could be sacramental, they could also be denounced by the religious establishment. Coffee, which had become a popular drink in Islamic coffeehouses, threatened clerics. Fearful that these new venues would lure their flocks away from the mosque, the imams tried to stamp them out.

Even in Christian Europe, coffee was greeted warily. Catholic priests attacked the "hellish black brew," a drink they considered only fit for Muslims. They failed to persuade Pope Clement VIII, who, in the early 1600s, rejected their entreaties: "We shall cheat Satan by baptizing it," he declared.

Food was also the raw material for myths and legends. Treasured by many as an auspicious fruit, the pomegranate took on darker tones in Greek myth. The goddess Persephone, who was spirited away to the underworld by Hades, the lord of the lower depths, was tempted to eat a "honey sweet" pomegranate seed. As a consequence, she was condemned to stay underground during the winter months and only ascend to earth in the spring.

Mint, a mythic herb, sprang up after Persephone beat her rival, the water nymph Minthe, and "tore her limb from limb," as French scholar Marcel Deti-enne recounts the tale. Hades, who had made Minthe his mistress, turned her remains into *menthe*, a "sweet-smelling plant."

Many plants were esteemed as much for their curative powers as for their culinary attractions. Before it was transformed into an everyday food, celery, for example, was valued for its restorative seeds and leaves. Its bitterness and pun-gent fragrance, largely bred out of the modern vegetable, made "water parsley" a popular medicine. The plant was hung in the rooms of ancient Greeks suffering severe illnesses. Years later in England, the herbalist Nicholas Culpeper praised celery as a tonic: the plant was "one of the herbs which is eaten in the spring to sweeten and purify the blood."

Celery never completely lost its medicinal aura. In Kalamazoo, Michigan, a center of vegetable cultivation in the late nineteenth century, companies marketed celery palliatives. The Kalamazoo Celery and Sarsaparilla Compound was promoted as a cure for "fever . . . all forms of nervousness, headache, and neuralgia . . . and female complaints."

"Spicie drugs," as the English poet John Milton called them, were coveted by ancient and modern traders. Spices were desired not just as seasoning but also as medicine. Sugar was once considered a cure-all, a drug to remedy the body's ills. Long before it was sweetening chocolate, tea, and coffee, sugar was being dispensed by medieval apothecaries. Influenced by Arabic pharmacology, sugar was prescribed for fever, dry coughs, chapped lips, and other ailments. Sugar infused syrups, tonics, powders, and other compounds.

Nutmeg—*mada shaunda*, or "narcotic fruit"—was an Indian folk remedy. To quiet irritable children, parents gave them small amounts of nutmeg. English nannies would later give babies the spice to make them sleepy.

In England, mulled wine, fortified with nutmeg and other spices, was given by doctors for chest coughs. Others used it to relieve the excesses of heavy dining and drinking. Lacing alcohol with the spice helped to "reduce the flatulence and dyspepsia resulting from such stimulating liquids," English folklorist L. F. Newman observed.

Food played another important role, as a symbol of social distinction. The upper classes paved the way for the adoption of many alien foods by making them emblems of status and wealth. Before many foods were popularized, they were the domains of the aristocracy. Chocolate, in its native Mexico the prerogative of the Aztec royalty, became a source of recreation for the nobility when it arrived in Spain. Jesuits reveled in the fashionable new drink.

The wealthy ostentatiously displayed exotic fruits to show off their positions. The regal pineapple was a centerpiece at dinner tables on English estates and depicted on Wedgwood china, sugar bowls, and teapots. The gentry grew luxurious pineapples in *pineries* (hothouses) during the cold months. Similarly, French royals prominently housed evergreen trees bearing oranges in fancy enclosures called *orangeries*.

In many cultures, some foods were assigned a lower status. Lentils, the "poor man's meat," may be fashionable today, but in the past they were often associated with the plebeian classes. This was the image of the common legume in ancient Greece: "When you cook lentil soup, don't add perfume," Jocasta says in *The Phoenician Women*. A rich man should shun lentils, Aristophanes counsels:

"Now that he is rich he will no longer eat lentils; formerly when he was poor, he ate what he could get." The Middle Eastern food historian Claudia Roden tells of occasions when her aunt offered guests a special lentil dish, pleading, "Excuse the food of the poor!"

If foods met a culture's practical material needs, there were fewer obstacles to their acceptance. For all of their other attractions, spices, for example, represented wealth. Black pepper, the dearest of the early spices, was the equivalent of capital in the ancient world. Imported from India, it was held in the Roman treasury and used as a means of exchange. The Portuguese, the Dutch, and other empires chased after it. In the heyday of spice consumption, the Middle Ages, rents were often paid in the lucrative aromatic. The expression "to lack pepper" meant that one was poor.

Saffron, which had adorned the Persian Court, was also lusted after in Europe. The spice was so precious that diluting it could lead to serious punishment. In 1444, one German offender was burned at the stake in Nuremberg for watering down saffron.

Food could also serve as an engine of economic growth. The common white potato often had a vulgar reputation. "The potato is criticized with reason for being windy, but what matters windiness for the vigorous organisms of peasants and laborers," the French philosopher Diderot sneered. However, potatoes also paid economic dividends. Feeding the commoners of Northern Europe, the tuber promoted a surge in population. As the historian William McNeill, who wrote his dissertation on the potato, pointed out, "[T]he spread of potatoes undergirded the nineteenth century industrialization by expanding local food supply, sometimes as much as four times over the caloric yield obtainable from grain harvests of the same fields." The potato, the scholar argues, sped Northern Europe's rise to "world dominion."

Other transplants sustained masses of people and met their nutritional needs. The peanut, a Latin American native carried to West Africa by the Portuguese, filled a major gap in the diet. Converted into spicy soups or stews, it provided critical protein.

The sweet potato, once a luxurious food for Europe's wealthy, has become a godsend for the poor of the Third World. High in vitamin C and easily grown, the plant is also a versatile food. In China, where the root grew in difficult terrain, it yielded the peasant four times as much as rice.

In the modern era, ingenious marketing was often required to persuade shoppers to try novel foods. The banana, which some feared would upset their stomachs, was such an item. United Fruit experimented in its test kitchens, searching for a breakfast dish that the banana could accompany. Cornflakes with milk and bananas was the company's candidate. Cereal boxes in the 1920s contained coupons offering free bananas.

Broccoli, which once had a predominantly ethnic market among Italians, was transformed into a national brand by the D'Arrigo Brothers Company. The company advertised the vegetable on the radio and labeled it "Andy Boy," after the son of one of the company's founders. The new brand had a dramatic impact on the mother of Charles S. Vizzini, a friend of mine. "It's not broccoli. It's Andy Boy," she enthused.

The odyssey of foods will doubtless continue. Banana leaves, the *New York Times* reports, are becoming standard items in Filipino restaurants. Quinoa, an ancient Andean grain, is now in such great demand that the supply in the producing countries is threatened. Consumers rush to snap up "Greek"-style yogurt, often without realizing that the word *yogurt* is of Turkish origin, and the product itself was perfected by the Turks. And soon we may be as conversant with the venerable fig as we are now with the once-unfamiliar pomegranate.

The tea I was enjoying had a tantalizingly sweet taste reminiscent of licorice. I had recently bought a box of Royal brand anise tea, an Egyptian import, and was sampling the soothing drink for the first time. Curious about my find, I asked an Egyptian acquaintance about anise, the spice that infused the tea. It was a "pharmaceutical," he responded, very pleasing to the stomach. Anise tea, I later discovered, has long been given to babies with colic.

The flavor of the tea is extracted from an ancient hot-weather plant, probably native to Egypt and the eastern Mediterranean. Anise's feathery leaves and clusters of yellow flowers are characteristic of the carrot family—for example, coriander, cumin, parsley, and fennel—to which it belongs. Its taste and scent derive from *anethole*, the fragrant oil contained in its seeds or fruits. The pale yellow oil gives off the telltale smell of licorice. Anise's sweetness—thirteen times that of sugar, according to scientist Harold McGee—is also derived from this oil. In addition to the pleasures it provides us, it also protects the plant by repelling insects.

Anise's allure over the centuries was based as much on its curative powers as on its flavor. John Gerard, a sixteenth-century English herbalist, was convinced of the spice's benefit to the stomach: "The seed wasteth and consumeth winde, and is good against belchings and upbraidings of the stomacke, allayeth gripings of the belly, provoketh urine gently . . . and stirreth up bodily lust." Its nickname, *solamen intestinorum*, or comforter of bowels, is a testament to its reputation.

In the days of the pharaohs, Egyptians believed that anise healed the body. Medical manuals prescribed it for stomach ills and recommended that the herb's seeds be chewed for toothaches. A drink of figs, honey, and anise "refreshes" the heart, according to one text.

Egypt supplied anise to ancient Rome, where it was a favorite spice. "Be it green or dried it is wanted for all conserves and flavorings," the Roman naturalist Pliny wrote. Roman cooks employed anise to make dishes both healthy and appetizing. Served in a wrapping of bay leaves, banquet cake was made fragrant with anise. Eaten at the end of a long night of feasting, the dessert was designed to help celebrants digest their dinner and to sweeten their breath. The Romans also exploited the sweet flavor of its seeds in other confections. After their military victories, General Quintus Fabius Cunctator rewarded the plebes with hard anise candy.

The Greeks also put great stock in anise. Pythagoras, who believed that anise banished gas and stomach pains, praised a bread fragrant with its seeds. Baked goods redolent of the spice are still widely consumed. Scandinavians and Germans traditionally make anise bread. Italians love anise biscotti, cookies that were originally served as festive sweets at weddings and other occasions.

During the Middle Ages, anise arrived in Europe from the East just as sugar, another exotic import, was beginning to make inroads in the kitchen. Tangy candies or confits were created by coating aromatic seeds (fennel, coriander, aniseed) with hard sugar, a practice, historian Tim Richardson suggests, that probably started with Arab apothecaries. At fancy gatherings, guests were offered a choice of these candies served on gold or silver dishes with the main banquet course or after the meal. Just as aromatic cake was for the Romans, the confits were meant as digestives and breath sweeteners.

The confits are the ancestors of our own anise sweets. The classic Anis de Flavigny hard candies, pea-size treats with a tiny green anise seed inside, were first produced by French Benedictine monks in 1591. In their abbey in the Burgundy village of Flavigny, the monks gathered heaps of anise seeds for their confections. More than two thousand years before, Roman soldiers had taken the herb to Gaul.

When the monasteries were dissolved after the French Revolution, several businesses took their place turning out pastilles. One family-owned company, now in its third generation, is currently making the candies by following the original recipe and techniques. Tumbling together in copper kettles for fifteen days, aniseeds are coated with successive layers of sugar syrup. Les Anis de Flavigny are sold today in such flavors as black currant, orange blossom, rose, and violet.

Alcoholic drinks flavored with anise have their roots in the Middle East. Doubly rewarding, they are at once intoxicating and relaxing for the stomach. Drinking the herbal liqueurs is restorative, Israeli journalist Amit Yariv wrote: "They are the Middle Eastern equivalent of chicken soup—a cure for all ailments."

Arak, the oldest of these refreshments, was invented by the Arabs, who pioneered distilling (*alcohol* comes from an Arabic word). The name, which means sweat or perspiration in Arabic, is an allusion to this process. It's an apt image for the droplets, which collect in the spout of the still before dripping out. The innovators, most probably Christians, produced the liqueur from fermented grapes. Aniseeds steeped in the alcohol provide the distinctive flavor and aroma.

Popular among Syrians, Palestinians, Iraqis, and other Middle Easterners, *arak* was perfected by the Lebanese. It continues to be made in the time-honored way, in copper stills, in mountainous Christian villages during the grape harvest. The artisanal drink is a fixture of the area's Sunday lunch. It is sipped with *mezze*, an assortment of olives, feta cheese, eggplant dips, and other starters that stimulate the appetite.

"There are drinks to get you drunk, and there are drinks to be savored with food," distiller George Haiby told the *New York Times*'s Neil MacFarquhar. "*Arak* from the village is like the sons of the village: pure. If you use good grapes, if you keep the entire process clean, if you distill the mash well, if you use good aniseed, everyone can make good *arak*."

In Turkey, people love *raki*, the country's equivalent of *arak*. Like other anise-based drinks, "lion's milk," as the Turks affectionately call *raki*, turns a milky white when diluted in a glass of water. This happens because its aromatic oils dissolve in alcohol but not in water. The convivial refreshment, which the Turks commonly sip with roasted chickpeas, sheep's-milk cheese, and other appetizers, has an intriguing history. Taverns and wine shops serving *raki*, historian Evliya Çelebi notes, sprang up in Istanbul during the seventeenth century. "Lion's milk" was in such demand, she said, that at least a hundred workshops were manufacturing it in the city at the time.

Anise drinks abound in the Mediterranean world. *Ouzo* in Greece and *pastis* in southern France each has its devotees (*pastis* means "mixed" or "confused" in the Provençal dialect). In Italy, *sambuca*, a similar liquor, has an Arabic imprint. After they conquered Sicily in the eleventh century, the Islamic colonists introduced an anise-flavored water known as *zammu*. Vendors offered customers glasses of cold water to which they added a shot of anise. Talking to Sicilian food writer Mary Ann Simeti, a local reminisced about the dying trade: "The sellers would walk around with clay pots like amphoras tied over their shoulders, or hanging from a yoke. They sold anise water . . . drinking water spiked with anise in clay pots to keep it cool." *Zammu* evolved into the alcoholic liqueur *sambuca*.

Anise refreshments epitomize the spice's sensual appeal. They "evoke an idyllic drowsiness," writer Regina Nadelson observes. Many centuries ago, the Romans credited anise with aphrodisiac powers. The fifteenth-century English king, Edward IV, was also a believer. He required that his sheets be perfumed with the aromatic—one more tribute to the captivating plant.

"MOON OF THE FAITH"
appreciating the apricot

Four radiant, yellowish-orange apricots were depicted on each of the cellophane packages stacked on a shelf in a Middle Eastern grocery near my home. An avid fan of dried apricots, I was drawn to the sheets of dried apricot paste imported from Damascus. *Amardine*, as it is called, is especially beloved in the Ramadan season, when it is used to make a juice that the faithful drink to break their fast or to savor during the festive time after sundown.

Translated into poetic Arabic, *amardine* means "moon of the faith." It is unlike your ordinary supermarket fruit roll that some call "shoe leather." According to Charlie Sahadi, owner of a vast Middle Eastern food emporium in Brooklyn, the Arabic delicacy has a "thickness" and "consistency" that ordinary fruit rolls lack.

The apricot, which was cultivated in China and Central Asia as early as 2000 BC, migrated with the country's traders, who traveled the Great Silk Road. The Chinese merchants, botanist Berthold Laufer suggests, very probably introduced the fruit to the Persians. They called it the "yellow plum" (*zardaloo*). Widely dispersed, it was spread throughout the Eurasian steppe by nomadic, horseback-riding tribesmen.

This member of the rose family, whose relatives include the plum, peach, cherry, and almond, is known botanically as *Prunus armeniaca*, a reference to the land from which the ancient Greeks believed it came. The Romans, who learned of the apricot in the first century AD, dubbed it *praecocum*, the "precocious one." They noticed that the fruit bloomed early in the summer. A sensitive plant, it was easily injured by early frost or strong winds. The fragile fruit has long been a favorite of royals and aristocrats. The apricot's beauty captivated poets like English writer John Ruskin, who described it "shining in a sweet brightness of golden velvet."

The conquering Arabs took the luxurious fruit from Central Asia to the Middle East. The caliphs, who ruled the vast Islamic empire stretching from the Gulf to Sicily between AD 750 and 1258, imported apricots from Tus in northeastern Persia to their capital in Baghdad. The chefs of the court created dishes for the *al-barqouq* ("apricot" in Arabic), which were adopted in the many Islamic dominions.

From the Persians, the Arabs had picked up the technique of adding tangy fruit, such as apricots and cherries, to liven up their meat dishes. One of the cookbooks of the empire called for apricots in a delicacy called *mishmishiya* (lamb and apricot stew): "Take fat meat. Boil it in a little water. . . . Take dried apricots and remove their pits and replace them with blanched almonds. And when the meat is done, throw the apricots on it, and raisins . . . a stick of Chinese cinnamon, mint, mastic, saffron, and jujubes, and sweeten it with sugar and honey." Middle Eastern cooks grasped the "special affinity," culinary historian Claudia Roden points out, "between lamb and apricots."

Passionate about sweets, the Arabs exploited the apricot for their sugary confections. A medieval syrup that blended its juice with sweet almonds was a forerunner of the apricot drinks later hawked in the Middle East by vendors or sold in cafés. The apricot also fit neatly into the repertoire of Arabic desserts. Stuffed with almonds or almond paste, the fruit complemented its nutty relative. Topped with chopped pistachios or almonds, one rich treat of pureed apricots and whipped cream was perfumed with either rose or orange blossom water.

Apricots flourished throughout the Islamic dominions. The Moors, who conquered Spain, planted apricots in Grenada. Syria was another bastion of the fruit. In the garden oasis outside Damascus, the nineteenth-century English naturalist Canon Henry Baker Tristram wrote, "The great apricot-trees were laden and bent down under strings of ripe, golden fruit. The lanes were strewn with apricots. Asses, mules, and camels in long strings carried heaped panniers of these 'golden apples.'"

To conserve the splendid produce throughout the year, the Syrians convert it to *amardine*. According to Middle Eastern food expert Sonia Uvezian, peasant women traditionally crushed apricots with their feet in stone troughs. They then extracted the pits and spread out the paste in the sun to dry.

Mohamed el-Shalati, whose Damascus company makes a popular brand of *amardine*, is one of many manufacturers who process and market the paste today. The "rotund, mustachioed, and avuncular" el-Shalati, as writer Ken Gould describes him, has sometimes gone to dangerous lengths to snare the fruit. He and his son, Ahmed, have traveled to Mataya, the apricot capital of Turkey, near the Syrian border, in search of their prize.

"Between avoiding Turkish army checkpoints and local brigands levying tolls on mountain passes, Mohamed and Ahmed have to cope with heat of more than 40 degrees C and narrow roads," Gould recounts. In el-Shalati's Damascus factory, the apricots are reduced to a pulp in copper pots and then put through huge sieves. Steady heating and stirring finally yields a paste that is dried under nets on the factory roof for forty-eight hours.

Most of us do not get to experience the glories of a succulent, ripe apricot. Instead, we make do with dried or canned fruit. We are deprived of this joy because modern shipping and marketing practices demand that the fruit be picked before it fully ripens on the tree. "I get docked for ripe fruit," grower George Bonacich tells fruit expert David Karp. As a result, shoppers are confronted with a pallid apricot. "Those harvested early to make them easier to transport are often a woolly, watery disappointment," English food writer Hugh Fearnley-Whittingstall observes.

A few farmers have attempted to break the mold and develop a fruit closer to the apricot's Eastern ancestors. John Driver, a Northern California agriculturist, has hunted for Central Asian varieties where the old Silk Road kingdoms were located. In this "hub of diversity," the home to the widest spectrum of the fruit, Driver found sweet, intensely flavored apricots in many shapes and colors: "There really is a tremendous amount of different apricots out there," he told Adam Gollner, a Canadian food writer. "Unlike Western apricots—invariably tawny or orange-yellow, occasionally flecked with reds—Eastern ones range in color from purple-black to cream-colored with a rosy blush. They can be small as a pea or as big as a tennis ball, as sweet as honey or [as] acrid as cat pee on burnt toast."

Driver took the seeds back to his Northern California farm and soon was growing several varieties. Because Eastern apricots usually required colder winters than California's, his achievement was all the more stunning. Driver marketed his apricots as "CandyCot Apricots: The Sweetest Thing on Earth," twice as sweet as the typical fruit. Contrary to industry convention, he shipped his products fully ripe. His apricots traveled in foam-padded boxes to prevent bruising. "Maybe I'm crazy, but I think the industry needs to reexamine how they're selling fruit," he told writer Karp. "If I were a consumer, this is what I'd want."

While we wait for a more ideal apricot, we can still appreciate the yearlong pleasures of *amardine*. I remember waiting expectantly while the sheet of apricot steeped in a bowl of cold water in my apartment. The liquid gradually took on a bright orange hue. I waited expectantly. Sipping the thick, rough-hewn drink, with its intense apricoty flavor, I felt a strong kinship with the English writer Edward Bunyard, who wrote a rapturous ode to the fruit: "[T]he Apricot has a certain Eastern lusciousness, a touch of the exotic which comes strangely into our homely country. In some Persian Palace whose quiet garden hears only the tinkle of a fountain, it would seem to find its right setting."

THE ARTICHOKE "UNDRESSED"

"Undressing" them, to use Greek writer Rena Salaman's felicitous image, is the first step toward understanding the intricate vegetables. Take off their tough outer bracts, watching out for the thorny tips, peel away more leaves, extract the hairy choke, and make your way to the heart. The artichoke is truly an unusual vegetable. "Nipped in the bud," as artichoke experts C. A. and A. C. Castelli observe, it is, in fact, the unopened bud of a flowering plant that can grow to five feet in height.

We nibble on the leaves and savor their fleshy meat. We devour the heart, the base of the flower. But these gifts are denied us if the tall plant is picked too late. The outer leaves will then have opened and blue-violet flowers will have sprouted from the choke, which is really a mass of undeveloped flowerets. It is now lovely but inedible.

While we Americans confine ourselves to the leaves and the heart, other cultures are more adventurous. Mediterraneans eat the stalks, chokes, the head, and even sometimes the whole artichoke. Americans favor the green globe artichoke, while purple shades and other shapes are more common in Europe. "Purple has a negative image," American growers told food writer Elizabeth Schneider. Moreover, we reflexively boil or steam our artichokes, rarely imagining other alternatives like roasting, stewing, baking, stuffing, or pickling them. A lemon and butter dipping sauce is frequently the limit of our dreams. The Romans, in contrast, feast on artichokes braised in olive oil that are fragrant with mint and garlic.

Although we are often chary of artichokes, many people in other cultures exult in them. Their arrival signals the coming of spring and the end of winter. The first artichokes of the season can be an occasion for celebration. Food writer Sarah Dickerman writes enthusiastically, "The rites that artichokes serve, of course, are spring's, the annual greening and regreening of the palate after the long winter."

Where does this prickly, peculiar vegetable come from? Some writers trace it to Italy, where the artichoke is beloved. It was not the artichoke, however, but the lesser-known cardoon, its parent, that the ancient Romans prized, so much so that they were willing to pay more for it than any other vegetable. Resembling a bulky celery stalk, the cardoon was enjoyed for its slightly bitter leaves and flavorful flower buds. The plant's classical name, *carduus*, is Latin for thistle, the family to which the early botanists assigned it. The Greeks also ate the stalks of the cardoon, which they called *kaktos*.

This thistle, which grew wild throughout the Mediterranean, probably originated in North Africa. Carthage supplied many of the cardoons sold in Roman markets. It was Arab or Berber gardeners, food historian Clifford West suggests, who developed the artichoke, another thistle-like plant, from the cardoon. The Arabs disseminated the vegetable throughout their territories. Islamic farmers, who had transplanted sugar, eggplant, and other previously unknown crops in Spain, also cultivated the "edible thistle." In Andalusia, the region in the south of the country under Moorish rule, the artichoke was especially esteemed.

From Sicily, where the conquering Saracens (Arab warriors) took them, artichokes spread to the Italian mainland, first to Naples, in the middle of the fifteenth century. The *al-kharshuf*—"thistle" in Arabic—became *carciofi* in Italian. Later, it moved north to Tuscany, where it became a popular food.

In Italy, the "noble thistle," as the English gastronome John Evelyn called it, was held in awe by the titled classes. Isabelle d'Este, a well-bred lady, sent a small basket of young peas and artichokes, "some novelties," to her brother in Ferrara to reinvigorate him after a long trip. This story, which Italian food scholar Gillian Riley recounts, illustrates a fashion, "a growing interest in the hitherto rare and exotic vegetable, treasured and exchanged by wealthy collectors as they would antique coins and jewelry."

The Italians believed in the health benefits of this "spring tonic," as food expert Faith Willinger called it. Now known as a good source of zinc, potassium, and vitamin C, it was reputed in older times to be a diuretic and a balm for the liver. Cynar, the bitter artichoke-based liqueur, is praised by its devotees

as a digestive. And, of course, it was said to heighten erotic desires. "The meat of artichokes cooked in broth is eaten with pepper at the end of the meal and with galanga [a plant in the ginger family] to increase amorous appetites," the sixteenth-century Tuscan doctor Pietro Andrea Mattioli wrote.

In a probably apocryphal story, Catherine de' Medici did something "scandalous": she consumed too many artichokes at her wedding in 1572. The Florentine noblewoman then became violently sick. "She felt as if she would literally explode," it was supposedly reported. Since it was frowned on for a respectable woman to partake of the aphrodisiac, de' Medici was being suitably punished.

Adept horticulturalists, Italian gardeners developed varieties of artichokes that captured the fancy of Europe's nobility. The French and Spanish upper classes embraced the import. Green and purple or red artichokes were on luxurious display at the King's Kitchen Garden at Versailles. French aristocrats prized the artichoke as not only beautiful but also exotic. *Avoir un coeur d'artichaut*, a delicious French phrase, means "to have an artichoke's heart." The expression, food writer Evelyne Bloch-Dano observes, "is used to describe someone fickle, who falls in love easily and often."

The "aristocrat of the Renaissance kitchen," as culinary essayist Jane Grigson portrays it, was given a prominent place in court cuisine. Bartolomeo Scappi, sixteenth-century chef to popes, served tiny artichokes, simply seasoned with salt and pepper, at court banquets in Rome during the month of February. The sumptuous artichoke was also lauded for its ability to stimulate the taste buds. "When it is flavored with wild mint, a small quantity of finely chopped garlic, pepper, oil, and salt, it awakens the appetite," seventeenth-century Italian gastronome Paolo Zacchia observes. "It can make a good drink, for it is appetizing."

The artichoke was not easily accepted in the United States. The educated aristocracy in the colonies knew them. A recipe for making "Hartichoak Pie" appeared in Martha Washington's *Booke of Cookery*. But it took outsiders, first the French and the Spanish, and later the Italians, to initiate us. In New Orleans, all three groups contributed to making the artichoke a vital part of the Crescent City's food culture.

Probably originally planted in mission gardens by Spanish friars, artichokes were first grown commercially in the San Francisco Bay area in the late nineteenth century by Italian farmers. First on the outskirts of the city, and then in Half Moon Bay, south of San Francisco, the *giardinieri*, mostly from northern Italy, planted artichokes, zucchini, fava beans, and other novel vegetables and herbs. This produce had appeal in the cosmopolitan port city, where colonies of French and Spanish settlers had earlier put down roots. Although some locals looked down on what they called the "dago gardens," the artichoke had considerable cachet among the well-heeled patrons of the city's expensive hotels and the upper-class restaurants on Nob Hill. Discerning buyers would soon find artichoke seeds advertised in Bay Area plant catalogs.

The Italian enclaves that sprang up in San Francisco and along the coast provided an eager market for the artichoke. "From Pedro Valley [now in Pacifica] up through North Beach, it was all Italian," early artichoke farmer Angelo Del Chiaro told writer Steve Turner. "And everybody ate them. We called them *carciofi*. And what we had left over, we sent to New York. The first guy to do that, I remember he just packed them in a steamer trunk and sent them express."

The Italians pushed south down the California coast in search of more land to grow their crop. Castroville, one hundred miles south of San Francisco at the edge of the fertile Salinas Valley, burgeoned into the center of the artichoke industry. The area, once dominated by farmers of Spanish origin, was given over to potatoes, grains, and dairy cows. Andrew Molena, a large-scale farmer, grew sugar beets, another key crop, on his landholdings in Castroville. When the sugar beet market weakened, he began looking for a steadier and more profitable product. He soon began leasing out his property to Italian immigrants, who planted the first artichokes in the Salinas Valley in 1922. Five years later, twelve thousand acres of the vegetable were being harvested around Castroville, which locals called the "artichoke capital of the world."

The conditions were ideal for artichokes, the cool, foggy air allowing them to flourish. "[The] fogs come in. They love that," Pat Hopper, director of the Artichoke Advisory Board, says of the plants. Summers were not too hot and winters were mild, and it rained infrequently. The thorny plants thrived over a long season in the sandy soil.

Borrowing money from the Bank of Italy in San Francisco (later, the Bank of America), five Italian farmers banded together in 1924 to form the California Artichoke and Vegetable Growers Corporation. The firm grew into Ocean Mist Farms, the country's largest artichoke producer. Years later, Italians, who pioneered the industry, still dominate it. Artichoke farming remains concentrated in the Castroville region.

In the early days, Castroville had a strong Italian flavor. Hugo Tottino, son of one of the company's founders, evoked the atmosphere in a conversation with writer Daniel Akkad: "He recalls a tight-knit community of Italian groceries that delivered bread daily, people speaking Italian in the streets, and growing families and workers sharing homemade lunches and wine."

The families labored arduously in the fields and in the packing sheds to build their business: "In those days, they'd work in the fields all day, then pack artichokes for shipping at night," Tottino told the *Los Angeles Times*'s Russ Parsons. Tottino said the wooden boxes in which the vegetables were packed, with the label "Ocean Mist Farms," looked like coffins, and that was what they were called.

The prosperity of the industry depended on finding markets in the Northeast, particularly in the large Italian community in New York City. Although the artichoke growers had made some inroads there, a formidable barrier stood in their way: organized crime. Ciro "Whitey" Terranova and other mobsters blocked the growers from successfully tapping the market.

By threatening and wreaking violence on artichoke purveyors, the Mafia chiefs gained a monopoly on the produce in the 1920s. The high prices they exacted especially injured the Italians, the largest and most avid buyers of the vegetable. Gangsters also assaulted the California growers directly. During the "Artichoke Wars," as the farmers called them, thugs terrorized the artichoke fields, attacking farmers and destroying plants. The villains demanded that the farmers agree to their demands or suffer the consequences. "We either accept the price or get our skulls cracked," as one farmer put it.

In New York, Mayor Fiorello La Guardia had had enough of the Mob's domination of the market. Near dawn on the frigid morning of December 21, 1935, the coldest day of the year, the "Little Flower," as he was affectionately known, climbed up the back of a flat-top truck and proclaimed a ban on the sale of artichokes, declaring that a "serious and threatening" emergency endangered the artichoke business. La Guardia laid down the gauntlet: "I want it clearly understood [that] no thugs, racketeers, or punks are going to be allowed to intimidate you as long as I am the mayor of the City of New York."

The mayor successfully broke up the monopoly, and artichokes began flowing into New York City.

The thistle, however, has never been an easy sell in the United States. Early growers had to set aside their own preferences and market to American tastes. The old-timers were especially fond of baby artichokes. These small, choke-less vegetables are not a different type of artichoke—they sprout at the bottom of the same plant that produces the larger, more familiar thistle—but since mainstream, non-Italian shoppers preferred the large-globe artichoke, the sellers had to adapt accordingly.

"Hey, this is America," farmer Michael Scaffini told writer David Plotnikoff. "Bigger is better, right?"

The vegetable still retains some of its exotic aura and ethnic associations. In fact, many find them peculiar.

"People don't know what they are," farmer Joe Pezzini says. "If you're Italian, then sure, you know what to do with them. If you're from the South, they're a hand grenade." Shoppers remain chary of the artichoke, veteran grower Tottino remarks. "They don't know how to cook them," he observes.

The artichoke's intricacies continue to confound us. In sophisticated precincts, sommeliers complain that eating artichokes can spoil the taste of a good wine. A chemical in the artichoke, cynarin, can make other foods or drinks taste sweet. "It's impossible to pair with wines," a San Francisco wine director told *New York Times* writer Amanda Hesser. "You fumble, you really do fumble."

Oh, what would its ancient admirers say?

THE "LASCIVIOUS LEAF"
the lure of arugula

Beware: Eating arugula can brand you an effete snob. A mere reference made by candidate Obama to the leaf during the primaries made him a target of Republican jibes. How did this once largely plebeian herb become a sign of elitism?

In earlier civilizations, rocket (its English name) was hardly the fashionable garden plant of today. It was more like an herb, whose sharp flavor was inseparable from its reputed healing and erotic powers.

Known in Latin as *eruca*, from the word for "harsh, rough," the plant was a member of the mustard family. Native to the Mediterranean, it was an unruly weed that was foraged from the fields by peasants, who made simple meals of greens and bread.

Rocket, whose leaves and seeds contain a peppery mustard oil, was said to have a fiery, potent nature. The Romans, who eventually cultivated the plant, extracted the oil. They savored its leaves accented with pepper and cumin and dressed with *garum*, a fermented fish sauce.

The literati extolled rocket as a sexual stimulant. "If those leaves of wild rocket, picked with left hand, are pounded and drunk in honey water, they serve as aphrodisiac," the naturalist Pliny wrote. To Ovid, the Roman poet, the plant was "lascivious."

The herb offered a multitude of benefits, other commentators said. "Rocket, eaten in a rather large quantity, arouses to intercourse; its seed has the same effect," the Greek physician Dioscorides stated. "It is diuretic, digestive, and good for the bowel. They also use the seed as a flavoring in cooked dishes."

Rocket was sacred to Priapus, the Greco-Roman god of fertility. Beds of the greens were planted around statues of the god. The leaf, Roman author Columella wrote, honored the deity: "Th'eruca, Priapus, near thee we sow, To arouse to duty husbands who are slow."

The people of the biblical Holy Land also ascribed virtues to rocket. "One of them went out into the field to gather 'oroth," the Second Book of Kings said, using another ancient name for the plant. At this time rocket was appreciated as a spice and also as a digestive, deodorant, and remedy for eye infections.

While rocket was regarded as a "hot" plant, lettuce was its polar opposite. To achieve an emotional balance, food historian Margaret Visser points out, the Romans paired the feminine, chillier lettuce with the masculine, libidinous arugula. A cousin of rocket, watercress, was assigned the same responsibility.

Called nasturtium or "nostril torment" by the Romans, watercress was thought to be an invigorating herb. The Greeks, Visser points out, suggested that the "dull and sluggish" should "eat cress." Convinced that watercress was a tonic, the Greek general Xenophon insisted that his troops eat it before battle.

As the leaf was transplanted to new lands, rocket's fame traveled with it. In twelfth-century Islamic Spain, syrups were enlivened with ground seeds from the plant.

In Europe, where the church forbade planting the sensual herb in monastic gardens, herbalists enthusiastically embraced it. The "seasoning leaf," as they called it, imparted strength and vigor. "Whoever taketh the seed of Rocket before he be whipt, shall be so hardened that he shall easily endure the paines," John Gerard declared in his sixteenth-century *Herball*. His contemporary, herbalist William Turner, recommended rocket as an aid "against the bitings of the shrew mouse and other venomous beasts."

Lettuce remained relegated to the frigid domain. It was a "cold and moist potherbe," herbalist Gerard wrote. Hotter, more bitter greens would revitalize the body. "Water-cress potage is a good remedy to cleanse the blood in the Spring . . . and consumes the gross humours winter hath left," seventeenth-century physician and herbalist Nicholas Culpeper said.

Italy was the culture most avid about rocket and other wild greens. Vendors in fourteenth-century Florence sold the greens on top of toasted bread. The fascination with racy rocket (*rucola* or *rughetta* in Italian) persisted. Seventeenth-century physician Pietro Andrea Mattioli observed that arugula "augments sperm and provokes men to coitus."

Rocket continued to be a staple of the poor Italian's diet. *Fava faglie* ("beans and greens")—mashed fava beans mixed with greens and flavored with olive oil—was a common repast. Rocket has gradually been assimilated into Italian cuisine and has lost its exclusive association with the peasantry. Today it might fill a frittata, adorn a pasta, or infuse a ravioli.

The "lascivious leaf," which some suggest was first planted in the United States by the Puritan colonists, has come out of the wilderness in the last twenty years. Its English name, *rocket*, brought with it by the early settlers, has given way to *arugula*. Botanists have celebrated it as a "specialty leaf vegetable." It now enjoys a certain cachet among sophisticated diners. Tamed and domesticated, it perks up salads, although it no longer arouses excitement or fear.

ASPARAGUS
scents and non-scents

An early hint of spring, the asparagus shoots break through the soil. The delicate vegetable, a member of the lily family that includes onions, leeks, and other plants, gives us seasonal joy. Now more widely enjoyed, asparagus was once the province of wealthy and leisured individuals.

The Romans were passionate about asparagus. They plucked shoots from the wild and, over time, domesticated the plant. In the process, the once thin and fragile stalks became thicker. Roman enthusiasm could lead to excess, however; upon seeing a grotesquely plump variety, Roman naturalist Pliny was revolted. "Now we see artificial kinds, and at Ravenna, three stalks weigh a pound," he wrote. "What monstrous gluttony." Pliny preferred a pristine asparagus: "Nature made asparagus grow wild."

The Romans ate asparagus with zest. They savored briny spears from stalks that had been steeped in a salt-and-vinegar solution. Young sprouts were delicious in a salad. A simple and enjoyable way of eating them, author Columella reported, was flavored with salt, pepper, and butter, and dressed with the juice of citron, an ancestor of the lemon.

But the appeal of asparagus was more than culinary. Its value as a laxative and diuretic, Pliny emphasized, made the vegetable "among the most useful foods." Asparagus, and especially the water it was cooked in, he added, also made a good aphrodisiac.

Wherever Roman legions marched, asparagus followed. The plant was sown along the Mediterranean and then in France. It later spread to England and to

other parts of Northern Europe. Emperors dispatched special fleets to transport the plant to distant regions of their realms. The rulers spared no expense in preserving the early rising vegetable. Chariots and fast runners carrying asparagus bundles sped off from the Tigris River for the Alps. The stalks were then frozen in the snow for six months, after which they were returned to Rome for the pleasure of revelers at the Feast of Epicurus, held in February.

Asparagus spawned a lively lore. The saying "quicker than you can cook asparagus" began with Emperor Augustus, who reportedly uttered it when ordering the immediate execution of one of his subjects. An amusing story about Julius Caesar's way of eating asparagus was also often repeated: when he took it with olive oil instead of butter, the leader became the butt of jokes.

During the Middle Ages, asparagus was largely invisible except in convent and monastery gardens. The fathers used it as a diuretic. It was rediscovered during the Renaissance, when Europeans tried to emulate the Romans by planting the vegetables they loved. During the sixteenth century, herbalists like John Gerard introduced the plant to their readers: "The manured or garden Sperage, hath at his first rising out of the ground thicke tender shoots very soft and brittle, of the thickness of the greatest swans quil, in taste like unto the greene beane."

Gradually, asparagus began to appear in markets. In one English town, "the poor people due gather the buddes or young shoots, and sell them." Hawkers peddled asparagus on English street corners.

The vegetable also acquired a new name. The Romans borrowed their Latin name *asparagus* from the Greek *asparagos*, a word that applied broadly to all tender, young shoots. By the seventeenth century, a new term had been conjured up. The English writer Samuel Pepys recounts "bringing with me from Fenchurch Street a hundred of Sparrowgrass." Two centuries later, asparagus reentered the English language.

The aristocratic classes were the most avid consumers of asparagus. In their infatuation, they mimicked their idols—the imperial Romans. French medical professor Michael Bicais compared his contemporaries' obsession with the Roman lust for the stalk. Asparagus "obliged the ancients to ferret them out greedily, and to attach a price to them, or to make them into something divine."

Royals demanded a constant supply of this "delicac[y] of princes" for their tables. King Louis XIV could feast on asparagus in December thanks to the "hot beds" in the palace gardens. At lavish gatherings, the nobility banqueted on rich asparagus dishes. A seventeenth-century Italian recipe for an asparagus pie was an example of this court cuisine. Flavored with cinnamon, rose water, raisins, figs, and ground almonds, the pastry made abundant use of sugar, cream, and egg yolks.

The Europeans, like the Romans, had faith in the healing powers of asparagus. They read the writings of the second-century Greek physician Galen, who lived in Rome, and subscribed to his gospel. Asparagus, he judged, was "healing, cleansing. . . . It relieves inflammation of the stomach, relaxes the bowels, makes urine, and helps the weak."

Botanists agreed. When the Dutch scientist Linnaeus was classifying the vegetable, he called it *Asparagus officinalis Linnaeus* ("of the dispensary").

The legend of asparagus's sexual powers persisted. Some prurient commentators warned readers of its dangers. "The decoction of the roots boiled in wine . . . stirred up bodily lust in man or woman," physician and herbalist Nicholas Culpeper wrote. As late as the nineteenth century, food writer Rebecca Rupp comments, girls' schools in France would not allow their charges to eat the vegetable for fear of encouraging their sexual appetites.

Asparagus had one major liability—the distinctive scent it induced in urine. It "affects the urine with a foetid smell . . . and therefore [has] been suspected by some physicians as not friendly to the kidneys," one observer remarked. Its scent, some said, could even reveal a romantic liaison. The "unpleasant odor," French writer Stanislas Martin quipped, "more than once betrayed an illicit dinner."

Proust surprisingly did not join in this chorus of disgust. The intoxicating smell, he said, turned "my chamber-pot into a vase of aromatic perfume." However, apostles of asparagus believed its odor had a healthful purpose: it was the body's way of purging "bad humors," a means of purification.

The preoccupation with the foul smell led to the discovery of the first amino acid in 1806. Searching for the cause of the odor, two scientists distilled asparagus juice into a concentrate they called *aspargene*. When they gave it to human subjects, the experimenters concluded that the substance was not the culprit. These people detected no smell in their urine. The latest thinking is that when we eat asparagus, a sulfur compound in the vegetable is, in most bodies, converted to a highly pungent chemical related to skunk spray.

Undeterred by its modest defects, the Europeans continued to ennoble asparagus. While green asparagus won the hearts of Americans, the white vegetable was the Continent's crown jewel. To grow it, mounds of soil were placed over the stalks. The covering blocked sunlight and prevented the plant from producing chlorophyll and turning green. Although the white asparagus was bigger and thicker than its cousin, Europeans were convinced that it was tenderer.

Chefs still dazzle their patrons with luxurious asparagus dishes. Consommé Argenteuil, one of many dishes named for a town that supplied Paris dining rooms with the vegetable during the nineteenth century, is one splendid example. The asparagus is cooked in a liquid suffused with egg yolks and whipping cream.

Agronomists are now attempting to breed a white asparagus that, unlike earlier efforts, would thrive in American soil. But can the white stalks ever equal verdant asparagus as an exhilarating reminder of spring? The Romans would have shaken their heads in disbelief.

THE "BUTTER PEAR"
the mysterious avocado

We had to be taught to eat and enjoy this once-exotic food. The avocado, the ancient fruit so vital to the indigenous peoples of the Americas, is now eaten by most of us as a party dip or restaurant appetizer. Most of the guacamole we scarf down is consumed during our annual bacchanals, the Super Bowl and Cinco de Mayo. How many of us have ever sampled avocado soup or savored the fragrance of an avocado leaf? Gladys Fernandez, a waitress at El Tamarindo, a Washington, D.C., Salvadoran restaurant, once told me that the avocado of her homeland *huele bien* (smells good).

In Latin America, the avocado is commonly treated as a basic staple. Families grow the tree in their dooryards. "Four or five tortillas, an avocado, and a cup of coffee—this is a good meal," according to a Guatemalan saying. In an earlier day it was dubbed the "poor man's butter."

A member of the laurel family—which includes cinnamon, bay leaf, and sassafras—the avocado plant shares their tantalizing aroma. The curious tropical vegetable, anatomically actually a fruit, has long been a source of puzzlement. It has been variously called alligator pear, avocado pear, butter fruit, and butter pear. In Mexico, where seeds dating back to 7000 BC have been discovered, the Aztecs called the tree *ahuacacuahatl*. The "testicle tree" bears fruits that hang in pairs from long stalks. The Spaniards shortened the name to *aguacate*.

The high-energy fruit, which grew wild in Mexico's highlands, was avidly pursued by the Aztecs. The Indians probably selected the larger avocados and concentrated on cultivating them. The tree's oily flesh was especially attractive

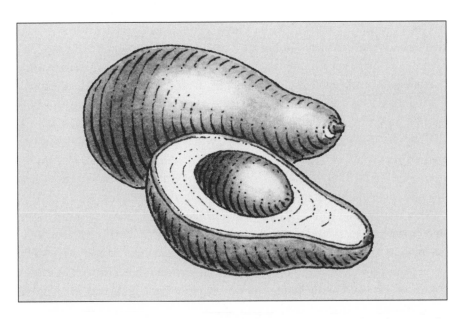

to a people who subsisted on a low-fat diet. (We now know that the avocado contains high quantities of "good" cholesterol.) Scientists have suggested that the fruit's high fat content gave it an evolutionary advantage. According to fruit specialist David Karp, they "theorize that this extravagantly rich pulp evolved to entice megafauna like mastodons and ground sloths to swallow the fruit whole and disperse the giant seeds."

The avocado offered other benefits for the aboriginal farmers. Since it was one of the few fruits that didn't ripen on the tree, the avocado could be harvested when convenient. Only when the fruit is plucked from the branch does it begin to soften. It happens then, food scientist Harold McGee explains, because it is cut off from a hormone in the leaves that prevents ripening.

Europeans were baffled by the avocado and groped for ways to utilize the strange fruit. "In the center of the fruit is a seed like a peeled chestnut," observed Fernandez de Oviedo, a Spanish chronicler of the Indies, in 1526. "And between this and the rind is the part which is eaten, which is abundant, and a paste similar to butter and of very good taste." Since the avocado resembled a pear, de Oviedo thought it pleasant to have with cheese as a dessert. José de Acosta, another Spanish writer, preferred taking his avocado with sugar, while other commentators recommended salt. Jesuit missionary Bernabé Cobo urged that avocado oil be employed for cooking and lighting. Cobo suggested that the fruits, like olives, be stored in brine.

Others remarked on the fruit's meatiness. Père Labat, a French priest who traveled through the Caribbean during the sixteenth century, observed wild pigs, carnivorous animals, gobbling up avocados on the ground: "These animals become in consequence marvelously plump, and their flesh contracts an excellent flavor."

Adding to its appeal was the similarity of avocado flesh to butter. English sailors called it "midshipman's butter," spreading it on hardtack biscuits in the 1700s.

The avocado was also invested with mythic power. William Dampier, an English buccaneer, passed on a popular superstition in an account of his "voyage round the world," published in 1697: "It is reported that this fruit provokes to lust and therefore is said to be much esteemed by the Spaniards."

The fruit gradually made its way to the United States. "Alligator pears" were first grown as ornamental plants in Florida in 1833. In California, horticulturalists pioneered the avocado industry. In the early twentieth century, Frederick O. Popenoe, owner of the West India Gardens nursery in Altadena, California, organized expeditions to Latin America to bring back budwood for grafting avocado trees. His associate Carl Schmidt returned with a plant that survived the great California fire of 1913. The tree, called the *Fuerte* ("vigorous"), was the foundation for avocado farming in the Golden State.

His son, Wilson Popenoe, a self-described "explorer" for the US Department of Agriculture, rode horseback thousands of miles through the Central American highlands, searching for tropical fruits. Part of his mission was to make the avocado a "staple foodstuff." Popenoe sent samples of budwood from the tree wrapped in moss to his sponsors in Washington.

Amateur farmers played a key role in avocado development. An unlikely innovator, a mailman who moved from Milwaukee to California, bred a new variety. After a chance planting of three hundred seeds, he produced a leathery fruit that was a cross between the Mexican and Guatemalan avocados. The Haas, a pebbly, black-skinned fruit, became a supermarket favorite. More durable than the more flavorful but thin-skinned Mexico avocado, it was eminently shippable. The Haas had another crucial advantage: it could be picked year-round. California farmers put their money on the Haas, which became the avocado of choice.

The introduction of avocados spurred a land boom in California. During the 1920s, real estate operators encouraged would-be farmers to plant the profitable crop. Sales brochures touted the avocado as a health food. "The Avocado is more than a dessert fruit or a relish . . . it is a Health fruit possessing unusual Vitalizing and Rejuvenating properties," according to one pitch. Growing avocados, real estate developer Edward Hart promised, would lead to a "heritage of Health to your children in a cluster of 'Green Gold.'"

As avocado farming expanded, the infant industry started looking for a way to market the largely unknown product. First and foremost, the fruit had to acquire a more palatable name. *Alligator pear*, spokesmen felt, was a liability. After pressure from the American Pomological Society and the USDA, the fruit was renamed *avocado*. A public relations campaign in the 1920s was mounted to rid the avocado of another negative association, with promoters assuring customers that the avocado was *not* an aphrodisiac.

The industry, then, had to determine the best audience for the fruit. As historian Jeffrey Charles tells the story, the marketers aimed their appeals to well-heeled women. During the 1920s, the California Avocado Society extolled the avocado in advertisements in the *New Yorker* and *Vogue* as the "aristocrat of salad fruits." Food writers commissioned by the organization wrote fancy recipes for avocado and grapefruit salad and avocado stuffed with lobster, which were distributed to grocery stores. Early advocates of the fruit had hoped to turn it into a basic staple, even a replacement for meat. "A pound of avocado equals a pound of beef steak," farmer William Spinks asserted in 1915. Now the industry was targeting consumers who desired good health and fitness. Avocado salad, Jeffrey Charles observed, "was now understood by nutritionists [to be] part of a healthy, lean regimen."

In post–World War II America, avocado farming was portrayed in the media as a relaxing and prosperous part-time vocation. Southern California, one columnist wrote sarcastically, became the symbol of the new lifestyle: "[I]t was made to appear that almost anyone out of the East could come to Southern California, collect an avocado tree or two, pitch a hammock between them, and wait for the fruit to ripen. When it did ripen, it immediately turned to gold. Security, prosperity, and happiness ever after."

For most of the early era of avocado marketing, little was said about the Central American origins of the product. It must have been presumed that a foreign association would have scared shoppers away. In 1970, a cover article in *Sunset* magazine, the preeminent booster of Western leisure, showcased the fruit, picturing the avocado on the cover and including a piece hailing guacamole: "Guacamole: Sauce of the Americas: It's endlessly versatile. It's a dip, a sauce, a dressing, a spread. It's guacamole."

No longer a cause for squeamishness, the avocado has arrived. At the Jolt 'N Bolt Coffee & Tea House in the Adams-Morgan neighborhood of Washington, D.C., health-conscious patrons relish avocado and hummus in pita and avocado BLT sandwiches. Not far away at Pho Viet, a Vietnamese café in Columbia Heights, the owners offer customers a traditional drink from their country— avocado and condensed milk. Clearly, the avocado is now familiar, not alien.

THE "CURIOSITY OF THE INDIES"
the baffling banana

At the Philadelphia Centennial Exhibition in 1876, an unusual fruit, wrapped in tinfoil, was on sale for ten cents. Billed as a "Curiosity of the Indies," the banana was being introduced to fairgoers.

The odyssey of the banana—assumed by many to have originated in Africa or Latin America—actually began more than seven thousand years ago in the tropical rain forests of Southeast Asia and New Guinea. Imagine fruits the size of your index finger filled with large, stony seeds; these are the wild ancestors of our supermarket banana. They lacked the succulent pulp of today's fruit, with "thin" and "mealy" flesh, according to botanist I. H. Burkill. Their buds, stems, and flowers were probably eaten as vegetables. But the plant was most serviceable for practical tasks. Its fibers were woven into nets and clothes; food was baked in banana leaves, and houses were thatched with them.

When variations in the original plant emerged that made it more appealing to eat, it is surmised, the forest dwellers concentrated on growing the new types. Mutants that were seedless and had rich pulp were gradually domesticated. The regular farming of bananas and root crops like yams transformed early cultures, paving the way for a more settled society.

Ancient farmers discovered that growing the banana plant was not difficult. The seedless fruit didn't need pollination. After a single stem, or "hand," of banana developed from its flowers, the plant died. To produce a new "tree" (the plant is technically not a tree, but rather the world's largest herb), planting a piece of its rhizome (cuttings from its shoots) was all that was required.

The first sightings by Europeans of the mysterious plant were on the Indian subcontinent. Alexander the Great's soldiers spotted bananas growing in India during their campaign in 327 BC. Alexander called the fruit a "fig," a name that Europeans later adopted. The earliest descriptions of the banana were colored by reports from the expedition's botanists. Theophrastus, the Greek botanist, described a "tree whose leaf is oblong in shape, like the feathers of the ostrich; this they [the soldiers] fasten on to their helmets."

In India, the banana came to symbolize purity and contemplation. Its name in Sanskrit, *kalpatharu*, means "virtuous plant." Buddha, the story goes, meditated in its shade. "The sages of India live on it," Pliny, the Roman naturalist, observed. When Linnaeus, the Swedish plant taxonomist, classified the banana in 1750, he gave it the Latin name *Musa* (from the Arabic *muz*, for banana) *sapientum*, "Of the Wise Men." The bountiful banana also represented fertility in Indian culture. When wedding his bride, the groom often blessed her with a present of the fruit.

Hybrids of the early Southeast Asian banana developed in India. Two types of the fruit took shape. One, the starchy plantain, has to be cooked to be enjoyed, and it is commonly eaten baked, boiled, or fried, like a vegetable. The other, the common banana, can be eaten raw and is often—but not always—sweeter than its cousin. The two, Burkill explains, are botanically very closely related: a plantain "is, as it were, a banana arrested in development before the starch in ripening is converted into sugar."

From India, the banana, probably transported by Arab traders, arrived in the Middle East. The plant fascinated Muslims, who embraced it as the Tree of Paradise from the Garden of Eden. Crusaders in the Holy Land were also impressed: "There is also another fruit called apples of Paradise," wrote Burchard of Mount Zion in 1282. "It grows like a bunch of grapes, having many grains [fruits]. . . . These grains are oblong in shape, sometimes six fingers, and as thick as a hen's egg."

The banana spread throughout Islam's expanding empire. From Egypt, where it was extensively cultivated, the plant moved west in the tenth century to North Africa, and then to Spain. Passionate about gardens, Spain's Moorish rulers cultivated bananas as well as groves of pomegranates, oranges, and lemons.

Both the banana and its close relative, the plantain, took root in Africa. More than twenty-five hundred years ago, historian J. R. McNeill theorizes, anonymous sailors carried bananas and other plants across the Indian Ocean to East Africa. He calls this journey the "monsoon exchange." The trees, in time, would dot the Indian Ocean shoreline. Visiting the region in the fourteenth century, Arab traveler Ibn Battuta discovered people in Mombasa (on the coast of what is now Kenya) savoring dishes of boiled green bananas and mangoes flavored with ginger.

As Arab traders pushed into the interior, banana trees emerged. By the time Portuguese voyagers reached West Africa in the fifteenth century, they found the coastal tribes harvesting a tree they called a *banema* or *banama*. The Africans incorporated it as a basic staple in their diet. For them, the banana—a high-yielding crop—was a crucial source of energy, far surpassing the potato. In most West African cultures today, the plantain, like other starches, is pounded into a mash called *fufu*. Often topped with a peppery sauce, this dish provides both spark and sustenance.

The Portuguese took the banana with them from West Africa as they established new beachheads in the islands of the Atlantic. Portuguese mariners carried slaves to their new sugar colonies, Madeira and the Canary Islands. The ships, historian Judith Carney points out, were stocked with bananas to provide a filling and familiar foodstuff for the captives. The Portuguese and Spaniards used the sugar islands as jumping-off points for their forays to the New World. The bananas followed.

In 1516 a Catholic friar, Tomas de Berlanga, took banana plants from the Canaries to the Spanish colony of Hispaniola. In the tropical climate of the Caribbean, bananas flourished as they never had in Spain. In the sixteenth century, as Spain acquired new possessions, bananas were planted in Mexico, Costa Rica, Ecuador, and other Latin countries.

European observers marveled at the curious fruit. The Spanish chronicler Fernandez de Oviedo was struck by how easy it was to peel the banana: "Inside it is all flesh which is very much like the marrow of the legbone of a cow." Another Spanish writer, friar José Gumilla, saw salvation in the plantain: "The plantains are the relief of all poverty; in America they serve as bread, as meat, as drink, as conserve and everything else, because they satisfy hunger in all these ways."

The slaves, and later the freedmen of the Americas, were especially fond of the plantain. In Jamaica, which Spain occupied in 1509, plantains were grown on the provision grounds that plantation owners set aside for their laborers. Later, after their emancipation, islanders grew the trees in their yards and gardens.

The plantain had a number of advantages over its cousin, the banana. To the slaves, it was more familiar, because in Africa it had been the more widely eaten of the two. Drawing on African tradition, the islanders re-created a dish akin to *fufu*. Unlike the banana, the plantain also lent itself to a variety of preparations as it ripened. Plantains, the British botanist Henry Barham pointed out, were quite versatile. "Roasted before they are ripe, they eat like bread; they are eaten boiled or roasted, and one roasted that is ripe, and buttered, eats very delicious."

In the United States, the banana was initially regarded as a luxury fruit—and a foreign one at that. Bananas began appearing in New Orleans markets during the 1830s and 1840s. The early trade in the fruit was haphazard and casual. Boats traveling to the Crescent City from the West Indies occasionally carried a few bunches on their decks. From schooners with tiny loads bought from small Caribbean farmers, descendants of slaves, the business gradually expanded into a vast industry controlled by large corporations. To provide a steady supply of America's first non-seasonal fruit to distant markets, the banana industry had to fashion an efficient, integrated operation. United Fruit Company, the banana giant formed in 1899, would own plantations, refrigerated steamships and rail lines, and its own distribution company.

The fruit itself presented an unusual set of challenges to the banana companies. Unlike many fruits that ripen best on the tree, the banana reaches its prime only after picking, starting to ripen immediately after it is harvested. In his study of the banana, Philip Reynolds explains how the fruit develops: "The necessity for infinite care in handling a bunch of bananas will be appreciated when it is realized that this fruit, when harvested, is practically a living organism drawing sustenance from its stalk, with sap flowing and tissues changing; that in the ripening process it generates heat within itself; that a few degrees of temperature above or below normal may stimulate too rapid ripening, or cause checked vitality and chill."

Seeking a variety to meet its needs, the industry seized on the Gros Michel, a breed native to Southeast Asia, which was growing in Jamaica. The plump banana was tasty and ripened to a vivid yellow color. Most important, "Big Mike" was a hardy traveler; its thick skin protected the fruit on its journey to market. In the early 1870s, a Cape Cod fishing captain, Lorenzo Don Baker, hauled the first load of "Big Mikes" from Jamaica to New England. The fruit companies soon converted their huge plantation tracts to growing this new variety.

Persuading shoppers to buy the novel item was another formidable task. Americans gingerly approached the banana. At a fancy dinner party in Boston in 1875, guests ate the luxurious fruit with knife and fork. To instruct readers, *Scientific American* published an article in 1905 on how to peel them.

The banana aroused other fears. Americans cringed about reports of snakes and spiders lurking in shipments of banana stalks. Tropical diseases, it was thought, might spread with the fruit. During a yellow fever epidemic that struck New Orleans, the largest entrepôt for tropical fruit in 1905, the city banned shipments of bananas in or out of the city. Americans also feared that bananas sold on the street might be harmful, but the *Literary Digest* assured its readers that the fruit's wrapper kept them "uncontaminated by dirt and pathogen germs, even if purchased from the pushcart in our congested streets."

Moreover, Americans were chary about raw fruit. They worried that the banana might be hard to digest and might upset their stomachs. Nutritionists and health experts calmed the public. The banana "may be served raw," an article in *Parents* magazine stated in 1920. "All its vitamins are surely retained if this is done. The stringy fiber on the outside of the peeled banana is scraped off with the blunt edge of a knife. Then the fruit, which Nature so thoughtfully gave a sanitary protective covering, is ready for consumption."

Early banana recipes also offered comforting cooked dishes, like banana pudding and pie, suffused with cream and butter.

Experts hired by the companies helped to popularize the fruit. United Fruit recruited doctors to proclaim the banana an ideal baby food. Researchers in the company's test kitchens, food historian Virginia Jenkins relates, searched for an attractive breakfast dish featuring the fruit. They decided on cornflakes with milk and bananas. In the 1920s, consumers began finding coupons for free bananas in their cereal boxes.

Culinary experts gave their blessing to the banana. The fruit "ranks with oranges in extent of consumption," Fanny Farmer, the popular cookbook author, wrote. She urged readers to try baked bananas at breakfast, a salad of cubed bananas and green peas with French dressing, and sautéed bananas with tournedos of beef.

In postwar America, the banana was gaining wider acceptance. But aggressive marketing was still needed. At the end of World War II, United Fruit began wooing shoppers with the Chiquita Banana radio jingle, which provided hints on how best to enjoy the fruit: "I'm Chiquita Banana and I've come to say, / Bananas have to ripen in a certain way, / When they are fleck'd with brown and have a golden hue, / Bananas taste the best and are best for you." A cartoon character, modeled after Carmen Miranda, the "Brazilian Bombshell," sang the ditty. The sultry figure, who carried a bowl of fruit on her head, also adorned recipe books and sheet music for the song, sent to public schools. In later years, United Fruit (renamed Chiquita) attached blue-and-gold stickers featuring her picture directly on the bananas.

Bananas have become so ordinary and plentiful that it's hard to imagine a time when they were unusual and scarce. In poor regions of the world, the fruit is still an essential staple. As scientist Kodjo Tomekpé told *Smithsonian* magazine, "Here in Africa, the banana is not about dessert or a snack. It is about survival."

HOLY BASIL

"She wrapped it up; and for its tomb did choose / A garden-pot, wherein she laid it by, / And cover'd it with mould, and o'er it set / Sweet Basil, which her tears kept ever wet." In these lines from "Isabella; or, The Pot of Basil," a poem published in 1820, John Keats portrays a grieving woman who buries the severed head of her murdered lover, Lorenzo, in a pot, covers it with soil, and plants basil on top. Faithful to his memory, she steadfastly cares for the herb. Nourished by her tears and the decomposing flesh, the plant ultimately blooms "thick and green and beautiful." The image of basil in Keats's poem is a jarring one. The herb's association with the primal emotions of life, love, and death is an unfamiliar one today. "Basil . . . was not always the innocent, delightful kitchen pot-herb that we know," anthropologist and food historian Margaret Visser observes.

In India, an ancient home of the plant, one important species called holy basil is planted in temple courtyards. Pots of the leafy bush are planted prominently on pedestals in the homes of devout Hindus. The faithful wear rosaries or garlands with beads made from its stems and roots. Women are traditionally responsible for tending the plant, the embodiment of the goddess Tulsi, the wife of Vishnu, the world's creator. Every evening, worshippers walk around the *tulsi* (the plant has the same name as the goddess), praying and chanting mantras. A lamp is lit, illuminating the holy basil throughout the night.

Holy basil, known as the "Destroyer of Demons," is believed to ward off forces of evil and to purify the air. The guardian of marriage, it also strengthens fidelity and promotes fertility. *Tulsi* is protector of both the living and the dead,

who are washed with holy basil water to ensure their path to heaven. Its leaves are often buried with the body. So venerated was the plant in colonial India that it became a touchstone of legal proceedings. The British colonial authorities required that oaths be taken in the presence of holy basil. Citizens were sworn in with leaves in their hands, which they would then chew and swallow.

Probably because of its sacred status, the tangy herb is only infrequently used in Indian cooking. An invigorating tea infused with basil, honey, and shredded ginger is a popular refreshment. Treated with awe and respect on the Indian subcontinent, basil is eaten with zest in Thailand, in stir-fries and curries. These playful Buddhists, lovers of coriander, lemongrass, and other aromatic flavorings, relish it as one more saucy herb in their repertoire. In a celebrated *ka prow* dish, holy basil leaves are strewn over chunks of stir-fried chicken, beef, or shellfish. Its anise accent blends with the sharp taste of garlic as well as the soy and red chilies in the sauce.

When basil reached the West, it arrived with mythic connotations, some of which echoed Eastern beliefs. (Sweet basil, the kind associated with Italian cooking, was the variety typically grown in Mediterranean lands.) The plant collectors in Alexander the Great's army, it is said, carried basil from Central

Asia, from Persia, India, or Afghanistan, to Greece. The Greeks named the herb *basilikon*, or "royal." (In Persia, it was given the honorific "royal leaf of the king.") Basil was so esteemed in Greece and other societies that only the king was permitted to cut it, and then only with a golden scythe, not with iron or some other ignoble metal.

In the Mediterranean world, as in India, basil is invested with awesome powers. The Greeks place pots of the talismanic herb on their doorsteps to stand guard against the "evil eye." In both Greek and Indian traditions, basil's powers were thought to be strong enough to keep mosquitoes and other insects at bay.

Its sunny exuberance made the plant ideal for the rites of courtship. In Italy, a pot of basil placed on the balcony signaled a lady's willingness to meet suitors. A man wooing a woman might wear a sprig of basil in his hair. The exchange of basil leaves between lovers was a promise of fidelity.

Although the herb was an emblem of romance, it could also convey intense grief. Sprigs of the plant, believed to have sprouted in Christ's grave, are still carried by Greek Orthodox women to the church to be blessed on St. Basil's Day, the first day of the New Year. Returning home, they scatter its leaves on the floor for good luck.

Curiously, basil carried with it the scent of danger. A scorpion, according to the Roman botanist Pliny, might spring from pounded basil placed under a stone. The insect, a symbol of lust, was said to be attracted to plants with a powerful aroma. In ancient and medieval lore, then, basil was the perfect remedy for a scorpion's sting. Like the scorpion, a fearsome serpent was intimately connected with the plant in Greek legend. The snake's name, *basilisk*, came from the same root as the Greek word for the herb. Touching the monster or being the object of its gaze was said to lead to death—and basil was the perfect antidote to its venom.

One Mediterranean region, the Italian province of Liguria (which includes the port of Genoa), was able to break the basil spell. The people of the northwest coast reveled in the flavor of the herb, which grew luxuriantly on its hilly slopes. Sailors who embarked from Genoa, food writer Waverley Root speculated, returned from their long voyages ravenous for fragrant cooking. Herb-rich dishes "offered [to] him . . . when he returned home restored for the old-time sailor the charm of the damp woods, of the verdure of the fields, of the sun on the mountain slopes, of the freshness of riverbanks."

Pesto blossomed into the favorite dish of the Italian Riviera. The basil-laden sauce, scholar Margaret Visser suggests, resembles *moretum*, a paste conceived in ancient Rome. It was made by pounding herbs like parsley and wild celery together with salt, garlic, cheese, and nuts. Olive oil and vinegar were then added to the mixture. Eaten with bread dipped in the sauce, *moretum* provided a simple, filling lunch.

Recipes for pesto, a word that comes from the Genoese *pesta* ("to pound or beat"), followed strict tradition. "The making of pesto in Genoa is a rite and must be done with mortar and pestle," food expert Giuliano Bugialli tells his readers. In the mortar, basil leaves, along with coarse salt and garlic, are crushed. As the Genoese proverb goes, *O morta o sa sempre d'aglio* (the mortar always smells of garlic). Cheese, traditionally Parmesan and Sardinian Pecorino, is beaten into the green sauce. Olive oil poured into the concoction produces a rich and fragrant medium for the pesto. Finally, crushed pine nuts, *pignoli*, impart their flavor to the sauce.

Today we take the pleasure of basil for granted. Happily, the herb no longer summons up the feelings of dread it once did. Listen to medieval herbalist Culpeper—after recounting a story of a scorpion, born in a person's brain as a result of smelling basil, the sage shudders: "I dare write no more of it."

"IT'S NOT BROCCOLI. IT'S ANDY BOY"

"It's not broccoli. It's Andy Boy," my friend Charles S. Vizzini's mother told him enthusiastically. The new brand had arrived in Brooklyn, and the Sicilian-born woman was delighted to be rid of the older, scruffy variety that had to be cleansed of ants. Of ancient Mediterranean vintage, this member of the cabbage family, bred for its clusters of undeveloped flowers still in the bud, was not swiftly adopted in America. Especially prized by ethnic Italians, broccoli was popularized in the twentieth century by the D'Arrigo Brothers, the company that marketed "Andy Boy," the first commercially branded vegetable in the United States.

Quite popular with the Romans, its name derives from the Latin word *brachium*, meaning "branch" or "arm." In Rome, farmers dubbed the vegetable's branches the "five green fingers of Jupiter." Over the years, Italian gardeners and horticulturalists domesticated new varieties. The Calabrese type is the basis for the familiar headed broccoli we eat today.

Southern Italians are especially fond of eating broccoli, steamed, sautéed in olive oil and garlic, or in a myriad of other ways. Noted for being voracious consumers of the vegetable, the Neapolitans were once called *mangia foglie*, or "leaf eaters." *Leaf* was synonymous with broccoli. The people of this port city enjoyed all parts of the plant—flowers, stems, and leaves.

Northern Europeans were initially mystified by broccoli. An early eighteenth-century gardening dictionary called it "sprout colli-flower" or "Italian asparagus." Steven Switzer, an English gardener of this period, spread the word about

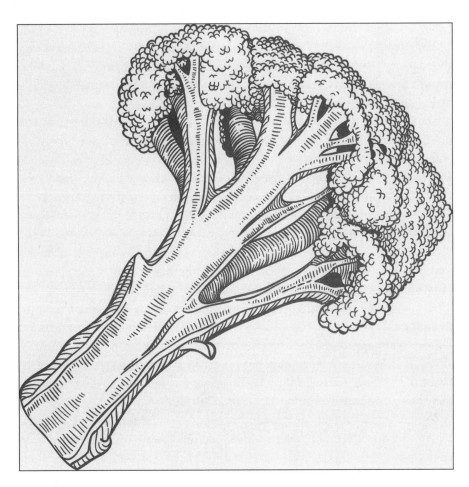

broccoli, one of what he called "foreign kitchen vegetables." The choicest broccoli came from the "sea coast about Naples and other Italian places," Switzer said, quoting an authority.

In America, broccoli initially had limited appeal. Connoisseurs like Virginia statesman John Randolph introduced it to the reading audience in a gardening treatise published in 1775: "The stems will eat like Asparagus, and the heads like Cauliflower." Jefferson tried planting broccoli seeds at his Monticello estate. As the Italian community in America grew, immigrants and their descendants, particularly those from the southern region, became broccoli's most fervent American fans.

Two Sicilian brothers played a decisive role in creating a broader, more-receptive market for the vegetable. Stephen and Andrew D'Arrigo, whose father owned a lemon farm in the Sicilian town of Messina, arrived in the United States in the early 1900s. They worked as "hods" (cobblestone carriers), shoe-factory workers, and at an assortment of other jobs before joining their cousins in running a Boston grape business, whose clientele was mostly ethnics making homemade wine.

Stephen, who moved to San Jose, California, to oversee grape shipments, was thrilled to find Italian farmers growing fennel, prickly pears, and broccoli—crops he knew from his native Sicily. The experience changed his life. Intrigued with broccoli, he attempted to grow the vegetable with seeds sent by his father. Heartened by his success, the brothers bought a twenty-eight-acre ranch in the area and began harvesting broccoli. They decided to leave the grape business and move out on their own, forming the D'Arrigo Brothers Company in 1924.

These early steps led to the entrepreneurs' major breakthrough: shipping iced broccoli in rail cars from California to the East Coast. Transported in 1925, this was the first such shipment of the vegetable in the country. The innovators were counting on marketing broccoli during the winter months, when it was sparse in East Coast states. They also were seeking to capitalize on the largely untapped market for the product among the Northeast's large Italian population, especially among the Southern Italians, who were most ardent about the vegetable. Except for a small amount grown in Brooklyn, broccoli was not readily available in the New York City area.

Gradually, the brothers increased their holdings in California's fertile Salinas Valley, to produce broccoli, celery, and other crops. They were intent on making their major product—broccoli—stand out in the retail market. Their ingenious solution: labeling the vegetable. In 1927, the company attached a pink wrapper to each bunch of broccoli. The Andy Boy label carried recipes and instructions for using the vegetable. It showed the cherubic face of Stephen's two-year-old son, Andy, who loved traipsing in the broccoli fields with his father. This marketing technique, the first commercial branding of a vegetable, increased recognition and sales among Italian consumers and, over time, in the wider national arena.

The D'Arrigos reinforced their branding with media and merchandising campaigns. Probably the first company to use the medium to promote a branded vegetable, in 1928 they advertised Andy Boy on a Boston Italian-language radio station. They expanded to English broadcasting in Boston, sponsoring "The D'Arrigo Serenaders," a musical program, on the WBZ station.

In their radio ads, the D'Arrigos extolled the vitamin- and mineral-rich vegetable to housewives. They were also the first company to provide on-air cooking instructions for a vegetable product. Richard Montgomery Mason, a radio producer who developed programming for the D'Arrigos in New York, Philadelphia, and Boston, credits the firm with educating an audience poorly acquainted with broccoli. Before the Andy Boy promotions, Mason said, "women didn't know . . . whether to throw the tops or the bottoms away."

The company also sent its sales representatives into grocery stores to train retailers in the proper handling of a vegetable that could easily wilt or spoil. D'Arrigo put up streamers and displays, handed out leaflets, and arranged demonstrations on how to prepare Andy Boy.

The marketing paid off. From twelve carloads of broccoli in 1924, D'Arrigo sales rose to more than one thousand carloads in 1945. The company was making strides in selling broccoli as more than just a largely ethnic vegetable.

A *New Yorker* cartoon that ran in 1928 showed a mother and her son at the table. The mother was pushing her son to eat some broccoli, saying, "It's broccoli, dear." Her son replied, "I say it's spinach, and I say the hell with it."

Broccoli has long had the reputation of being a vegetable that's "good for you"—not a food to be savored in its own right. Children have had to be persuaded to eat it. Andy Boy helped to dispel this severe image and make the vegetable an object of warmth and affection.

HEAD OF ITS CLASS
the cabbage

The Romans revered it. "Cabbage is a vegetable that surpasses all others," wrote Roman statesman Cato—an opinion that would jolt many of us today who either ignore cabbage altogether or dismiss it as a lowly vegetable.

Enjoy it raw, dipped in vinegar, Cato urged his readers. Cabbage also helps with digestion, he added. Cato preached that eating the leaves would prevent the ills of excessive eating and drinking: "If you wish at a dinner party to drink a good deal and to dine freely, before the feast eat as much raw cabbage with vinegar as you wish, and likewise after you have feasted, eat about five leaves. It will make you as if you had eaten nothing and you shall drink as much as you please." Cabbage was also curative. "Put crushed cabbage leaf on all wounds and tumors," Cato advised. "It will cure all these sores and make them well without pain."

The vegetable the Roman extolled was not the modern cabbage. The large leafy plant, more like kale and collards, was headless. The Latin name of the curly leafed kale and its sister, the smoother-leafed collard, means "cabbage of the vegetable garden without a head."

In later years, the cabbage lost some of its luster. The Roman satirist Juvenal scoffed at the poor man supping on his "nauseous dish" of cabbage while his patron devoured "excellent fish" garnished with olives. Lucullus, a government official, argued that the vegetable was ill suited for gentlemen.

The Roman invaders brought the large-leafed cabbage to Britain. Migrating through Europe, transported by merchants, sailors, and armies, it soon sprouted in monastic gardens. In Northern and Central Europe, the hardy plant thrived

better than any other vegetable in the chilly climate. By the end of the Middle
Ages, cabbage had become the mainstay of the peasant diet. Cheap and filling
meals were constructed around it. The Irish concocted "champ," buttery mashed
potatoes laden with cabbage, a Halloween favorite. French and German women
made soups and stews that melded potatoes, pickled pork, salted goose or duck,
and cabbage leaves.

Medieval physicians used cabbage leaves to stanch infections. They applied cabbage plasters to ulcers. The sulfur in cabbage, which caused its smell, made it an effective healing agent. In the maritime age, cabbage protected sailors on their dangerous voyages. Ships' doctors put cabbage compresses on wounds. On Captain John Cook's first expedition in 1769, forty crew members were saved by the prophylactic.

Cook, who planted cabbage in New Zealand to use for future voyages, was an enthusiastic convert. Containers of pickled cabbage were loaded onto his ships, and his crews were directed to eat the rations. The vitamin C–rich vegetable, Cook believed, would keep them from getting scurvy.

Cabbage came to the rescue during long European winters when little fresh produce was available. The German tribes devised a method of preserving cabbage by fermenting it in a salty brine. The end result was sauerkraut. (Centuries before, the Romans had pickled cabbage in a solution of sour wine, vinegar, and salt.)

Originally, sauerkraut was prepared at home. In Holland, historian Sue Shephard points out, tubs of steeping cabbage sometimes sat in the warm living rooms of homes before being shifted to the pantry or cellar. In time, workshops were processing it. The British navy was a major customer.

By the seventeenth century, the cabbage family had taken on its now-familiar form. The cabbage, whose leaves were now tightly folded to make a head, had evolved through several stages from the scraggly wild plant that grew on the rocky coastlands of Northern Europe and the Mediterranean. Through selectively breeding cabbages for distinctive features, a diverse group was developed. The cauliflower, which Mark Twain called a "cabbage with a college education," featured a head of undeveloped flower buds and stems. The kohlrabi, a cabbage with swollen stems, was also cultivated (the German word *kohlrabi* means "cabbage turnip"). Mark Twain likewise satirized Brussels sprouts, another family member, which stood out because of the budding heads on its stems. Eating a Brussels sprout, he wrote, was to rob the cabbage of its young.

Cabbage found a new home across the Atlantic. During the eighteenth century, Peter Kalm, a Swedish traveler in New York State, was struck by an odd dish offered by his landlady: "An unusual salad tastes better than one can imagine ... cabbages ... cut in long thin strips." His Dutch hostess was serving a salad her fellow nationals had introduced to the New World. *Kool sla*—the Dutch words, respectively, for "cabbage" and "salad"—was served both cold and warm. The warm salad consisted of shredded greens cooked in butter and oil, accented with vinegar, onion, salt, and pepper. Taking the English word for cabbage, *cole*, Americans started calling the dish *coleslaw*.

Cabbage, first planted in North America along the St. Lawrence River in 1540 by French explorer Cartier, was later grown along the Hudson River by Dutch settlers. English colonists took it to Virginia, where it was planted in the gardens of Washington and Jefferson. Collards, a favorite of the African slaves, became a staple of the Southern diet.

"Sauerkraut suppers" were introduced by the Pennsylvania Dutch, German-speaking immigrants who arrived in the United States during the eighteenth century. The church gatherings became a fall tradition wherever the newcomers clustered. So tied were they to their beloved cabbage that Southern soldiers during the Civil War called the Pennsylvania Dutch "sauerkraut Yankees."

Sauerkraut anchored Pennsylvania Dutch meals and highlighted festive dinners. It accompanied pork in the fall, salt pork in late winter, and fish in the early spring.

The ethnics celebrated Thanksgiving with turkey and sauerkraut. New Year's Day, however, demanded pork and sauerkraut, because, as the saying went, "the pig roots forward."

The European peasant dish gradually gained wider acceptance, until it was branded as alien during World War I. The Pennsylvania Dutch and other German speakers were pressed to call sauerkraut "liberty cabbage." Poet Charles Ziegler came to its defense:

> "Liberty Cabbage" now's the name
> But the thing remains the same.
> Has it not the old aroma?
> Is not "Liberty" a misnomer?
>
> Why discard the name as hellish
> When the thing itself you relish?
> You may flout it and may scold—
> No name fits like the old.

Who would have thought—a war of words over the humble cabbage?

THE WILD CAPER

As I embarked on this project, my wife, Peggy, mentioned that capers, the subject of my quest, were central to tartar sauce. She was right. To my surprise, I learned that capers are a common ingredient in recipes for the dish. I realized what an asset capers are to the relish. Gastronome Nigel Slater explains their contribution: "In one knife-sharp hit, this sauce of mayonnaise, gherkins, mustard, and capers continually sharpens an appetite that would soon be dulled after mouthful after mouthful of crumbed or battered food." Capers add zip to this basic accompaniment to fish, just as they spark the smoked salmon and herring of Scandinavia.

Most cultures, even ones without a reputation for spices, seem to desire some sort of verve in their food. The English, for example, were avid for capers. In the eighteenth century, they developed a creamy caper sauce to go with lamb or mutton. During Tudor and Stuart times, merchants imported barrels of capers. When capers were unavailable, cooks replaced them with buds of nasturtium or those of the broom shrub. Desperate for capers, some turned to a recipe from Mary Eaton's *The Cook and Housekeeper's Complete and Universal Dictionary* (1822): "An excellent substitute for capers may be made of pickled green peas, nasturtions, or gherkins, chopped in similar size, and boiled with melted butter."

The source of this tangy pleasure is a spiny shrub that originated in the arid terrain of Central Asia and is now especially prevalent in the Mediterranean. The caper is the green, closed bud of this plant. (The plant also produces a berry that is enjoyed by some, but here we use "caper" to mean the more familiar bud.) The

bush grows well in harsh soil and in hot, dry climates. It often grows wild along the Mediterranean coast, thriving in the salty air. The sprawling shrub sinks its roots deep into cracks in the ground and in rocky crevices. It clutches old walls and clings to ruins. Caper bushes were found growing in the Roman Colosseum and springing up along Jerusalem's Western Wall.

The farmers of Pantelleria, a tiny island between Sicily and North Africa, cultivate an exquisite caper on the volcanic slopes of this hot, windblown land. The plant flourishes between the black lava rocks.

The preparation of capers for market is a delicate, laborious task. In the early morning during the growing season, typically between May and August, workers gently pick the flower buds. They search for the smallest, tightest ones, considered the choicest (often referred to as "nonpareil"). They must also move gingerly to avoid being scraped by the protective thorns that frequently guard the buds. The Turks aptly refer to the caper as the "cat's claw." The caper is also known as the Flinders rose because of the similarity of the two plants.

Time is at a premium during the harvest period, as the buds must be picked quickly, before they open up. (After budding the caper displays white and purple flowers that give way to the caper berry.) To avoid spoiling, they then have to be immediately steeped in drums of salty brine. Further curing and pickling is required for the caper, which contains mustard oil, to lose its bitterness and achieve a pleasing pungency. Ultimately, the buds are packed for shipment in salt (the ideal preservative for flavor) or vinegar.

The caper has a rich, ancient tradition. Clay tablets dating from 130 BC found in Crete reveal that capers were used to flavor olive oil. However, the caper used to be esteemed even more for its medicinal rewards than for its piquant taste. The Greeks, who imbued sauces and stews with capers, believed the bud to be a remedy for rheumatism, flatulence, and other ills. The Roman naturalist Pliny recommended eating capers to ward off palsy and spleen ache. Capers, recent research has shown, are rich in antioxidants and vitamin C.

Other cultures have also held them in high regard. The Frenchman Ambroise Paré, a Renaissance physician, observed that "capers are good in that they sharpen the appetite and relieve bile." In the seventeenth century, Evliya Çelebi, who wrote of her travels in Turkey, extolled the virtues of the caper: "This pickle is very beneficial since it heals diseases and makes one sprightly, fit, and energetic."

Southern Italians and Sicilians have taken to the caper with gusto. The eighteenth-century Neapolitan author Vincenzo Corrado was enthusiastic about the bud's versatility. The caper is a "good condiment, not only for salads [and] salumi [cold cuts], but with cold foods, sauce, in meat ragu, in both stuffings with or without meat."

The cooks of the region excel at marrying the invigorating caper with other strong, assertive flavors. My favorite version of pasta puttanesca ("prostitute's pasta") is made with a sauce laden with capers, olives, anchovies, and garlic. (The more familiar presentation of the dish also comes with a tomato sauce.) Cookbook author Paula Wolfert suggests adding raisins and pine nuts, hallmarks of Sicilian cuisine. Ladies of the evening, the story goes, whipped up this plate for a quick, hearty repast between clients.

Sicily's classic relish, caponata, is unthinkable without capers. Sweet and sour, it is a blend of olives, tomatoes, eggplant, and capers, enhanced with a little sugar and vinegar. Other Mediterranean regions have also made ingenious use of the bud. In Provence, a paste is made from pounding olives, capers, and anchovies. Tapenade, which gets its name from the regional dialect's word for "caper," is a delightful tangy and salty spread.

Some are still unpersuaded of the caper's virtues. In one episode of *The Sopranos*, the family's Russian maid pointed to a jar of capers in the refrigerator and declared, "Special capers from Italy. Soprano kids don't like them."

FROM ARABIA
TO SCANDINAVIA
a cardamom chronicle

Although few of its devotees realize it, the aroma of chai, the popular spiced tea they find so addictive, usually comes from an ancient spice—cardamom. The seductive fragrance of cardamom also permeates households in Saudi Arabia and neighboring lands during Ramadan. Far away in icy Scandinavia, the Swedes, Norwegians, and Finns are equally ardent about the spice.

Native to India, cardamom has long been a magnet for explorers. Lined with coconut and palm trees, India's Malabar Coast has lured mariners, adventurers, and traders hunting for cardamom, black pepper, and cinnamon. Phoenicians, Romans, and Arabs, among the many seekers, have landed on these lush southwestern shores. From these beachheads, they ventured inland toward the Cardamom Hills, in whose rainy evergreen forests spices grew abundantly.

Large leafy bushes of cardamom flourish in their high altitudes and shady areas. "It luxuriates in mists and fogs and cooling breezes," remarked George Watt, an English botanist. From the base of this rhizome, a member of the ginger family, stems sprawl out along the ground. Light-green pods, the cardamom's "fruits," sprout on the stalks. Inside each pod are the coveted spices, fifteen to twenty small, sticky black seeds. When the seeds are roasted, they release oils that produce a captivating fragrance, suggestive of lemon and eucalyptus. British food writer Diane Henry says that the aroma reminds her of roses and licorice.

Trading empires clashed in their zeal to control India's spice treasures. The Portuguese were the first of the European powers to send their fleets to the Indian Ocean. Determined to dislodge the Arabs, who had long commanded the region's sea lanes, they built trading posts and "factories" (for storing and processing the spices) along the Malabar Coast in the early sixteenth century. Before long, Portuguese caravels were hauling spices, along with indigo, rubies, and coconut oil, back to Lisbon.

The "Queen of Spices" was especially desirable because it could be used in so many alluring ways. Cleopatra, it is said, burned the spice in her chambers to woo Marc Antony when he visited Egypt. The Greeks and Romans prized it as a perfume.

In India, cardamom played a sacred, ritualistic role. Early Hindus honored the god Rama by offering him a drink flavored with ginger and cardamom. The Indians also relished cardamom in their food. The spice is a key element in many of the *masalas* (spice mixtures), as well as in curry powder. Its aroma permeates rice dishes like *pilau*, the South Asian version of pilaf.

Cardamom is most prominent in Indian sweets, a fixture of weddings, holidays, and parties. *Kheer*, a rice pudding often sprinkled with pistachios, almonds, and raisins, has the intense fragrance of cardamom. Indian tea also gets its intensity from cardamom. The sweet, milky drink called *masala chai* is spiced with it, the cardamom flavor providing a foil to the bitterness of the tea.

The same qualities—intoxicating aroma and flavor—that made the spice a popular ingredient also gave cardamom a medicinal allure. The Ayurveda, the traditional system of Indian medicine, recommended cardamom for promoting digestion and increasing the flow of saliva. It was also supposed to clean the teeth.

Chewing *paan*—a combination of spices that often includes cardamom, and is wrapped in a heart-shaped leaf—is a venerable custom that continues to be a refreshing and healthy pastime. To sweeten their breath and to help them digest their meal, Indians chew cardamom seeds as an after-dinner cleanser. "They mix it with their betel [a kind of leaf] to give it a pleasant scent," the seventeenth-century Portuguese physician Garcia de Orta said.

The doctor also described cardamom's curative powers. "They say it draws out inflammations from the head or stomach." Cardamom's eucalyptus scent also made it an attractive remedy for respiratory ills. "The Indians use it a great deal to open the nasal passage and to clear the head," de Orta noted.

Other cultures have placed their faith in its cleansing powers, as well. The Roman gastronome Apicius concocted a powerful *digestif* for diners that was a blend of cardamom, mint, cumin, and black pepper.

The world's third most expensive spice (after saffron and vanilla), cardamom was considered a royal prerogative in India. In the court, it was customary to of-

fer guests the spice as a gesture of hospitality. Extending his palm, the host would offer a few pods to visitors, who were expected to grasp them with two fingers.

India's Moghul emperors carried the pods coated in edible gold and silver in a silver cask akin to a snuffbox. The royals and their retinue chewed on them all day to freshen their mouths.

A similar practice prevailed in China. To purify themselves, mandarins prepared for an audience with the emperor by nibbling on cardamom.

The Arab world also fell in love with the spice. Centuries ago, their *dhows*, small vessels propelled by the monsoon winds, sailed across the Arabian Sea to India. They returned from the Malabar Coast with loads of cardamom and other spices. Cardamom, they discovered, married well with coffee, the drink Arabs had created.

Bedouins, nomadic tribesmen in the Arab states, introduced the cardamom habit. Traditionally, a split green pod was placed in the coffeepot spout. Today the roasted beans are boiled with ground cardamom. The drink is then poured from a brass pot with a long, curving spout into small cups.

Sharing coffee is a hallmark of social gatherings and festive occasions in the Arab world. The luxurious spice is meant to elevate these events and to express hospitality. To mark a particularly special event, like a wedding, cardamom is lavishly added to the coffee.

During the month of Ramadan, cardamom consumption in Saudi Arabia and its neighbors soars. Preparing coffee during the day binds families together. At dusk, when the fast is finally broken, a cardamom-infused cup of *qahwa* is a pleasure to be savored.

Arab artists have long extolled the glories of cardamom. In the 1960s, Samira Tafiq, a singer known as the "passionate Bedouin girl," had a big hit with her recording, "Pour the Coffee and Don't Spare the Cardamom."

Arabian countries no longer import their cardamom from India, but, oddly enough, from Guatemala. Saudi Arabia, the world's largest user of the spice, is the Latin American country's biggest market. The export of cardamom, first planted in Guatemala in the early twentieth century by German settlers, is highly profitable. "Cardamom is the heart of our economy, and Guatemala is the biggest exporter [of the spice] in the world," Otto Chavarria, a prominent *cardamomero* from the mountainous province of Alta Verapraz, told journalist Larry Luxner. "In this province, cardamom is even more important than coffee."

Because the Saudis covet the greenest and plumpest pods, Guatemalan workers carefully pick and sort the spice pods by color and size—an arduous process. "Cardamom pods are like Christmas trees," Dr. Luis Pedro Torrebiarte, president of the Cardamom Growers Association in Guatemala, told Luxner. "The greener and bigger they are, the more they're worth."

Not far from the Gulf nations, in Ethiopia, cardamom is inseparable from tea drinking. Nations in the Horn of Africa have long traded with India and Arabia. Cardamom, one of the fruits of that trade, is roasted in Ethiopian households to flavor tea. When Ethiopians traveled to America, they brought their enthusiasm for cardamom with them. Packages of the "tea spice" line the shelves of their grocery stores.

The spice also journeyed to an unlikely location—the countries of Scandinavia. Some speculate that the Vikings, extensive travelers, transported the aromatic there from Constantinople. In these northern lands, families stock their cupboards with cardamom, which imparts a sweet fragrance to breads, cakes, pastries, and other treats.

Kardemummakaka, a Swedish coffee cake, is scented with cardamom. It is also essential to Swedish sweet breads. *Julekake*, a Norwegian Christmas bread studded with candied fruit and raisins, is made with the spice. The Finns bake a *pannukakku*, a pancake fragrant with cardamom. It "billows from the oven like a giant Yorkshire pudding," as journalist Robert Jurney describes it.

During the frigid holiday season, Scandinavians celebrate with cardamom-infused refreshments. Swedish mulled wine, *glogg*, is a blend of red wine, cardamom, cloves, cinnamon, ginger, and orange peel. It is reminiscent of heavily spiced medieval drinks like mead.

Cardamom also enlivens savory dishes in Northern Europe. Swedish meatballs are flavored with the spice. Germans season pickled herring with cardamom and use it in some varieties of sauerbraten.

When Scandinavians emigrated to America, they brought their passion for cardamom with them. Its aroma filled the room when newcomers and their friends gathered for coffee. Cardamom-spiced breads and cakes were a fixture of these occasions.

Cardamom continues to be reincarnated. In pursuit of ever-new flavors and fragrances, modern marketers have resurrected it. Sellers of aromatherapy products purvey cardamom oil to stave off fatigue and stress. Perfumes emit its aroma. The now-shuttered Elettaria (Latin for cardamom), an Indian restaurant in New York City, offered the Eighth Wonder cocktail, a blend of cardamom-infused bourbon, lemon juice, and sweet vermouth.

Chai, the tea often infused with cardamom, is being offered in varied forms—iced chais, smoothies, shakes, cocktails, and even chocolate bars. "Chai is a high-profile replacement for those who don't drink coffee," Don Reynolds, owner of Port City Java in Wilmington, North Carolina, told the *Nation's Restaurant News*.

Meanwhile, back in India, a company has unveiled a cardamom-flavored toothpaste. It is marketing the mouth freshener of old as a healer of gums and a remedy for tooth infection, proving the timeless appeal of this spice.

THE CARROT PURPLE

The orange carrot, now so familiar, was once a novelty. In fact, this young up-start was first cultivated a little more than four hundred years ago. Until then, the purple variety was dominant. Although we consider the carrot immutable, it has been continually reinvented through the ages.

The weedy wild carrot is the oldest form of the plant. Scientists have uncovered wild carrot seeds at Neolithic campsites in southern Germany and Switzerland dating back to 2500 BC. Unlike other members of its family—like dill, anise, coriander, and parsley, with their characteristic umbels (clusters of flowers) and aromatic seeds and roots—the carrot was not quickly cultivated. Its sisters, mostly grown in the Mediterranean and used as aromatics and medicines, seem to have been more highly valued.

The wild carrot, which has a tiny, thin root, is the forebear of today's robust, fleshy vegetable. The plant, which sprouts prolifically in the fields and roadsides, came to be known as Queen Anne's lace. Since it was avidly chewed by the animals, it was also known as "cow's currency." Wild carrot also rapidly goes to seed. To protect its bounty of seeds, the plant's umbel closes, forming a "bird's nest," giving it another popular nickname.

Its pretty white flowers and striking umbels, sometimes with more than twelve thousand petals, make it especially attractive. In its center, a purple flower often springs up. The royal shade was said to have come from a single drop of blood that fell from Queen Anne's finger when she pricked it while sewing lace.

The wild carrot was an unappealing food because of its bitterness, although its acrid taste did win it favor as a medicine. The plant, whose botanical name, *Daucus*, is derived from the Greek word for "burn," was a popular diuretic and stomach soother. The seventeenth-century English herbalist Nicholas Culpeper praised its benefits to the body: "Wild carrots belong to Mercury, and expel wind and remove stiches in the side, promote the flow of urine and women's courses, and break and expel the stone . . . it helpeth conception." The flower was said to cure epilepsy.

The carrot has been long regarded as an aphrodisiac. The Greek name for the wild root was *philtron*, the word for "loving." Many years later, the carrot retained its erotic mystique. Men in 1870s Tehran, food writer Jane Grigson reports, swore that carrots stewed in sugar enhanced their potency.

To noble ladies, the wild carrot also provided an alluring adornment. During the seventeenth-century reign of England's King James I, women of the court decorated their hair, their hats, and their dresses with its feathery fronds.

How did this primitive plant come to be domesticated? An expedition of Russian agronomists found a wide variety of carrots—both wild and cultivated, and many a vivid purple—growing in Afghanistan in the 1920s. The domesticated carrot, they concluded, was first grown in mountainous terrain, where the ridges of the Hindu Kush mountains and the Himalayas meet, in the tenth century AD.

Farmers of the region, it is surmised, were unhappy with the scrawny, fork-rooted wild carrot. Through a process of selection, they were able to cultivate a tastier vegetable with thicker, smoother roots that was also more easily harvested.

"Eastern carrots," purple and yellow—the yellow likely a mutant of the former—moved west from Afghanistan. They were introduced to the wide reaches of the Islamic empire by travelers and merchants. From Afghanistan, carrots traveled to Iran, where they were reported in the tenth century. These "Eastern carrots" cropped up in Syria one hundred years later. From North Africa, the Moorish conquerors of Spain introduced them to their new colony. In this kingdom known as Andalusia, Ibn al-Awwam, an Arab agriculturist, observed them. The purple carrot, he found, was "more succulent" than the yellow. He also highlighted the carrot's other desirable attributes. It was a "diuretic" plant that "increases the sexual appetites" and "delights the heart."

In these oldest carrot heartlands, the root vegetable assumed a prominence, even a grandeur, that would be puzzling to us. In Afghanistan and neighboring Iran, elaborate rice pilaf dishes typically served at weddings, fancy parties, and other special occasions highlight the carrot. *Qabili pilau*, Afghanistan's national dish, is "nearly always made for guests and other special occasions much more than any other pilau," Afghan food expert Helen Saberi points out. The plate of layered basmati rice mixed with scrumptious chunks of lamb is adorned with raisins and brilliant orange strips of carrot. The name for this Afghan variant on pilaf reflects the intense dedication and effort that goes into it. *Qabili*, Saberi notes, means something "well executed or well done."

An Iranian pilaf, *morasa' polow*, is an equally extravagant delicacy in which the carrot is featured. The King of Persian dishes, as it has been called, is topped with jewel-like decorations—pistachios as emeralds, barberries as rubies, rock candy as diamonds. Layered in the rice are carrots, glazed with sugar and resplendent with a saffron sheen. A must for weddings, Iranian food expert Margaret Shaida observes, it promises the couple a plentiful future. Carrots star in another Iranian specialty, *haveej polow*, which is made like the *morasa'*. Author Shaida points out that unlike its jeweled sister, it generally graces the "less opulent" wedding.

Regarded less as a root vegetable than as a sweet in Iran, the carrot is blended into Persian jams and syrups. The Persians have conjured up a carrot jam that has the look of orange marmalade. It has the fragrance of sweet cardamom, rose water, and sour orange peel. Almonds, frequent companions to carrots in Persian dishes, contribute their flavor to the confection. The jam, Shaida explains, is meant as a dip, not as a spread for bread. The carrot sweet is served over ice cream and also spooned into tea.

In India, another cradle of the ancient root vegetable, cooks in the Punjab, the country's breadbasket, invented a carrot halvah that is now popular throughout the nation. Unlike the familiar Middle Eastern halvah, which is dry and crumbly, the Punjabi sweet is more like a thick pudding. (*Halvah* derives from the Arabic word for "something sweet.") Glazed with sugar and slowly cooked in milk and a buttery ghee, the winter carrot treat is a rich repast. Cardamom lends a sweet spiciness to the pudding. The halvah is garnished with almonds, a hallmark of the food that Muslim migrants brought to North India.

The peregrinating carrot left the Mediterranean and took root in Holland, France, and Germany during the 1300s. A century later, Flemish exiles fleeing persecution in Holland transplanted the vegetable to England. English diplomat Thomas Elyot warmly received the new arrival: "Parsneppes and carrettes . . . do nourish with better juyce than the other rootes." The purple carrot would become a common garden crop in Western Europe.

Initially, the carrot was cloaked in mystery. Many did not know what it looked like. "Carrots are red roots sold by the handful in the market," a Parisian man instructed his new wife in the fourteenth century. (What we today describe as "purple" was typically termed "red" in that era.)

After an early embrace, Europeans grew dissatisfied with the purple carrot. The issue was not flavor, because the pigment had no appreciable effect on taste. The purple carrot's disadvantage was that its color seeped into sauces, soups, and stews, turning them a brownish purple. The color also leaked onto the cook's hands. The yellow variety soon supplanted it.

But the reign of the yellow carrot was short-lived, and an orange root soon took center stage. Dutch agronomist Otto Banga documented the change. During the 1950s, Banga examined still-life paintings in the Louvre and other museums and detected an intriguing pattern. By the seventeenth century, orange carrots had become more prominent in Dutch painting. He noted, for example, a bunch of long, pale yellow-orange carrots in a kitchen scene drawn by P. C. van Rijck in the early 1600s. During the course of the seventeenth century, Banga found a deeper orange shade in the carrots portrayed.

Banga argued that the paintings proved the Dutch had bred an orange carrot, selecting plants that had grown up in the population of yellow carrots and improving on them. "Unlearned vegetable growers," he suggested, were the pioneering cultivators. The mostly female farmers in time produced four orange varieties, from which all similarly colored modern types descend.

Carrots were no longer simply carrots. Systematic breeding and classification of the vegetable originated in the seventeenth century. Carrots were categorized by the size, shape, and length of their roots, factors that increased their yield.

No one has definitively solved the puzzle of the orange carrot. We know that it achieved Western supremacy, but we don't know exactly why. The color took hold in Holland, it is argued, because of Dutch nationalism. This carrot reputedly honored William of Orange and his House because the orange variety was developed during his reign. It was also excellent nourishment for farm animals. The Dutch attributed the creamy yellow butter made from their Holsteins' milk to a diet of orange carrots.

But what explains the orange carrot's wider appeal? University of Wisconsin geneticist Philipp Simon offers a commonsense speculation that may be the most convincing: "The orange must have tasted pretty good or they might have gotten rid of it."

The once-alien carrot has become a staple in the food of many cultures, each of which has placed its own unique stamp on it. Carrots lend themselves to stews and soups but also to sweeter treatments. Dishes were also conceived that capitalized on the flavor of what many experts dub "the second-sweetest vegetable." In eighteenth-century Europe, food writer Jane Grigson observes, this was not unusual: "When new vegetables came in, they were viewed without savoury prejudice."

In Europe, cooks seized on the carrot to sweeten dishes when sugar and other alternatives were scarce or too costly. Frugal Europeans, some say, sometimes ground up the root to make sugar. Recipes for carrot pudding were regularly published in English cookbooks of the seventeenth and eighteenth centuries. This pudding, a likely ancestor to America's pumpkin and sweet potato pie, is a custardy confection. Food historian Charles Perry observes that "it looks like a pie, only with a slightly crunchy topping instead of crust. It cuts like cake, except that there's a thin layer of custard on the bottom. The texture is a cross between bread pudding and a moist cookie."

Hannah Glasse, the famous eighteenth-century English food writer, devised a recipe for carrot custard in puff pastry. She lavished eight eggs, half a pound of melted butter, and half a pint of cream in the dessert. She burnished it with nutmeg and three spoonfuls of orange blossom water, a fragrance introduced from the Middle East.

In her *American Cookery* (1796), the first American cookbook, Amelia Simmons prepared her carrot pudding with equal flair. She accented hers with cinnamon instead of nutmeg and perfumed it with rose water, another Middle Eastern exotic.

Throughout Europe's two world wars, carrot sweets filled the void when sugar was rationed in England. During World War I, the Ministry of Food circulated recipes to housewives for carrot pudding and carrot cake, as well as flan, toffee, fudge, and marmalade made from the root.

The carrot has played a major role in the culinary traditions of Eastern Europe. One of the few sweet vegetables in the frigid shtetls of Poland and Russia, the carrot carried auspicious associations in Jewish communities. The Yiddish word for carrot, *mehren*, also means "to increase and multiply." Carrots, which resemble gold coins when sliced, kindled hopes for good fortune and prosperity. Carrots, apples, raisins, and honey, fixtures of the Rosh Hashanah New Year's table, were tokens of a sweet happiness to come. Often replacing turnips in holiday rituals, carrots feature in a stew that pairs them with prunes or other dried fruit. The dish, known as *tzimmes* (from the German "to eat"), frequently suffused with cinnamon and honey, conveys the festive holiday spirit. Jewish food writer Faye Levy figured out a way to accentuate the sweetness in her *tzimmes*.

After enjoying *carottes glacées* (carrots cooked slowly in sugar and butter) in France, Levy used this technique to prepare the carrots for her stew.

There is a striking resemblance, some suggest, between this Eastern European stew and a dish from an ancient culture with an equally deep love for the carrot. A classic Persian stew, or *khoresh*, also marries carrots and prunes. Perhaps the idea reached Poland with the medieval Jewish merchants who forged commercial ties between Europe and Central Asia. Some of the traders married Poles and left their mark on the food. Remains of carrots have, in fact, been dug up in Krakow's main market square. Even if the speculation is far-fetched, it does demonstrate the shared affinity of disparate cultures for the bountiful carrot.

The modern carrot continues to evolve, especially in the hands of American agriculturists. Feeling the pressure to develop and market new products, growers have ceaselessly transformed the vegetable. In the 1950s, carrots, which were first sold in bulk, began to be sold in the United States in cellophane bags. The "cello carrot" required no change in the carrot's appearance. "It had to look like a carrot and that was enough," geneticist Dr. Philipp Simon points out. The latest marketing innovation, baby carrots, demanded a reconfigured product and a change in emphasis on the kind of carrot grown.

Mike Yurosek, a California farmer, revolutionized the industry by dreaming up the "baby carrot" idea. Tired of throwing out four hundred tons of imperfect carrots a day at his Bakersfield packing plant, he pondered how to make more-efficient and profitable use of his crop. Freezing firms bought his carrots and cut them into cubes, coins, and other shapes. "If they can do that, why can't we, and pack 'em fresh?" he calculated.

After first cutting carrots by hand in his own kitchen, he bought an industrial green-bean cutter from a failing frozen-food company. The machine turned out two-inch pieces of the root. By 1989, Yurosek had built a mechanized operation to turn out his product. Marketed as baby carrots, the miniatures are not young vegetables at all. "They're grown-up carrots cut up into two-inch sections, pumped through water-filled pipes into whirling cement-mixer-size peelers, and whittled down to the niblets Americans know, love, and scarf down by the bagful," journalist Elizabeth Weise wrote.

The "fresh-cut" segment of the carrot industry, which includes baby carrots and items like carrot chips, carrot sticks, and shredded carrots, is the fastest-growing and most profitable. Baby carrots, the business's "sweetheart," as scientist Simon calls them, have spurred growers to concentrate on harvesting a long, thin, narrow vegetable. A shorter, fatter root is less suitable for process-ing the high-value product.

"Prior to baby carrots, the ideal length for a carrot was somewhere between six and seven inches," Simon notes. An eight-inch carrot, a "three-cut," can produce three two-inch babies. Further lengthening the carrot is a boon to the farmer. "You make it a four-cut, and you've got a thirty-three percent yield in-crease," Simon says.

Because fresh carrots must be mass-produced in elaborate, large-scale facili-ties, the industry is now the preserve of large corporations with deep pockets. Two firms, Bolthouse and Grimmway, control the market.

The production of carrots may be rapidly changing, but carrot tastes remain stubborn. Most of us remain wedded to the orange carrot that has only burst on the scene comparatively recently. "Purple and yellow carrots were eaten more than a thousand years [ago] in Afghanistan and seven hundred years ago in Western Europe," geneticist Simon says. Simon, who directs the US Department of Agriculture's vegetable-breeding program at the University of Wisconsin-Madison, is America's leading scientific breeder of carrots.

Simon studied potatoes as a graduate student. "This was the job that was available," says the scientist, who grew up in rural Wisconsin. "I would have been glad to work in wheat." Simon later stumbled into carrot research because of his interest in genetics. The wide spectrum of colors among carrots piqued his curiosity. What genetic factors, he wondered, explained this phenomenon? "I got interested because it was unusual," he said. He jumped into his investigation before he realized that colors were of "nutritional significance."

In an early experiment, Simon sharply increased beta-carotene, the pigment in the orange carrot. Carotene is also used by the body to manufacture vitamin A. The deeper orange root he produced contained four times as much of the coloring as the standard carrot. Manipulating the vegetable's hue, he was learn-ing, conferred significant health benefits. "About thirty percent of the vitamin A we consume comes from carrots," Simon told a reporter in 1995. "It used to be fourteen percent about twenty-five years ago, but it has increased due to the higher beta-carotene levels in carrots today."

Like beta-carotene, the pigments responsible for other colored carrots also guard the body just as they shield plant cells during photosynthesis. Lycopene, the coloring in red carrots, protects against heart disease and may help to keep prostate cancer at bay. The xanthophylls in yellow carrots help ensure healthy eyes. The anthocyanins, which make carrots purple, are strong antioxidants.

The strange-colored vegetables, Simon recognized, had to be modified before they would be accepted. The purple carrot his laboratory acquired from Turkey, for example, had several handicaps. Since it was not as tasty as the orange, Simon crossed the two to make a more flavorful variety. The hybrid had another advantage: it resisted disease that the purple was victim to. "We were fascinated by dark purple carrots from Turkey, but back in Wisconsin, they literally melted in the face of sclerosia, a pathogen that attacks many carrots, but not orange ones," Simon observed. "We didn't even know this disease was still around."

Turkey's purple carrot is responsible for one of the country's most popular refreshments. Şalgam is a cool summer drink that relies on the root vegetable for its flavor. To make it, pickled carrots and turnips are fermented in barrels. Served in large glasses with a side dish of pickled carrots, it complements spicy kebab dishes. Şalgam also helps to settle the stomach, its fans say, and softens the effects of raki, the intoxicating anise-flavored Turkish beverage. Ersu, a Turkish company, has begun bottling black carrot juice, extracted from what we would call purple carrots, for export to the United States and other countries. In one of my last conversations with Simon, the carrot expert mentioned bringing two cases of purple carrot drink back from Turkey. A bit uncomfortable with the flavor, he stashed the bottles in an office closet.

Oddly colored vegetables are a hard sell in America. Burpee's Purple Dragon Carrots and All Blue Potatoes were "flopperoos," George Ball, the seed company's chairman, told the Wall Street Journal. "The sight of blue is unappetizing to many people," he said. "I couldn't give them away."

Dr. Simon is still struggling to break down American resistance to multicolored carrots. The purple carrot, however flavorful, makes consumers nervous, even though the shade has no effect on the taste.

Before sampling his vegetables, Simon found, people would ask, "Are they really carrots?" or "Are they safe to eat?" "We've become married to the colors we associate with particular foods," he learned. "We eat with our eyes, to some extent."

THE NUTTY FRUIT
the captivating cashew

The bountiful evergreen captivated the Jesuit priest: "It furnished food and household remedies for the poor, a refreshing beverage to the sick, a sweetmeat for tables richly served, and resin and good timber for industrial uses." The cashew tree that excited Father J. S. Tavares on his travels through Brazil in the early 1900s is parent to the familiar nut. It also bears an unusual-looking apple—a mystery to most Westerners, but a delight to people of the tropics. To them, a Mexican friend told me, the fruit is "famous." Many Latinos throw the nut away and eagerly hold on to the apple.

In the tropics, brilliant red and yellow fruits resembling bell peppers dangle from branches of low-spreading evergreens. Attached to these apples are green, kidney-shaped nuts that some have likened to small boxing gloves. The object of much affection, the cashew is a member of the curious family of plants that includes poison ivy, as well as the mango and pistachio. All exude irritating, sometimes harmful liquids.

In the international economy, it is the cashew nut, not the fruit, that excites the most interest. The cashew is an expensive item because it demands such careful handling. Inside the shell are acrid and injurious oils that protect the nut from insect invaders. Bite into this "blister nut" at your peril, as it will cause severe burns on your mouth and lips. As a result, in order to be fit to eat, the cashew must be roasted, its shell extracted, and the harmful liquids removed. This is why shoppers never see the nut in its shell.

Native to northeastern Brazil, the hardy cashew tree grows wild on the coastal sands and in the Amazon forest. Easily spread, its colorful apples attract birds, and the nuts entice bats. The fruit, which floats easily, travels down waterways to new seedbeds.

The cashew is deeply embedded in the folkways of the country's Indians. It attracted the Tupi-Guarani Indians, who called it *acaju*, or "to pucker the mouth." They harvested the tree's apples and squeezed from them an invigorating, astringent juice. The Indians fermented the fruit to make a "fragrant and delicious wine," wrote the sixteenth-century Portuguese plantation owner Gabriel Soares de Souza. The cashew, the Guarani believed, also had healthful qualities. The fruit's juice, de Souza observed, was thought to be good for the "conservation of the stomach," adding that the Indians ate the nuts in the morning "for a good breath."

The cashew remains a popular remedy in Brazil. In the Amazon today, cashew juice and tea made from its bark are used to treat diarrhea.

Equally important, the tree served as a guidepost. The Guarani measured time by determining how long it took the cashew apple to ripen. They calculated their ages by counting the nuts on the tree.

Portuguese colonists learned from the Indians how to take advantage of the trees. They were taught how to burn off the caustic liquids in the shell by roasting the nuts over an open fire. They also acquired a taste for the potent cashew brew. By distilling the wine into brandy, they heightened its punch. In Brazil's "big houses," the brandy became the slave master's drink of choice. Sent home to Portugal, toasted cashews were adopted as a tasty after-dinner treat.

Venturing along the coasts of India and East Africa, the Portuguese spice traders planted cashew seeds on the shores. Possibly first introduced to prevent erosion, the sturdy tree took root. Cashew seeds escaped, and semi-wild thickets of the trees soon formed.

First planted in Goa, the hub of the Portuguese commercial empire, the cashew migrated through much of South India. All along the southwestern coast, people adopted *caju*, the Portuguese name for the tree. The fruit was also known as the "Portuguese mango."

The cashew captivated Dutch writer Jan van Linschoten, who lived in Goa during the 1580s. "They are of a pale green and thicke, with white blossoms like Oringe trees, but thicker of leaves, yet not so sweete of smell. The fruite is in greatnesse and forme like a Goose Egge, or a great Apple, verie yellow & of good

savor, [moist or] spungie within, and ful of juice, like Lemmons, but without kernels: sweet of taste."

He urged his readers, however, to be cautious about the nuts: "For wher the apples have a stalke, these Cajus have a Chestnut, as big better and more savorie to eat, but they must be rosted. When they are raw and unrosted, you must not open them with your mouth, for as soon as you put them to your mouth, they make both your tongue and your lippes to smart." Happily, the roasted nuts, he points out, "provoke lust."

Infatuated with the cashew fruit, the Goans made a hard liquor from the apple. In Goa, a cottage industry sprang up in the villages to produce *feni*, the cashew drink whose name comes from the word for "froth." During the festive harvest season, farmers and distillers, often working together in family units, labored feverishly. In the lush green cashew groves, the apple harvest today often continues in time-honored ways: "After being plucked from the tree or those fallen underneath the tree, the apples are crushed laboriously with the feet as in the case of thrashing the paddy," one participant wrote. Enjoyed for its intoxicating punch, *feni* is also considered a drink with laxative, diuretic, and other powers.

In recent years, large distillers have been cashing in on the *feni* market. Dissatisfied with *feni*'s image as a local country toddy, they are positioning it as a drink for tourists and young sophisticates. There may even be a global market for the liquor, some promoters believe. *Feni*, some think, may become the equivalent of Mexico's tequila.

In Mozambique, the cashew nut was long neglected in favor of the more pleasurable apple. In 1895, food writer Julia Morton notes, the government condemned the cashew tree as a "source of vice and ruin." To curtail drinking, it even outlawed cashew cultivation for a time.

Both Portuguese colonies made use of the cashew in their cooking. Cooks sprinkled the nuts on sweets like rice pudding, and adorned pilafs, biryanis, and other rice dishes with them. Ground cashews thicken rich sauces. A symbol of prosperity, the golden cashew marks celebratory gatherings. *Caju barfi*, a nut fudge covered with edible silver foil, is served at weddings. *Poori*, a puffy bread, is made from cashew flour for the summer festival honoring Ganesha, the elephant god.

In Mozambique, which has a large Indian population, cashews also infuse curries. Ground cashews are an important ingredient in *matapa*, a classic dish of shrimp or crab and greens, flavored with chilies and coconut milk.

However, it was the profitable nut, not the seductive fruit, that ultimately became the focus of commerce in India and Mozambique. The advent of cashew-shelling machinery and the establishment of plantation farming increased output. In addition to the nut itself, its acrid oil developed into a major export item. The oil is used for brake-lining lubricant, waterproofing, varnish, and other industrial products.

By the 1950s, India had achieved supremacy in the world cashew market, and it is still the largest exporter of the nut today. But the subcontinent was only one of several destinations for the wandering cashew. Searching for spices in Southeast Asia, the Portuguese transported the plant to Malacca, the trading crossroads they seized on the Malay Peninsula. By the seventeenth century, it had no doubt reached China. The familiar chicken and cashew dish of Chinese restaurants reflects the culture's fondness for the nut.

Ironically, Brazil, the cashew's birthplace, was a latecomer in capitalizing on its resource. While India and Mozambique were advancing in their production methods, Brazilian peasants were handling the nut in the most primitive ways. An American missionary in 1963 lamented their efforts: "They burn them over wood fires on perforated kerosene-tin sections, allowing the fire to flame and scorch them atrociously before quenching in sand and then cracking on any stump or stone. Unsightly, unclean . . . they sell because they are the only nuts our people have."

Finally, Brazil organized a more efficient system of growing cashew trees, processing the nuts, and extracting their valuable chemical by-products for the export market. In the midst of this modernization, the age-old appetite for the nut lives on. Cooks grind cashews into *vatapa*, a puree of dried shrimp, coconut milk, chilies, and peanuts—a traditional Brazilian sauce.

The custom of collecting cashew apples and converting them to tasty uses remains a vital part of Brazilian life. A young Brazilian immigrant I met remembers learning the hard way not to eat the fruit until it is perfectly ripe: "Your tongue falls off" if you partake of the unripe, astringent apple. In the villages, preparing the cashew is a family activity. Mothers squeeze a refreshing juice from the apples and make *doces*—sweets—from them. Jellies, jams, and apples in syrup are common household treats.

The cashew fruit has followed the path of the Portuguese and Brazilian diasporas. Groceries and cafés in ethnic enclaves in Newark, Boston, Providence, and other cities purvey the cashew drink to their nostalgic patrons. Latin shops display rows of containers featuring a picture of the nutty fruit. Some upmarket groceries are even beginning to carry the product. Those who have only been acquainted with the familiar nut can now savor the tart, slightly pineapple-ish juice of the captivating cashew.

THE CELERY CURE

It was not always a delicious garden vegetable. Long before breeders transformed the plant, celery was prized for its aromatic qualities and its health-giving properties. In the ancient world, it was picked because of its strong scent and bitter taste. The Greeks and Romans valued the herb's seeds, leaves, and stalks. Wild celery, which is known as *smallage,* was notable for its fibrous texture and thin, hollow stalks.

A member of the fragrant Umbelliferae family, which includes coriander, parsley, fennel, and other plants bearing parasols of flowers, celery was named for its distinctive qualities. The words for celery in Greek and Latin echoed terms for crispness and bitterness. Celery's name, some suggest, may also have been a generic one affixed to plants that grew in a swampy location. In *The Iliad,* Homer depicted horses nibbling on celery leaves and shoots in the marshes of Troy. The plant loved the wet soil near the sea. Wild celery drank in the moisture from the salty marshes and tidal flats in its native Mediterranean. Celery's crispness derives from this affinity for water.

Later, when taxonomists classified celery, they gave it an evocative name, *Apium graveolens. Apium,* or "liked by bees," refers to the powerful attraction its white flowers have for insects. *Graveolens,* or "heavily scented," also highlights celery's fragrance.

In early civilizations, celery was popular as a tangy condiment. Greeks perked up wine with crushed celery seeds. Apicius, the Roman gourmet, recommended garnishing sauces with its leaves, and noted that sprinkling ground celery seeds

over fish enhanced its flavor. The Roman author Columella suggested pickling celery stems with vinegar and wine.

It was also thought that those who were sick would benefit from the herb. A diuretic described by Hippocrates was a vinegary solution of celery, water, and honey. Crowns of wild celery, the Roman poet Horace wrote, prevented hangovers. Roman banqueters wore these leafy crowns to keep from being intoxicated. The Persians came to believe that the vapor of celery-seed oil was a remedy for headaches.

Celery was often hung in the rooms of Greeks with severe illnesses. The plant was also reputed to help the dead. Romans wore wreaths of celery leaves at funerals, and the plant adorned Greek tombs. Some believe that celery's strong, potent fragrance made it especially appealing for funereal settings.

Celery also honored the might and valor of the living. According to the Roman author Pliny, the mythic hero Hercules wore a crown woven of olive fronds, willows, and celery to salute his physical prowess. Celery was an obvious ornament for feasts, festivals, and victory celebrations. Great achievements were marked by evocations of this botanic symbol. When the Greeks founded a city for their capital in Sicily, they called it Selenium, or Celery City. Selenium's coins were decorated with celery leaves.

In medieval Europe, celery retained its reputation as a medicinal herb. Apothecaries prescribed wild celery as a diuretic and a laxative. Boiled celery leaves also made a handy poultice. Writing in the sixteenth century, English herbalist John Gerard saw little culinary—but much curative—use for the plant: "Water Parsley . . . is seldom eaten, neither is it counted good for sauce, but it is profitable for medicine." The English name for the herb reflected these beliefs. The Latin root of *celery* conveys something that is "quick-acting"—likely a reference to its role as a speedy remedy.

Celery was also invested with erotic powers. Love potions made from celery juice had a strong following. Giacomo Castelvetro, a seventeenth-century Italian refugee in London, emphasized celery's ability to stimulate sexual appetites: "It is warm and has great digestive and generative powers, and for this reason young wives often serve celery to their elderly or impotent husbands." The aphrodisiac was also favored for its more general invigorating capacity. Nicholas Culpeper, the seventeenth-century English herbalist, described wild celery as "one of the herbs which is eaten in the spring, to sweeten and purify the blood."

By the seventeenth century, the first halting steps were being taken, mostly by anonymous gardeners, to remake celery and transform it from an intensely pungent herb into a tender vegetable. They gradually domesticated wild celery, selecting more desirable types and breeding them. The focus now was less on the aromatic leaves and seeds than on improving the stalks. Thicker, solid stalks started to replace the thinner, hollow stems. The vegetable was becoming fleshier and less stringy.

Crucial to these changes was the technique of blanching, or whitening, celery. If its stalks could be sheltered from the sun, horticulturists figured, the vegetable would lose its bitterness. When soil was piled around it, a whiter, more appetizing celery would no doubt emerge. In Italy, where the blanching process was first developed, "in early autumn the celery plants are dug up and earthed up close together in a trench," the writer Castelvetro observed. "Showing about four fingers above the earth," the plants are "left for fifteen to twenty days. They will then have blanched and become good to eat."

Blanching was perfected by Jean-Baptiste de la Quintinie, Louis XIV's gardener at Versailles. From the kitchen gardens, white, succulent celery sprang up that royal cooks preferred to the green, more bitter variety. Celery would soon capture the fancy of European gastronomes. Castelvetro praised it as a digestive. Raw stalks seasoned with salt and pepper, he wrote, made a nice after-dinner refreshment. Domesticated celery, English botanist John Ray contended, was superior in flavor to its wild ancestor. The vegetable "becomes milder and less ungrateful, whence in Italy and France the leaves and stalks are esteemed as delicacies, eaten with oil and pepper."

As salads came into vogue in Europe, celery was promoted as a choice ingredient. "Our Winter Sallets are likewise greatly improved by blanch'd Sellery, which is an hot herb," English horticulturist Richard Bradley observed. John Evelyn, the English vegetable connoisseur, extolled the "high and graceful taste" of celery that had been peeled and sliced and dressed with "Oyl, Vinegar, Salt, and Peper."

Evelyn proclaimed that celery, once "a stranger with us," deserved a prominent position in the homes of gentlemen. In America, celery enjoyed a lofty status among the well-to-do many years before it became a supermarket staple. During the Gilded Age after the Civil War, celery, food writer Rebecca Rupp points out, was displayed on the dining tables of the rich in "towering" glass or silver vases.

So familiar to us today, celery was for a long time an uncommon vegetable in many American households. In the late nineteenth century, immigrants from Holland pioneered its entry into a national market. Hailing from a land with a long tradition of celery farming, Dutch farmers started growing the crop in the "mucklands"—the moist fields of Kalamazoo, Michigan, the "celery city"—and its environs. The wet soils, like those of the Netherlands, were ideal for the crop. "They come from a country reclaimed from the sea bed, protected by dykes and dredged by ditches," a Michigan celery grower put it. "Unlike the American, the Hollander delights to work this low wet land."

The farmers worked the soil as it had been done in their homeland. Wearing "klompers"—wooden shoes with tight metal rims, somewhat like snowshoes— they trod through the earth. Their horses were also fitted with wide wooden shoes to keep them from sinking into the mud. "I've seen horses go down clear up to their belly," recalled Bob Greendyke, the son of an early celery farmer.

The immigrants toiled twelve to sixteen hours a day. "It's no genteel, light work or child's play," Frank Little, a Michigan celery historian, wrote. The immigrants waded into swamps and turned them into fertile ground. Trenches were dug to drain off excess water from the flatlands. The labor, Little added, was "long and violent, or rather patient wrestling with many and sundry tamarack stumps, above ground and below."

Their large families were an asset to the Dutch farmers. "Families sometimes arrived in the fields as early as two in the morning and worked until about seven a.m., moving through moonlight as they lifted the blanching boards and set them out as planks to walk on, jammed their knives into the earth and sliced the celery at the roots," journalist Judith Lin observed. Their strong Calvinist work ethic intensified their efforts. The newcomers willingly cultivated fields that local farmers shunned. "American farmers had little use for this poorly drained land, and thus . . . sizeable acreages remained idle awaiting development," sociologists John Jakle and James Wheeler pointed out.

Following the European method, Dutch farmers were blanching their celery to produce a "white" or "yellow" variety. They were in pursuit of a vegetable sweeter and more tender than the green version. Pale yellow, *Wall Street Journal* reporter Mark Russell noted in a 1985 article, was the "ideal color" for Americans in an earlier era.

Kalamazoo celery soon reached a broader audience. Vendors began selling bunches on the street corners of "Celery City." Salesmen climbed on trains stopping in Kalamazoo and offered passengers the novel item. A new railway snack was born. The fame of the city's product spread. "Fresh as dew from Kalamazoo," the celery was snapped up by restaurant and hotel kitchens. They featured it prominently on their menus.

Health-conscious Americans were also turning to celery for invigoration and for a solution to their maladies. Kalamazoo was at the forefront of merchandising celery palliatives. Kalamazoo Celery and Sarsaparilla Compound was touted as a cure for "fever . . . all forms of nervousness, headaches, and neuralgia . . . and female complaints."

Kalamazoo's mania mirrored the country's celery enthusiasm. An 1897 Sears and Roebuck catalog advertised a celery brew as a "great nerve builder."

An array of other items produced in the "Dutch City" traded on the vegetable's appeal. Kalamazoo Celery and Pepsin Chewing Gum, Celery Tar Soap, and celery pickles were among the products produced there.

Across America companies were concocting celery drinks to quench the public's thirst for an effervescent, healthy beverage. Regional bottlers marketed celery phosphate, celery cream, celery and iron, and a variety of other sodas. James Mayfield, a partner of Coca-Cola inventor John Pemberton, opened a Celery-Cola facility in Birmingham, Alabama, in 1899. The drink was soon distributed nationally.

Lake's Celery, a drink created in Jackson, Mississippi, in 1887, was a special favorite of writer Eudora Welty. In her short story, "The Little Store," Welty remembers riding her bike as a child to purchase the treat on summer afternoons. "You drank in the premises, with feet set wide apart to minimize the drip." The drink's name, she said, was self-evident. "What else could it be called? It was made by a Mr. Lake out of celery."

Dr. Brown's Cel-Ray soda, first manufactured in 1869, is a survivor of this celery-mad era. As the story goes, this drink was the brainchild of Dr. Brown, a physician from the Williamsburg neighborhood of Brooklyn, who created a tonic infused with celery seeds, seltzer, and sugar to nurture sick children. Sold in trademark green bottles, the refreshment gained a fervent following in Jewish delis, where customers relished it as a foil to pastrami, corned beef, and other briny, spicy fare. "Generation after generation was weaned on this stuff," enthused company vice president Harry Gold. Columnist Walter Winchell dubbed it "Jewish Champagne."

As its ethnic devotees dispersed from their old neighborhoods, so did this talismanic soda. Transplants from Jewish enclaves clamored for the drink. "With them they take their tradition, with the tradition comes the deli," Alice O'Leary, an advertising account executive for the company in the 1970s, observed. Posters advertising the product played on these yearnings: "Imported from the old neighborhood," one said. "We missed you too." Dr. Brown's Cel-Ray tonic promised "prompt, temporary relief of the minor pain of nostalgia," the company advertised.

Recent devotees of the drink know little of its former medicinal allure. In the 1920s, the US Food and Drug Administration (FDA) forced the company to change its label. The government feared that customers would mistake the product for a pain-relieving elixir. Once marketed as a "tonic," it is sold as a soda today.

Another celery center was growing up in an unlikely location—a hardscrabble section of Florida. Like the Kalamazoo growers, the innovators were immigrants. Andrew Duda and other Slovak Lutherans fled religious persecution in the Austro-Hungarian Empire during the early twentieth century, coming to America. In 1912, Duda settled in Cleveland, where he and fellow ethnics worked in factories and on truck farms. The newcomers, many of whom were former farmers, soon tired of city life. They dreamed of forging a self-sufficient community united by their faith. "Let's take our children on the farms where there will be less temptation of the world and the wickedness of the large city," one émigré said longingly.

Hearing of vacant land in Florida on which they could plant vegetables, Duda and several other Slovak adventurers set out for Seminole County in central Florida, a few miles northeast of Orlando.

Once planted with citrus, the land had been abandoned when the orange crop was decimated by severely cold weather. Hoping to find bountiful acreage, they instead discovered a harsh area of thick woodlands and wetlands. Joseph Mikler, one of the early arrivals, expressed his bitter disappointment: "It was cold, there was water everywhere. My wife had expected warm weather and groves of oranges. But there was nothing, only woods."

The only buildings available to live in were old shacks that had once housed sawmill and turpentine workers. Paul Wehr, who chronicled the history of Slavia, the name the farmers gave to their community, described the conditions: "The shacks . . . were equally divided between boards and cracks and served not so much to keep out the cold and rain as to delay their passage." To make ends meet, Andrew Duda worked as a lumberman, dragging cypress logs out of the swamps with the help of mules and oxen. He tried to grow celery, but returned to Cleveland in 1916 after his efforts failed. His plan was to save enough to eventually return to Florida to buy land.

Andrew returned ten years later and bought a forty-acre plot. The early years were arduous and brutal—the mucklands had to be cleared, and the soil tilled with a plow and mule—but the effort paid off. Celery, it seemed, flourished in the damp soil and cool climate. "Celery used to grow like crazy in the muck," Karen Jacobs, the coordinator of the Museum of Seminole County History, observed. By 1930, Florida was turning out a third of the country's commercial celery crop.

With the help of his three sons, Andrew Duda brought out his first celery cash crop in 1926. From these early seeds, the Duda celery business sprouted. Duda Farm Fresh Foods, which markets the Dandy brand and a host of other celery products, rose to become America's largest producer of this crop.

By World War II, farmers growing celery in California were overtaking Florida and Michigan growers in the industry. Celery farming was increasingly concentrated in the Golden State, whose attractive soil, climate, and large tracts of land gave it an edge. Once typically a fall vegetable, celery could now be grown year-round in California for a national market. Supermarket chains, which pressed growers for a reliable annual supply of celery, accelerated this trend. Duda now grows most of its celery in California.

Along the way, greener celery began replacing the blanched vegetable. Vulnerable to fungus, the latter variety also demanded a costly, labor-intensive process. Consumers loved the color. This product, they were convinced, was healthier than its predecessor.

Deep green celery developed gradually over several decades of research and breeding. Hybridization, Duda breeder Larry Pierce notes, produced celery varieties of "mixed blood." Gradually, a truly green plant was perfected. The earlier pale green or yellow green celery started to disappear from grocery stores. The new breed was so intensely green that its stalks could not even be blanched white.

Older shoppers were not so quick to embrace the novel item. "Why does no one grow white celery anymore?" read a typical message to Duda. The skeptics, breeder Pierce discovered, had used celery primarily for making soup. The "mellow," less stringy celery he was developing was less suitable for their purposes.

Duda has relentlessly responded to and molded consumer preferences. Capitalizing on its extensive seed-research program, the company is constantly bringing new varieties to market. Alert to shoppers' desire for quick, ready-to-eat vegetables, Duda sells packs of celery sticks, and markets already sliced and diced celery.

"Convenience is king," observes Greg Tirado, plant manager of the firm's facility in Oxnard, California, about the "fresh-cut" business. Hotels and restaurants are attractive targets for the company. Pierce devised the Dandy Celery Straw, a stalk with a hollow center—aimed, of course, at Bloody Mary drinkers. Marketers had found a new function for the ancient garden herb.

THE BATTLE OVER THE BEAN
the puzzling chickpea

I had always thought of the chickpea as an unassuming bean. While I had enjoyed the pleasure of chickpea dishes like hummus and falafel, until I began digging into its story, I hadn't realized the strong feelings the lowly legume had aroused over the ages. I was astonished to learn that the Roman orator Cicero's name came from the Latin word for chickpea (*cicer*). (His family was not alone: the families of other Roman statesmen—Fabius, Lentillus, Pisus—were also inspired to name themselves after beans.) Nations have vied with each other for the right to claim falafel and hummus as their own.

The chickpea also carries a stigma, which I discovered during one of my many journeys to the Ironbound, a Portuguese-Brazilian neighborhood in Newark, New Jersey, a favorite haunt of mine. On one visit, I stopped for lunch at a bakery-café that makes delicious country soups like *caldo verde* (kale and potato) and wonderful egg custard pastries.

My curiosity was piqued by a new item in the display case, a chickpea and cod salad, so I asked a woman standing next to me about the unusual dish. She said that the salad was called *Meia-Desfeita*, which means "half an insult." Later, I pieced together the story behind its name. The two unlikely bedfellows represented clashing cultures. The salt cod was a subsistence food for generations of Portuguese. The chickpea, known as the *grão-de-bico*, or "granule with a beak," was associated with the hated Moors who had conquered Portugal and Spain.

Both scorned and adored, the chickpea was an ancient crop that sustained many early civilizations. The poet Homer evoked the chickpea in a simple

rustic setting: "Just as dark-fleshed beans and chickpeas leap off the threshing floor sped by shrill wind and a strong winnower, so bitter arrows ricochet off the breast-plate of noble Menelaus and fly far off." Domesticated in the Fertile Crescent more than ten thousand years ago, the wild chickpea was native to southern Turkey and nearby Syria. The plant, a two-foot-high bush, sprouts pods whose seeds are the chickpeas we eat. The legume's ancestors presented problems for the early settlers. The pods, for example, easily popped open, spreading seeds over the soil. Farmers, scholar Jared Diamond suggests, latched on to a "non-popping" mutant from the wild and steadily improved it. They also bred a larger and sturdier seed.

This legume, invaluable to early agriculturists, thrives in the most marginal soil and produces a high yield. Ideal for hot, dry climates, the plant sinks its taproots deep in the ground. A superb nitrogen fixer, the chickpea replenishes the soil for future crops. It is also easily sown, ripens fast, and can be stored indefinitely. In early settlements, chickpeas were cultivated along with, or in rotation with, wheat, barley, and rye. Together with livestock—sheep, goats, pigs, and cattle—they provided what Jared Diamond calls a "balanced package" of nutrients. The cereals and legumes offered essential amino acids and proteins, rewarding the population with energy and vitality.

Farmers had apparently stumbled onto a plant especially rich in trypto-phan, which increases the growth of serotonin in the brain, researchers have concluded. The chickpea helps to "induce accelerated growth." The legume diet, they conclude, leads to "higher ovulation rates, more frequent births, and better-fed infants."

From their vivid imaginations, the ancients conjured up pictures of the vital bean. *Cicer arietinum*, the Latin name for chickpea, compared the legume to a ram (*aries*) with its distinctive curled horns. A papyrus school text found in Egypt called the chickpea "hawk face" because of its beaked appearance.

A versatile food, this "poor man's meat" could be roasted, boiled, salted, pounded into a mash, or made into a soup. Cooked with bacon and packed in clay pots for export by the Romans, it was a constituent in what food historian Waverley Root called the first pork and beans. The chickpea was a key element in peasant grub—what the Roman poet Horace described as an "economical diet of onions, pulses, and pancakes" that kept you healthy and full.

Eating the bean, however, might mark you as a person of low status. In Rome, food historian Ken Albala points out, a *fricti ciceris emptor*, or buyer of roasted chickpeas, was synonymous with someone poor. The chickpea was also con-sidered demeaning because it was used as fodder for animals. In his play, *The Acharnians*, Greek author Aristophanes praised the legume because it helped to fatten pigs. Bean dishes were relegated, in one medieval Middle Eastern recipe collection, to the "Book of the Misers."

It might have been disparaged, but the chickpea was also touted for its erotic powers. The Roman naturalist Pliny called it the "pea of Venus." The Greek physician Galen wrote that "it has been believed to stimulate sexual urges at the time as being generative of semen."

The chickpea became a staple of another ancient civilization's diet. In India, where the chickpea was not cultivated until five thousand years after its appear-ance in the Fertile Crescent, it enriches many of the *dal* or legume dishes beloved by the country's vegetarians. *Channa*, as it is called, is simmered for many hours and stewed in a spicy sauce, or *masala*. Milled into a pale flour called *besan*, it is used to make a batter for *pakoras*, vegetable fritters. Packaged snacks like *sev* (fried vermicelli) are also prepared with *besan*.

The people of Punjab, India's rural heartland, are especially devoted to the chickpea. It adds fiber and bulk to many of the province's dishes. Street vendors ladle out *chole*, a spicy chickpea stew flavored with tomatoes. Accompanied by *bhatura*, a puffed bread, it makes a fortifying repast.

The chickpea was also one of the earliest street foods in the Middle East. Throughout the history of the region, merchants have wooed hungry crowds with the tasty beans. In Damascus during the Ottoman Empire, vendors selling roasted chickpeas shouted *Ummen-naren* ("Mother of two fires"), assuring the crowds that their wares were well roasted. In the Syrian city, sellers offered their customers fresh green chickpeas. Paper cones of salted chickpeas with a squeeze of lemon juice are a popular Egyptian treat today.

Modern-day ethnics have also embraced the bean. In the early decades of the twentieth century, immigrant Jews in New York City eagerly awaited the arrival of vendors selling chickpeas and other street foods. In his memoir, *The Walker in the City*, author Alfred Kazin was enthralled by "paper spills of hot yellow chickpeas." "I still hear these peddlers crying up and down the streets (in Yiddish) '*Arbes! Arbes! Hayse gute arbes! Kinder! Kinder! Hayse gute arbes.*' (Chickpeas, Chickpeas. I've got good chickpeas! Children! Children! I've got good chickpeas.)"

The chickpea, I discovered, also has a rich Italian heritage. On a summer evening during one of the weekly *festas*—saints' feasts celebrated in Boston's North End Italian neighborhood—my wife, Peggy, and I wandered through the throngs of revelers. We watched as the statute of the saint, draped with dollars, was carried through the street. We listened as a raucous band belted out Italian favorites from the 1950s. The streets were crowded with food stands. There was the unmistakable smell of fried dough, the cracking sound of cherrystone clams being opened, and the sizzle of sausages, peppers, and onions frying. And, of course, there were salted chickpeas for sale.

In the Middle East today, the chickpea fritter called *falafel*—a fixture of street stands, delis, and sub shops—has become a quintessential street food. Claimed by both the Israelis and the Palestinians, falafel has become the focus of fierce contention. Its ancestor, the *ta'amia*, is a fava-bean croquette that the Copts, the Egyptian Christian sect, regard as their own. They developed the meatless snack as a Lenten repast. During this holy period, Copts offer the *ta'amia* to friends as an act of penance. Gradually, the popularity of the croquette spread beyond the Coptic community. It has evolved into an Egyptian national street food sold at stands throughout the country.

As the *ta'amia* migrated from Egypt to other parts of the Middle East, it was reinvented. It was renamed falafel, probably from the Arabic word for "spicy," *mefelfel.* In Palestine, the vegetarian burger was now prepared with chickpeas instead of fava beans. When Jewish settlers arrived in Palestine in the late nineteenth and early twentieth centuries, they discovered that the locals were fervent about falafel. Since the familiar Eastern European foods were ill suited to their new homes, they searched for a different culinary identity.

The Jews gradually began borrowing from the Arabs: "If you were given the choice between falafel and gefilte fish, which would you choose?" Middle East scholar Najwa al-Qattan asked *New York Times* reporter Jodi Kantor. Since falafel had the aura of peasant food, it also appealed to the early Zionists' socialist sentiments, Middle East food authority Claudia Roden points out. Nonetheless, Israeli falafel had its own distinctive character. It was served with a choice of garnishes—pickles, turnips, eggplant—from a salad bar.

The arrival of Jewish immigrants in Israel from Arab nations in the 1950s strengthened falafel's national standing. Jews from Yemen, in particular, were attracted to the falafel trade. The newcomers "made it possible to incorporate elements like falafel without referring to them as Palestinian," Rutgers professor Yael Zerubavel commented to Ms. Kantor.

Falafel is now symbolic of Israeli culture. A popular song, "And We Have Falafel," written in 1958, illustrates its assimilation. "It used to be when a Jew came to Israel he kissed the ground and gave thanks, / Now as soon as he gets off the plane, he has a falafel," was one of its catchy lines. A popular postcard sold in Israel depicts a pita stuffed with a falafel that is decorated with the country's national flag. The card proclaims, "Falafel—Israel's National Snack."

Falafel conflicts are likely to persist. Israel's appropriation of the food still touches a raw nerve among Palestinians, who feel that they have been robbed of a national snack. "You stole everything else from us; now you want to steal falafel," a Palestinian woman exclaimed at a conference of Israelis and Palestinians.

Another classic chickpea-based appetizer has also precipitated a food fight in the Middle East. Until recently, the competition over hummus was a playful one. Chefs from both Lebanon and Israel have vied for the distinction of who could make the heftiest spread. The 2009 contest was billed with the slogan, "Come and fight for your life, you know you're right." The Lebanese won with a product that weighed over ten tons.

A more contentious rivalry has erupted as the Association of Lebanese Industrialists has taken their nation's claim to a protected status for hummus to the European Union Court. If the dip won recognition as being Lebanese, their rivals would be prevented from promoting it as an "Israeli" product. "If we don't tell the Israelis that enough is enough, and we don't remind the world that it's not true that hummus is a traditional Israeli dish, they [the Israelis] will keep on marketing it as their own," association executive Fadi Abboud declared.

Both sides have summoned strong arguments to make their case. "We were the first country in the world to industrialize the production of hummus, and [to] export hummus when Israel was barely five years old," Lebanese spokesman Abboud asserted. The chickpea dip, Israelis have responded, is too ancient and widespread to be claimed by any nation. "Trying to make a copyright claim over hummus is like claiming for the rights to bread or wine. Hummus is a centuries-old Arab dish—nobody owns it, it belongs to the region," Israeli journalist Shooky Galili contended.

It is easier to determine the genealogy of the chickpea than it is to trace the origins of hummus. The dip we know, a luscious chickpea puree suffused with the flavors of lemon, garlic, olive oil, and, most important, sesame *tahini*, is markedly different from the nutty, herb-laden dish of the first recorded recipe from thirteenth-century Egypt. The instructions for making *Hummus Kasa* (chickpea blanket), as translated by Middle East food scholar Charles Perry, call for the cook to pound the beans "fine" after boiling them. Then vinegar, pepper, mint, parsley, thyme, walnuts, hazelnuts, almonds, pistachios, caraway, and other ingredients are added.

Whatever its origins, hummus was probably perfected by the Lebanese, the Middle East's consummate restaurateurs. With culinary flair they elevated a basic food into something grand. Hummus metamorphosed into a convivial dish to be savored as part of *mezze*, an elaborate assortment of appetizers offered at restaurants ranging from tangy eggplant salads and creamy yogurt spread to grilled beef and lamb sausages. The *mezze* blossomed with the rise of open-air cafés in Zahle, a mountainous region of northeastern Lebanon known as the "Switzerland of the Middle East."

As the renowned Middle East food writer Claudia Roden tells the story, "Zahle, the resort where Lebanon's favorite riverside restaurants are situated, acquired a mythical reputation for gastronomy. In 1920, the first two cafés opened by the river. They gave away assorted nuts, olives, bits of cheese, and raw vegetables with the local *arak*. Gradually, the entire valley became filled with open-air cafés, each larger and more luxurious than the next, each vying to attract customers who flocked from all over the Middle East with ever more varied *mezze*. The reputation of the local mountain village foods they offered spread far and wide." In time, restaurants throughout Lebanon adopted the winning formula.

The beloved bean traveled with the Arabs to new destinations, where it again was invested with strong emotional associations. The chickpea, for example, was woven into the cultural fabric of Sicily, an island invaded by the Saracens in the ninth century AD and ruled by them for two hundred years. Vendors still sell salted chickpeas, and Sicilians are fanatical about *panelle*, a street snack, likely of Arabic origin, made from the bean. The rectangular slice sprinkled with parsley is a fritter made from chickpea flour.

The bean, the tale goes, played a dramatic role in a fabled event called the Sicilian Vespers. In retaliation for the abuse of a young girl by a French soldier, Sicilians set off on a murderous spree during the Church of Santo Spirito's vespers service. They targeted their victims by their inability to correctly pronounce *cicero*, dialect for chickpea, and pronounced "chee-chair-o" in Sicily. Failure to do so was an unmistakable sign of guilt, since the French can't pronounce "h."

In Spain, another occupied land, the Moors popularized the chickpea. For the Spaniards, the garbanzo, as they called it, became an everyday, high-energy staple. "The garbanzos are the vegetable, the potato of the land," English writer Richard Ford observed in 1846. Dishes like chickpeas and spinach still are listed on restaurant menus.

Because of its Moorish heritage, however, the chickpea sometimes acquired a bad reputation. A thirteenth-century cookbook discovered by scholar David Gitlitz relegated the bean to the world of "country people" and "gluttons." The bean, it was thought, was not an appropriate food for noble Christians.

Like the Moors, Spanish Jews also paid a price for their fondness for chickpeas. When courts began investigating the authenticity of *conversos*, Jews and Muslims who had converted after the Inquisition, their dining customs were often presented as evidence. During a trial held from 1520 to 1523, *conversa* Isabela Garcia was charged with preparing a Sabbath meal of "chickpeas, onions, spices, and honey."

In America, the chickpea has been smoothly assimilated. Once unusual, hummus is now a common party snack. Mass marketers are inventing new hummus blends to reach ever more diverse customers. The Holy Land Company in Minneapolis, food journalist John T. Edge discovered, was turning out tubs of hummus for grocery stores in jalapeno and guacamole flavors. "I'm making an American product," the Kuwaiti-born executive told Edge. "And this is what Americans want. Flavors and varieties and guacamole."

"Hummus and tabbouleh are sold in every deli in America," notes Charlie Sahadi, the Middle Eastern food magnate who remembers when they were considered exotic foods.

In some parts of the world, however, the chickpea still retains negative overtones. In France, after the nation's humiliating exit from the 2010 soccer World Cup, some politicians looked for scapegoats among the players, many of whom were from immigrant backgrounds. According to the *New York Times*, one official jeered that they were "guys with chickpeas in their heads instead of a brain."

"FOOD OF THE GODS"
chocolate

Have you ever seen the tropical cacao tree that is native to the rain forests of Central and South America? Even a photo of it? The image is arresting. How many of us associate chocolate sweets with an evergreen whose pods, orange or red, do not hang from stems but jut out directly from its trunk and branches? These striking fruits spring up after the cacao's white and pink flowers have bloomed.

The cacao's seeds, purplish beans that are buried in the pulp of the pod, excited the curiosity of explorers. On a ship in the Gulf of Honduras in 1502, Columbus spied a dugout canoe, most likely Mayan, whose passengers were carrying a load of peculiarly shaped beans. "They seemed to hold these almonds at a great price; for when they were brought on board ship together with their goods, I observed that when any of these almonds fell, they all stooped to pick it up as if an eye had fallen," his son, Ferdinand, recounted. He did not know that the almond-shaped objects were, in fact, cacao beans.

The Aztecs in Mexico were fascinated by the bitter, acrid beans. From these seeds, they conjured up an invigorating, even intoxicating—but definitely not sweet—drink. The Aztecs called the tree *cacao* and the refreshment *cacahuatl* (*atl* means "water"). Much later, the botanist Carl Linnaeus placed this plant in the evocatively named genus Theobroma, or "Food of the Gods."

In the beginning, the chocolate drink had a mystique about it. A mysterious stimulant, its pleasures were the prerogative of the elite. The cacao beans in this ceremonial beverage would one day be transmuted into a commonplace candy.

The Aztecs, the wandering tribe who built their empire in Mexico's dry highlands, assimilated cacao into their aristocratic culture. The coveted seeds, symbols of wealth and power, were used as currency, as "happie money." Aztec chiefs took them as tribute from tribes they held subject. Huge storehouses were bursting with the treasure. Montezuma was said to have been paid 980 sacks, or 24,000 beans, yearly.

The Aztecs developed ingenious techniques for processing the raw cacao. They fermented the pods, extracted the seeds from the pulp, then dried, toasted, and peeled them. The beans were then ground long and laboriously on a three-legged stone called a *metate*. The grounds were used immediately to make a savory drink by adding cold water, or were molded into cakes and stored. The *cacaoatl* was crowned with a glorious foam. Spanish friar Bernardino de Sahagún observed that the chocolate vendor was expert at this delicate task: "She adds water sparingly, conservatively; aerates it; she makes it form a head, makes foam; she removes the head, makes it thicken, makes it dry, pours water in, stirs water into it."

The drink would repel modern-day fanciers of creamy, sugary hot chocolate. Its makers highlighted the bitterness of the bean and enhanced the flavor with a variety of infusions. Vanilla, honey, chili, maize, and pungent flower pastes were among the condiments. The drinks came in many hues, Father de Sahagún noted: "flowered chocolate, flavored with green vanilla, bright red chocolate . . . black chocolate, white chocolate."

Mostly reserved for royalty, the celebratory drink was a form of conspicuous consumption, a reminder to underlings of the aristocracy's exalted status. Montezuma's retainers, the conquistador Bernal Diaz recounts, honored him at a banquet with lavish offerings of the potion: "[T]hey brought more than 50 great jars of prepared good cacao with its foam, and he drank of that; and the women served him drink very respectfully."

Mexico's Spanish colonizers gradually adopted the Indians' cacao habit. "The main benefit of this cacao is a beverage which they make called Chocolate, which is a crazy thing valued in that country," remarked a wary Jesuit, José de Acosta, in 1590. "It disgusts those who are not used to it, for it has a foam on top or a scum-like bubbling." Suspicions broke down, anthropologist Sophie Coe points out, as Latin men, who married or cohabited with native women, became accustomed to the flavor.

The chocolate drink the Spanish had fallen in love with in Mexico became a national passion. Savoring a frothy cup of thick hot chocolate grew into a breakfast ritual. Laced with sugar, it lacked the astringent flavor of the original. The refreshment substituted the subtle fragrance of cinnamon and almonds for the fire of chili. Unlike the Aztec version, it was drunk hot instead of cold. The Spaniards named their drink *chocolatl*. Until the manufacture of the solid sweet in the middle of the nineteenth century, "chocolate" simply meant the liquid treat.

The Spanish jealously guarded their product, their most profitable New World export. To maintain their monopoly, they kept its source a secret from their European rivals. They continuously expanded their chocolate empire, establishing plantations in new colonies in the Caribbean and Latin America. The settlers also planted thousands of acres of sugarcane, an essential ingredient for their favorite indulgence.

Although it would spread in time to the middle classes, chocolate was primarily an aristocratic recreation. The elites pioneered the chocolate fashion. The Spanish royalty imbibed it in court, and the nobility aped their superiors. The clergy, especially the Jesuits, reveled in the delicacy and popularized it in their travels to monasteries throughout Latin America and Europe. Keen students of the chocolate market, the friars also traded in the commodity.

The chocolate mania presented the church with a difficult dilemma—how to reconcile the sensual appeal of the sweet with Catholic doctrine. Clerics pondered whether chocolate was a drink or a food. During the sixteenth century, Pope Gregory XIII twice declared that chocolate, because it was a drink, didn't violate the fast.

After a hundred years of supremacy, the Spanish lost their stranglehold on cacao. In the eighteenth century, Catholic monarchies in Portugal, France, and Italy elbowed their way into the business. They, too, colonized tropical lands to feed the hunger for chocolate. In this era, chocolate remained tightly linked to the monarchy and aristocracy. It "became the drink of the European aristocracy, as much a status symbol as the French language, the snuffbox, and the fan," historian Wolfgang Schivelbusch observed.

Morning chocolate at breakfast or, ideally, in bed suited the lifestyle of the idle rich perfectly. Artists painted scenes of the indolent, drinking the refreshment in their boudoirs. The indulgence was tinged with the erotic. "People seek to be fortified through chocolate in order to perform certain duties," a seventeenth-century text said.

Doctors and scientists touted chocolate's erotic powers. Chocolate "vehemently incites to Venus, and causeth Conception in women, hastens and facilitates their Delivery," Antonio Colmenero de Ledesma, a seventeenth-century Spanish physician, wrote. Henry Stubbs, an English physician of the same period, was lyrical about the "great use of chocolate in Venery [sexual desire], and for supplying the Testicles with a Balsam, or a Sap."

Soon, another drink would compete with chocolate. Emerging as the favored drink of the Protestant middle classes in Northern Europe, coffee fostered alertness, energy, enterprise—all qualities that these entrepreneurial societies valued. Freethinkers derided chocolate as the symbol of a corrupt church and an opulent aristocracy.

In the meantime, chocolate was on the threshold of change. Businessmen seized the commercial potential of the sweet, turning it from a luxury product into an inexpensive consumer good.

In 1789, Joseph Fry, a British manufacturer in Bristol, England, used a steam engine to grind cacao beans. A Dutchman, Conrad Van Houten, developed an ingenious method for making chocolate a more appetizing drink. In 1848 he extracted a third of the cocoa butter from chocolate with a mechanical press. Cocoa powder was the end product. Using a blend of milk, sugar, and cocoa powder, his version of cocoa was thinner and milder than the Spanish hot chocolate. The aristocratic drink had been stripped of its luxurious richness.

The excess cocoa butter left over from the Van Houten process was also put to ingenious use. It fattened up a new product: the chocolate bar. Blended with sugar, it was added to cocoa powder. The resulting smooth paste could be easily molded. In 1847, the Fry Company turned out the first chocolate bars with this technique.

By the end of the nineteenth century, chocolate was growing more affordable. Providing an inexpensive, nourishing product for the working classes had been the dream of the Quaker manufacturers—the Frys, Rowntrees, and Cadburys—who dominated the British chocolate industry. Believers in temperance, they hoped that chocolate would wean workers away from drink.

Modern chocolate has lost many of the qualities it possessed as a luxurious pleasure. But even though it has become a quickly consumable candy rather than a voluptuous drink, it still has a powerful hold over us.

"SWEET WOOD"

cinnamon

Young men should be wary of women "whose feet abide not in their home" and who invite them back to their cinnamon-scented beds. These temptresses, the Hebrew proverb says, offer an amorous evening: "Come, let us take our fill of love until the morning." In the ancient world, cinnamon and its lower-status sister, cassia, were prized for their aromatic powers. (When I can reasonably pinpoint which of the two spices is being referenced, I will use their individual names; otherwise, I will use the generic term *cinnamon*.) But it was rarely used in that age to season food, and only then to flavor wine.

The Bible's Song of Solomon called the Eastern spice "one of the chief perfumes." "Your robes are redolent of myrrh, aloeswood and kasia," an anonymous poet said, addressing a royal bride. In addition, cinnamon played spiritual and ceremonial roles. The Lord commanded Moses to anoint the holy tabernacle with the oil of cinnamon. Gold-encased cinnamon, the Roman naturalist Pliny wrote, adorned his city's temples. Sappho, the Greek poet, evoked the atmosphere of a wedding in Troy: "Myrrh, cassia and frankincense rose in smoke . . . all the old women wailed and the men raised a fine cry."

The ancients embalmed their dead with cinnamon, and it was burned at funerals. After the Roman emperor Nero's pregnant wife died (from being kicked in the stomach by her husband), Nero ordered that all of the city's cinnamon be gathered and then burned in the funeral pyre.

Cinnamon could also be a cosmetic. The elegant men of Rome massaged their faces and perfumed their hair with *malabathrum*, an oil drawn from the leaves of *tajpat*, a relative of the cinnamon tree.

Cinnamon was also avidly sought because of its medicinal value. The spice was a key ingredient, the Greek physician Galen noted, in the antidotes for treatment of poisonous bites. The compounds evolved into all-purpose drugs.

So coveted was cinnamon that the spice became a luxury item. Pliny estimates it was worth fifteen times as much as silver. Since spices were so magical, many believed they emanated from an Edenic place. "Rare cinnamon," the Roman poet Prudentis claimed, originated in Paradise.

Others wove fabulous tales about the spice's mysterious origins. The Greek historian Herodotus passed on these stories in his chronicles. He traced cinnamon to the birds' nests in the steep heights of Arabia: "The Arabians say that the dry sticks . . . are brought to Arabia by large birds, which carry them to their nests, made of mud, on mountain precipices which no man can climb. . . . People cut up the bodies of dead oxen into very large joints, and leave them on the ground near the nests. They then scatter, and the birds fly down and carry the meat to their nests, which are too weak to bear the weight and fall to the ground. The men come and pick up the cinnamon. Acquired in this way, it is exported to other countries."

Cassia, Herodotus recounted, came from an equally terrifying location in Arabia. Cutters of the bark braved "winged creatures like bats," which flew menacingly around a lake in which the tree grew.

Other accounts placed the fragrant spice in "Cinnamon Country," the region of the Horn of Africa. Queen Hatshepsut of Egypt, the story goes, sent five ships to explore the Land of Punt, present-day Somalia, in search of spices and other riches. The boats returned laden with cinnamon, gold, ivory, and incense. Ethiopia was another nearby land fabled to have treasures of cinnamon.

Contrary to these tales, cinnamon did not grow in Arabia, Somalia, or Ethiopia. Their dry climates and inadequate rainfall were not congenial for the spice. The merchants were hiding the true source, keeping potential competitors out of their business and boosting the prices of their product. The spice's reputed locations were, in fact, trans-shipment points on its long voyage from the East.

The Arabs, who named it *dar sini*, or wood of China, knew where the cassia was coming from. It was native to Southern China and Vietnam. Cinnamon, on the other hand, was grown first in Sri Lanka, the tiny island off the tip of India that the Arabs called Sarandîb. Both spices were prepared from the dried bark of

tropical evergreens, tall trees that, in the wild, can tower as high as forty or fifty feet. Members of the laurel family, which includes the avocado and bay laurel, these trees when cultivated are cropped to form low bushes.

Cinnamon, which comes from a Greek word, *kinamon*, or "sweet wood," has a thinner bark and more delicate flavor than cassia. Besides having a thicker bark, cassia has a more intense, pungent taste. Today's spice connoisseurs regard cinnamon as the true spice and cassia as an impostor. When we buy cinnamon, we may actually be getting cassia, or a mixture of the two spices.

The Chinese have long been enthusiastic about cassia, their earliest recorded spice. The trees grew wild in large forests in the high mountains of the tropical south, but the plant was quickly domesticated. An ingredient today in Chinese five spice powder and a flavoring for braised meat, cassia was revered for its purifying fragrance. It was used to cleanse the air of temples after the burning of the dead, and was valued as a meat preservative. A taste of the Bark of Life, the Chinese believed, ensured immortality. Eating a mixture of toad's brains and cassia for ten years, the Chinese philosopher Baopuzi counseled, would enable one to walk on water and live forever.

Quills of curled-up cassia were sent west. (The Greeks called the quill a *syrinx*, or pipe; later the Italians introduced the word *cannella*, or "little tube," which came from their word for cannon, to describe it.) The spice was also transported in ways that would astound us today. Twigs and branches of the tree were one mode, or a whole tree might even be shipped. The physician Galen provided Emperor Marcus Aurelius with a box of cassia for his medical treatment. The box, Galen wrote, was "shipped from the land of the barbarians, four and a half cubits long, in which was a whole cinnamon tree of the finest quality."

Cassia probably arrived in Greece and Rome by the seventh century BC. But how did it get there from Asia? Trying to guess the spice's route has been a rich area for speculation. Pliny thought he had the answer about its secret transporters: "[They] carry it over vast tracts of sea, upon rafts, which are neither steered by rudder, nor impelled by oars or sails. Nor yet are they aided by resources of art, man alone, and his daring boldness, standing in place of all these." The sailors, most likely Indonesians, followed the monsoon winds in their outrigger canoes.

Building on clues from Pliny and from other sources, historian J. Innes Miller fleshed out the rest of the story. In his version, the mariners sailed the Indian Ocean to the island of Madagascar. From there, they traveled up the coast of East Africa, probably to an entrepôt across from the island of Zanzibar. Arab or Phoenician traders purchased the spice there and then oversaw its journey to the Red Sea and, ultimately, to the Mediterranean.

What reward did the sailors get for their labors? Pliny commented in characteristically sardonic form, "In return for their wares, they bring back articles of glass and copper, cloths, buckles, bracelets and necklaces; hence it is that this traffic depends chiefly upon capricious female fidelity to fashion."

Centuries later, modern spice traders battled for control of the lucrative cinnamon commerce. The tiny island of Ceylon (Sri Lanka), with its treasure trove of wild cinnamon, beckoned to the Portuguese empire builders. Control of Sarandîb, as the Arabs called it, would give the Iberians a monopoly on the luxury spice. The island's bark, more delicate than China's pungent cassia, was regarded as the "true" cinnamon. It was stripped from hardy evergreens that bore white flowers and black berries and grew in the island's forests.

The Portuguese had already built forts and trading posts along the spice-rich Malabar Coast of southwestern India. Moreover, their empire's Asian capital and chief entrepôt, Goa, was conveniently close to the coveted island.

An ancient trading center, Ceylon had enthralled visitors, like the thirteenth-century Arab geographer al-Qazwini: "The island of Silan . . . is large. . . . Here is Mount Sirandib upon which Adam was thrown down from Paradise. The wonders of China and the rarities of India are brought to Silan. Many aromatics not to be found elsewhere are met with here, such as cinnamon, brazilwood, sandalwood, nard, and cloves."

More than a hundred years later, the famous Arab voyager Ibn Battuta observed the "whole of the coast . . . covered with trunks of wood brought down by the rivers."

The Portuguese seized Ceylon in 1536 and forced the king to deliver an annual tribute of cinnamon. The king, now a dependent, had once been the master of his dominion's spice. The *salagama*, a hereditary caste of cinnamon peelers, were exploited by the Portuguese to perform the arduous labor of gathering and preparing the aromatic for market.

Bursting with the spice, the "cinnamon fleete" sailed from Goa, where the cargo had been hauled, for Lisbon. Besides cinnamon, the vessels also carried exotic goods like ivory figurines, mats, crystal, and straw hats. The most precious of the products weighed down the ships. In 1610, Captain Jean Mocquet, according to historian Anthony Disney, wrote that steering was a "great deal of trouble because the ship had cinnamon almost as far as the middle of the mast."

The lure of cinnamon produced a frenzy among the Portuguese. "At the scent of this cinnamon the kingdom loses its people," Sá de Miranda, a sixteenth-century poet, writes. Michael Ondaatje, the Ceylon-born Canadian author, believes that the thirst for conquest was whetted by cinnamon's intoxicating aroma:

"Captains would spill cinnamon on the deck and invite customers to smell Ceylon before the island even came into view."

The import acquired great prestige among Europe's upper classes. "Synamome," the fifteenth-century naturalist John Russell proclaimed, was for "lordes," while cassia was for "commyn people." On the Continent, cinnamon was not only popular in the kitchen but also an appealing tonic, a sedative for childbirth, and a breath sweetener. The Portuguese sold Europeans a liqueur distilled from the half-dried bark.

The Dutch expelled the Portuguese and took over Ceylon in 1656. The new occupiers were as obsessed with cinnamon as their predecessors had been. "No lover is as jealous of his mistress as the Dutch are of their trade in spices," a French writer commented in 1697. However, while the Portuguese had been trader-adventurers, the Dutch were unrelenting businessmen. When prices of cinnamon dropped, the profiteers burned the spice in the Netherlands. Ultimately, the Dutch transformed the haphazard industry into a ruthlessly efficient system. They built plantations to reap greater profits from their crop.

Cinnamon lost some of its luster as the spice was transplanted to new lands, like the Indian Ocean islands of Mauritius and Réunion. Gradually, cinnamon became less scarce, and was no longer the exclusive province of the aristocracy.

Might the fabled spice also grow in the New World? Columbus thought so. "I believe I have discovered rhubarb and cinnamon," he crowed. In 1540, Gonzalo Pizarro, brother of the Spanish conquistador Hernando, set off on an ill-fated expedition in search of cinnamon. In quest of La Canela, the Valley of Cinnamon, he led two thousand soldiers through the mountains of eastern Ecuador. Two years later, Pizarro gave up and returned with only eighty men. There were plants in Latin America that resembled cinnamon and had a similar fragrance, but the cinnamon of Asia did not exist there. The Spanish were forced to export the spice to their colonies. Some of their subjects—like the Mexicans, who flavored both coffee and hot chocolate with cinnamon—became avid users of the aromatic.

In an age of cinnamon buns and cinnamon toast, it often feels that the once-coveted spice has lost its magic. One group of Washington newcomers, however, seems to revel in cinnamon. The Ethiopians, heirs of an old spice-trading culture, are passionate about it. Cinnamon, cloves, and cardamom scent their tea. Cinnamon adds zest to their rice and stews. For these immigrants, cinnamon is more than just a pleasing flavor; it is a heavenly perfume.

THE "NAIL INCENSE"
uncovering the clove

The steamy tropical air of the Indian Ocean port was thick with spicy fumes. Aromatic droplets fragrant with cloves filled the atmosphere. A recent college graduate teaching in Dar es Salaam, the capital of Tanzania, I walked through the harbor during a brief sojourn on the island off the coast of the East African nation. Although Zanzibar was formally part of Tanzania, it had a culture all its own. I had often discussed the spice island's history in my classes at a secondary school outside Dar. A number of my students, many of whom wore the distinctive white caps of Islam, hailed from the predominantly Muslim society.

Looking around the harbor, I watched port workers hauling large bags of cloves, the chief export of what was then the world's largest producer of the spice. Cans of coconut oil rested on the dock. A ship headed for Bombay waited in the harbor.

At the time, other than gazing at the peculiar objects in the family's spice jars and knowing that they pierced the skin of my mother's ham, I knew little about cloves. What were they, actually? Where did these spices come from? Why were they so prolific in Zanzibar?

Over the ensuing decades, I gradually pieced together some basic details about the clove. In simplest terms, the clove is the unopened flower bud of a tall tropical evergreen. This member of the myrtle family, which can tower to thirty feet and live for a hundred years, is often graced by a leafy canopy. Cloves thrive on tropical islands like Zanzibar, where they can receive a maximum of heat and humidity. The evergreen enjoys the breezes but must be shielded from too-strong winds.

Six to eight years after planting, the tree bears its first crop. Harvesting the buds is a delicate and painstaking process. They must be picked when they are pink, before their flowers open. The buds are then laid out in the sun to dry. In the process, they turn into the familiar reddish-brown spice. The nail-shaped buds are coveted because their oil glands produce the spice's intoxicating scent.

In their fascination with the clove, cultures have conjured up a variety of names for the spice. The old French word, *clou*, from which our English name derives, means "nail." The medieval hand-forged nail, with its distinctive metallic prongs, bore a striking resemblance to the folded petals of the clove bud. Long before this, the mystified Greeks dubbed the spice *caryophillon*, the "petal of a nut plant."

People in the West had only the vaguest idea of where cloves and the other "spicie drugs," as the poet Milton called them, came from, or even what they looked like. They were somewhere in the remote Orient, in dangerous lands on the edge of the world. The East, it was imagined, was also an Eden filled with riches and precious aromatics. Mysterious and fantastical, the Spice Islands in the Eastern Sea possessed a powerful mystique. All of this enhanced the value and aura of spices.

Bizarre stories of the spice kingdoms abounded. An early account by Ibrahim ibn Wasif-shah was one such tale: "Also somewhere near India is the island containing the Valley of Cloves. No merchants or sailors have ever been to the valley or have ever seen the kind of tree that produces cloves: its fruit they say is sold by genies. The sailors arrive at the island, place their items of merchandise on the shore, and return to their ship. Next morning, they find, beside each item, a quantity of cloves. . . . The cloves are said to be pleasant to the taste when they are fresh. The islanders feed on them, and they never fall ill or grow old."

The traders—Indians, Chinese, and Arabs—who knew where to find them kept their source a secret. They had no interest in sharing information with potential poachers. Since it was believed that spices, like all plants, could grow only in one location, the desire to pry open their hiding place was all the more ferocious. The concept of transplantation was an alien one, even to distinguished scientists like the seventeenth-century German naturalist Georgius Rumphius, who spent five decades in the East Indies working for the Dutch East India Company. "Lord God, when assigning each country its proper wealth, kept the cloves within the limits of the Moluccan region, whereupon no human diligence can remove them," he wrote.

Cloves actually grew in one isolated area in the Molucca Islands, the Spice Islands east of Indonesia. They were located on five tiny volcanic islands of this chain. Ternate and Tidore, the most prized of these isles, were thrilling to observe. Each was a "rugged, towering volcanic cone forested with clove trees and encircled by treacherous coral reefs," writer Charles Corner noted. A "cannonshot" from the ocean, as the Portuguese physician Garcia de Orta put it, the clove trees were nourished by moist breezes and fed by monsoon rains. The wild spice trees gave the forest a delightful aroma.

Although they esteemed the lofty spice trees, the Moluccans had little appetite for the cloves themselves. The evergreen had a deeper, more emotional meaning to the islanders, as many marked the birth of their children by planting one of the trees. A child's fortune, they believed, was determined by the clove's progress.

China was the oldest civilization conversant with the clove. Indonesian sailors carried spicy wares from the Moluccas to the Celestial Kingdom. The Chinese invented colorful names for these imports. "Chicken-tongue aromatic" was an early term; later, the clove was known as "nail incense."

The Chinese respected the clove's curative powers. Guessing correctly that it was a potent anesthetic, people employed the spice to treat toothaches. Moreover, it enjoyed a reputation as a breath cleanser. In the seventh century AD, the government's official pharmacologist, Su Gong, directed those seeking an audience with the emperor to sweeten their mouths with cloves. Incenses and perfumes were also distilled from the tree's flowers.

In Indian culture great stock was placed in the clove as both an antiseptic and an anesthetic. The "strong-scented plant," as it was known in Sanskrit, was supposed to ward off bad breath and indigestion. "One who wants clean, fresh fragrant breath must keep nutmeg and cloves in the mouth," an Indian text prescribed. Preparations containing cloves were attractive solutions for treating tooth decay, bad breath, and poor gums. Even in modern-day India, sophisticated women suck on cloves to sweeten their breath. "You will often see fashionable young misses take out little silver boxes from their little silver purses, remove cloves and cardamom from them, and delicately place these spices on their tongues when mouth fresheners seem suddenly willed for," culinary writer Madhur Jaffrey observes.

Europe's trading empires would not sit idly on the sidelines and allow their Asian and Arabic competitors to gobble up the spices of the Moluccas. The Portuguese, who were already hauling black pepper, cardamom, and cinnamon from India, set their sights eastward toward the treasure trove of more expensive aromatics: cloves, nutmeg, and mace. Seizing Malacca, the bustling port on the Malay Peninsula near Singapore, was their first objective. Dhows from India and Arabia and Chinese junks, pulled along by monsoons and trade winds, stopped at the entrepôt to buy and sell the market's enticing products. The port, Portuguese official Tomé Pires wrote, "is at the end of the monsoons, where you find what you want, and sometimes more than you are looking for."

From Malacca, cloves and nutmeg from the Spice Islands were carried west to the Mediterranean, often in Muslim vessels. The middlemen exchanged their spices with Venetian buyers in Alexandria and other ports. The "merchants of Venice" then sold the items to customers in Paris, Nuremberg, and other medieval cities.

By taking Malacca, the Portuguese would control the lucrative traffic to and from this commercial crossroads. Their Venetian rivals would, in turn, lose their grip on the spice trade. "Whoever is Lord of Malacca has his hand on the throat of Venice," Tomé Pires observed. At the same time, the Iberians could fulfill their burning desire to wreak revenge on the hated "Moors." The Muslims, who were now interfering with the trading ambitions of the Portuguese, had dominated their country for more than three hundred years. This was not simply a war for spices: it was a fight to the bitter end between Christians and infidels.

In 1511, the Portuguese mobilized a vast force—fifty ships, eight hundred soldiers, eight hundred Indian archers—to conquer Malacca. The armada bombarded the port, waged a brutal campaign on land, and quickly achieved victory. The occupiers savored their rout. By overthrowing the city-state's ruling Muslim sultan, the Portuguese had established a Christian beachhead in a growing Islamic region.

Soon after their conquest of Malacca, the Portuguese were plucking cloves at their source in the Moluccas. They maintained control of the islands for a hundred years. Some wondered, however, whether the conquest of the clove was worth the price. "Cast your eyes over the numberless scattered islands of these eastern seas," the sixteenth-century Portuguese poet Luis de Camões implored his readers. "Find Ternate and Tidore—identify its burning peak, throwing out waves of fire—and there you will see the fiery clove trees, bought at the cost of Portuguese blood."

The trade in cloves and other spices was also changing Europe's culinary habits. The leisure classes were consumed by what historian Fernand Braudel called a "spice orgy." At the fancy tables of the aristocracy, stews and roasts fragrant with cloves were served. A fifteenth-century cookbook called for cloves, saffron, ginger, cypress root, cinnamon, sugar, and nutmeg to flavor a rabbit dish. The more elaborate and lavish the display of spices, the greater the status and prestige of the host who offered the luxuries to his guests.

The English, great lovers of pies, were adding spices from the East to savory pastries. Food historian C. Anne Wilson notes a typical Elizabethan recipe for minced pie: "Shred your meat (mutton or beef) and suet together fine. Season it with cloves, mace, pepper, and some saffron, great raisins and prunes." The French used cloves to give flair to their stews. Alexandre Dumas prescribed "three big onions, two with a clove stuck in each of them, the third with a clove of garlic" for pot-au-feu.

Cloves were essential to medieval drinks. Young or old ale, the English poet Chaucer writes, profited from cloves and nutmeg. A sixteenth-century recipe for spiced wine demanded "a gallon of wine, an ounce of synamon, two ounces of ginger, one pound of sugar, twentie cloves bruised, and twentie cormes of pepper big beaten: let all these soake together one night."

Cloves were also invested with a variety of curative powers. "Cloves give a clean breath, free the wind, and cure upset stomach," the Dutch physician Bernardus Paladanus asserted. Ground cloves were used to dress open wounds and to sharpen the eyesight. Since it resembled an erect phallus, the clove was often reputed to be an aphrodisiac. During the Middle Ages, when there was widespread fear of airborne pestilence and fetid odors, nobles wore pomanders ("apples of amber"), metal balls containing a mixture of cloves and other spices, around their necks for protection. They breathed in the pleasing aroma through an opening carved in the charm.

Back in the East, the battle for the control of spices raged on. A more ruthless nation was determined to depose the Portuguese. Intent on seizing the cloves and nutmegs for themselves, the Dutch ousted the Iberians in the early seventeenth century. The Netherlands dominated the Spice Islands for two hundred years. Learned commentators like Rumphius, who had been documenting the natural life of the Moluccas for the Dutch, justified the dominance of the vigorous and enterprising Northern Europeans over their "inferiors": "The Creator of nature created them not so much for these savage Inhabitants, as for the European and northern climes: for since Cloves have a hot essence, surpassing even Pepper in heat, but not in dryness, it appears that this first fruit cannot be of much service in these hot countries, but all the more so in the cold, northern world."

Having won the military victory, they set out to establish a firm monopoly on the islands' aromatics. Holland fixed the price for cloves and brooked no interference with that objective. In the company's cold-blooded calculation, restricting production was the most efficient means to this end. The Dutch limited clove-growing to one island, Amboyna; the trees on the others would simply have to be destroyed. There was no other way "to rid us of the overabundance of cloves and the burden of the unreliable Moors [the Muslim inhabitants of the islands], than to destroy their clove trees and level them to the ground," the Dutch official Aert Gysels said. Launching the policy of "extirpation" in 1625, the colonists cut down twenty-five thousand trees on Amboyna. Selling and possession of cloves, except on Amboyna, were made punishable by death.

Up to now, the focus of the clove wars centered on the Moluccas. But what if spices, contrary to myth, could be grown in locations other than their place of origin? A French colonial administrator, aptly named Pierre Poivre, punctured this legend, thus paving the way for new forms of competition.

Poivre, who had studied theology, philosophy, and art as a young man, served as governor of the Indian island colony of Isle de France (present-day Mauritius). Resentful of the Dutch stranglehold over spices, he was eager for his motherland to share in the wealth: "[T]he possession of spices which is the basis of Dutch power in the Indies was grounded on the ignorance and cowardice of the other trading nations of Europe," he argued. The indefatigable Poivre organized countless expeditions to spirit away clove and nutmeg seedlings from the Moluccas. If he was caught, he risked imprisonment or death.

Poivre did not succeed, but his followers were victorious. The spice thieves achieved their leader's goal of making Ile de France a "nursery" for cloves. By the end of the eighteenth century, the first crop was harvested there. Clove plantations soon sprang up on the French islands of Réunion and Seychelles. Not to be outdone, the English transplanted cloves to Malaysia.

A new arena for clove cultivation emerged off the coast of East Africa. A mere twenty-five miles from the coast of Tanzania, the island of Zanzibar had long been a commercial outpost and a resting place for a medley of peoples—Africans, Persians, Arabs, and Indians. Zanzibar was taken over in the early seventeenth century by the Arabian kingdom of Oman, which was strategically located at the juncture of the Persian Gulf and the Indian Ocean.

Sultan Seyyid Said, who moved his capital from the Arabian Peninsula to Zanzibar, planted the first clove seeds on the grounds of his palace. From the initial two or three plants, groves of evergreens spread over the island. Cloves "speedily became a favorite, and in 1815, the aristocratic foreigner almost supplanted the vulgar coconut and homely rice necessary for local consumption," the British explorer Richard Burton observed. The clove industry was built on slavery. Slaves hauled in from East Africa worked large estates, some with as many as ten thousand trees.

Zanzibar now dominated the world's clove market. Bringing in brass wire, muskets, gunpowder, and textiles, and taking out the aromatic buds, ivory, sesame, and other African exports, ships from America and Europe thronged the port. Salem, Massachusetts, the capital of the US spice trade, exported cloth made in the city's factories to the island.

The East Indies, the clove region that Zanzibar had eclipsed, ultimately regained its prominence. An addiction to clove cigarettes in Indonesia created an insatiable demand for the spice. *Kretek*, a mixture of two parts tobacco and one part shredded cloves, the story goes, originated as a cornhusk-wrapped treat in the late nineteenth century. The cigarette got its name from the crackling sound the burning cloves produced. Regarded as a cure for sore throat and asthma in its early days, *kretek* was initially sold in pharmacies. This fragrant cigarette spawned a huge industry complete with large companies, brand names, and advertising. Later, the hand-rolled cornhusk wrapper was replaced with white paper, and the cigarette was available with a filter or without, turned out by sophisticated machinery.

To satisfy the craving for the pungent incense, Indonesia looked to Zanzibar for raw material. In 1930, seven thousand tons of cloves were shipped to Indonesia from the island. Since *kretek* smokers were convinced that the Zanzibar clove made the best cigarette, Dutch adventurers stole seeds from Zanzibar two years later to transplant to their colony. Once clove-free, Zanzibar ended up rescuing Indonesia, which by the 1980s was growing and consuming two-thirds of the world's spice supply.

Tons of cloves may be going up in smoke, but some of the spice is still being used to ease our pain and suffering. During a recent dental operation, I detected the scent of cloves. A pharmacy in my neighborhood, I discovered, carried clove oil for relief of toothaches. "All dentists know about clove oil," the pharmacist told me. Calling spices "drugs" at last made sense.

THE "WINE OF THE BEAN"
coffee

How many of us imagine Ethiopia when we think of the origins of coffee? More likely, we associate the drink with Brazil, a latecomer to the bean, which only became a dominant producer in the nineteenth century. Thousands of years ago, the ancestors of today's coffee plant grew wild in the country's highland rain forests. Ethiopia is the birthplace of *Coffea arabica*, the most important and widely cultivated coffee species.

Shaded by the forest canopy, Ethiopian coffee grows on large, leafy shrubs. Small white flowers with a tantalizing jasmine fragrance bloom on the branches of the evergreens. After the flowering, bunches of "cherries," first green, then yellow, red, or crimson, sprout. These vivid fruits enclose the bean from which the coffee drink is made.

The wild coffee of ancient Ethiopia was not enjoyed as a drink but was most probably picked and eaten as a snack or food. The beans were roasted and crushed, mixed with butter, and shaped into hard balls. Wandering tribesmen nibbled the berries for a jolt of energy. But how did the Ethiopians figure out that the plant offered this reward? Myths of coffee's discovery abound in the country's folkways. In one popular legend, a shepherd noticed his goats frisking around after chewing on the fruit of a strange plant. Whatever the true story, word about the intoxicating shrub spread quickly.

In time, coffee became a valuable item of trade. Arab merchants likely carried sun-dried berries across the Red Sea from Ethiopia to Mocha, a port in the

Arabian land of Yemen. After it started cultivating coffee in 1543–1544, Yemen then became the primary exporter of the bean. Planting seedlings appropriated from Ethiopia, Yemeni farmers carved out terraces in the mountains that rose above the sea. The crop flourished.

A vibrant commercial network emerged along the Red Sea. Loaded on camels, the dried berries were transported from the terraces to middlemen in the towns, usually Arabs or Indians, who handled the merchandising. The coffee was transported from Mocha or other ports in small vessels, or *dhows*, to outposts along the Red Sea or the Gulf. Egypt was a profitable destination. Dealers bought coffee at the large Cairo bazaar and distributed their wares to Damascus, Tunis, Istanbul, and other cities. The Ottoman Empire, which ultimately stretched from the Middle East to the Balkans, developed into the center of the burgeoning coffee trade.

An Islamic brotherhood in Yemen, the Sufis, popularized coffee drinking. The mystical sect, who sought an immediate, personal relationship with God, incorporated the intoxicant in their worship. Coffee kept the Sufis awake and intensely focused in their all-night gatherings, called *dhikrs*. Sharing the drink, which their leader ladled out of a large red clay vessel, the groups swayed, sang, and chanted *Allah akbar* ("God is great").

As the Sufis roamed the Middle East, the coffee mystique followed. Astute businessmen soon capitalized on the enthusiasm by setting up coffeehouses. Gradually, coffee drinking lost its religious associations and was transformed into an opportunity for lively sociability. In cultures where wine drinking was forbidden and which lacked a restaurant culture, coffeehouses filled the void. Patrons, who sat on long benches called divans, spent their evenings kibitzing and debating the issues of the day. Some played backgammon and other games. They called the addictive drink *gahwa*, Arabic for "wine."

The new outlets threatened the social order. Clerics worried that the venues would lure their flocks from the mosques to impure diversions. "Things reached such a point that the coffeehouses were filled by professors, hypocritical misfits [Sufis], and idlers," sixteenth-century historian Ibrahim Peçevi wrote. The Muslim hierarchies set out to eliminate these gathering places.

In Mecca, Arabia, in 1511, the ruling pasha prosecuted the coffeehouses before a jury of judges versed in Islamic law. Physicians, Stewart Lee Allen notes in his coffee history, "testified that coffee caused mental alterations in the drinker and was therefore a type of wine." The judges declared the sale and drinking of coffee illegal. In the wake of the ruling, angry crowds burned coffee in the street

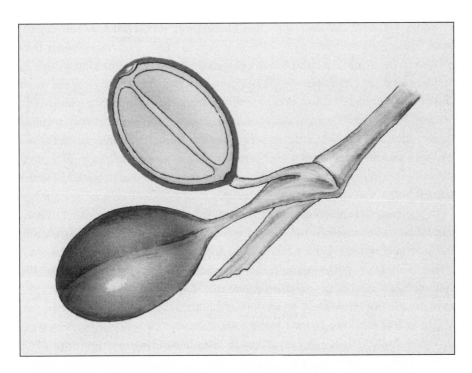

and attacked vendors and customers. Mobs in other cities wreaked havoc on coffee shops. A century later, Sultan Murad of Turkey banned coffee and ordered the closing of the "mutinous places of the people." For the second offense, the violator was to be sewn up in a leather bag and thrown into the Bosporus.

In spite of all the dissension, coffeehouses survived and assimilated into Islamic society. Coffee, which had originated in East Africa, now had the stamp of Arabia. Arabs who developed the techniques of roasting, grinding, and brewing the bean played a major role in popularizing the drink. When Linnaeus, the plant taxonomist, chose a name for the species, he called it *Coffea arabica*.

Even in the bean's heartland, Ethiopia, coffee had been greeted with suspicion. The Ethiopian Orthodox Church condemned coffee drinking by its congregants. The taint of Islam was a large factor in the church hierarchy's disapproval.

"Christians have a prejudice against it, because it is used so frequently by the Mohammedans," Nathanial Pearse, a European visitor to Ethiopia in the early nineteenth century, observed. During the same period, historian Rita Pankhurst notes, other travelers were confronted with the coffee taboo. When two Germans asked if they could make the drink in a Christian home, they were suspected of being Muslims and refused.

In the twentieth century, coffee was finally given its blessings by the church. Many Ethiopian families now perform a special coffee ceremony when they partake of the drink. An elaborate ritual, with precise steps of roasting, grinding, brewing, and serving *buna* (its Ethiopian name), the event binds gatherings of family and friends. "At home, people don't drink alone," my Ethiopian friend Emebet Tsiga (also known as Amy) told me. In America, she observed, you just "grab coffee and drink it." Her family in Addis Ababa religiously observes the tradition several times a day—after lunch, work, dinner, and church. In a room where the fragrant aroma of coffee blends with incense, she said, the smell of the roasted beans is as important as their taste.

By the early seventeenth century, Europeans were discovering coffee. Venetian traders were transporting the beans from the Middle East and distributing them throughout the Continent. Early coffee shops advertised the "Oriental" origin of their product. In London, signs displayed Turkish coffeepots or the Sultan's head. American merchants, who had strong Middle East connections, were pioneering traders and promoters of the drink in Europe.

Just as had occurred in the Middle East, European opponents of coffee tried to frighten people in an effort to dissuade them from using the import. In 1677, physicians from Marseilles pronounced coffee to be evil: "the vile and worthless foreign novelty . . . the fruit of a tree discovered by goats and camels . . . burned up the blood . . . induced palsies, impotence and leanness . . . hurtful to the greater part of the inhabitants of Marseilles." Culinary historian Claudia Roden suggests that the doctors were probably manipulated by local wine merchants.

As coffee moved west, it also faced the ire of the religious establishment. Priests in the early 1600s implored Pope Clement VIII to ban coffee drinking by Christians. Coffee, they argued, should be reserved for the infidels of Islam.

The pope was not persuaded. "Why, this Satan's drink is so delicious that it would be a pity to let the infidels have exclusive use of it. We shall cheat Satan by baptizing it," Clement responded. The drink that the priests denounced as a "hellish black brew" has become a morning essential for many of us.

Once dubbed the "stinking herbe," coriander has fallen in and out of favor. Native to the Mediterranean, the herb—both its tangy leaves and its earthy, citric seeds—has attracted flavor seekers from Asia to Latin America.

Coriander, whose seeds were unearthed in the tomb of the Egyptian pharaoh Tutankhamun's tomb (perhaps an offering), is an ancient herb belonging to the carrot family, a group that includes parsley, anise, dill, fennel, and cumin. These plants have a common characteristic—a cluster of flowers that looks like a "parasol," food expert Harold McGee observes. Pinkish flowers bloom in umbels on the plant, which can shoot up as high as two feet. Coriander, which thrives in warm, dry weather, also has the distinctive feathery greens of its species.

"The best coriander, as is generally agreed, is the Egyptian," wrote Pliny, the Roman botanist. The plant, which grew wild along the Nile, perked up many dishes. Recipes from Alexandria call for squash to be spiced with pepper, coriander seed, and cumin, and for grilled fish to be prepared in a sauce made from wine, pepper, raisins, and the herb. The Egyptians also infused wine with garlic and coriander to enhance its potency.

Coriander was an invaluable medicine and tonic. The feverish in Egypt, scholar Lise Manniche points out, were advised to add it to a lukewarm bath to cool their brows. Coriander, Pliny said, worked as "an antidote for the poison of the two-headed serpent both taken in drink and applied. . . . Spreading sores are also healed by coriander with honey or raisins. . . . [I]t is also taken in drink with rue for cholera. Intestinal parasites are expelled by coriander seed."

Egypt's neighbors, the Israelites, were familiar with the herb. The Book of Exodus in the Bible likened coriander to manna: "And the House of Israel called the name thereof Manna; and it was like coriander seed, white." In biblical times, the herb was commonly placed on the Passover table.

The Romans soon warmed to the Egyptian spice. Coriander seeds were already being sold in Pompeii's shops in the first century AD. Egypt's conquerors baked bread fragrant with coriander seeds and prepared a piquant sauce from the herb to go with oysters.

Coriander was also thought to promote health and energy. Roman statesman Cato urged the ill to eat the green leaves to awaken their appetite.

Another ancient empire, the Persian, was a heartland for coriander. The Persians, who revere herbs, still invigorate rice dishes and stews with its leaves. A verdant omelet, a *kookoo*, is filled with the aromatic leaves. It is one of the festive dishes served at Persian New Year celebrations.

The Chinese borrowed coriander from an old trading partner, the Persians. *Yuan cai*, or "fragrant vegetable," was esteemed for its spiritual powers—eating the seeds with a pure heart was a path to immortality. Anticipating the views of many modern health experts, the Chinese believed that coriander could soothe a turbulent stomach or intestine. It was also used as a remedy for ptomaine poisoning.

In the East, other civilizations were also captivated by coriander. In India, the nineteenth-century English botanist George Watt observed that "the leaves are eaten by natives like a vegetable." The ground seeds are an essential ingredient in the masalas, the Indian spice blends that add fragrance and heat to chicken, lamb, lentil, and vegetable dishes. Aromatic leaves decorate curries and are blended into chutneys.

Thai cooking would also be unimaginable without coriander. In Thailand, where the herb may have arrived from China, soups and salads are redolent with its leaves. Aurai, the former chef at Sala Thai in Washington, D.C., explained to me that coriander seeds are ground into Thai curry pastes. Coriander roots also add their aroma to these spice mixes. Aurai, who misses the superior herb of her homeland, lamented that she must make do with "Chinese coriander" rather than the hard-to-obtain Thai variety.

Coriander arrived with the Roman armies who invaded Britain. English cooks adopted the spice, seasoning steak, kidney, and oyster pies with it. Bakers made bread fragrant with coriander seeds.

The English and other Europeans sought new ways to capture the alluring aroma. After banquets, hosts offered their guests *confits*, sugar-coated coriander

seeds and other spices, as *digestifs*. The French extracted oil from the seeds to make Eau de Carnes, which served as both liqueur and cologne.

Medieval Europe fell in love with coriander, cumin, saffron, cloves, and other Oriental spices. Chefs imitated the spice-laden recipes recorded in the cooking manuals of the Arab empire, whose leaders ruled from Baghdad between AD 750 and 1250. "Put the meat in the oil . . . with fine-milled dry coriander, and fry lightly until browned," one recipe directed. "Then cover with water, adding green coriander leaves, cinnamon bark."

By the end of the seventeenth century Europe had started to sour on spices. Coriander, once so revered, was now the object of disdain. In 1597, the English herbalist John Gerard called it a "very stinking herbe" with leaves of "venomous qualities." Writing around the same time, French writer Olivier de Serres was similarly dismissive: "[I]ts leaves, rubbed between the hands, smelled like stink bugs."

Commentators, anthropologist Helen Leach argues, seized on the origin of the herb's name to disparage it. *Coriandrum*, its Latin name, came from the Greek word for "bug," *koris*. A nineteenth-century vegetable manual made the connection between the offensive odor of the spice and its etymology explicit: "Some writers say the leaves are used for seasoning but this statement seems odd, as all the green parts of the plant exhale a very strong odour of the wood-bug, whence the Greek name of the plant."

But was this the reason the Greeks and Romans used the word? It's more likely, anthropologist Leach contends, that those who already disliked the spice were looking for a justification.

Some modern cookery authors have gone even further, likening the smell of coriander to that of the bedbug. Margaret Visser notes that "the green leaves of coriander are said to smell like squashed bed-bugs." Herbalist Allen Patterson was struck by how similar the two fragrances were: "The herb's sweet, cloying smell is as close as one is likely to get to that traditionally distinctive odour."

In a television interview in 2002, author Julia Child added her voice to the chorus of disgust. She told Larry King, "Cilantro and arugula, I don't like at all. They're both green herbs; they have kind of a dead taste to me." Asked if she would ever order it, Child responded, "Never. I would pick it out if I saw it and throw it on the floor."

In a recent article, food-science expert Harold McGee contends that the coriander revulsion may not be so irrational after all. Molecules responsible for the plant's scent, he points out, are also found in bugs and in soaps and lotions.

A new generation of cooks and diners has rediscovered the delights of coriander—or should I say *cilantro*, its now-popular name. Cilantro evokes the inimitable fragrances of Thai and Mexican food, not the unpleasant stench the older name conjured up.

THE "BITTER BERRY"
reclaiming the cranberry

The venerable cranberry is clouded in myth, in tales of Puritans and Indians, and in stories of the first Thanksgiving. While we pay homage to this symbol of a by-gone era of simplicity and self-reliance during the holiday season, we know little about the actual history of this strange fruit. The cranberry is a North American original, one of three major fruits—along with the blueberry and the Concord grape—native to our continent.

The Indians discovered its evergreen shrubs amid the beach plums and bay-berry bushes in coastal New England. The viny plant, which bears crimson ber-ries, wound through marshes and swamps. The Wampanoag tribe of Cape Cod, a cranberry heartland, named it *ibimi*, or "bitter berry." The Native Americans prized the cranberry for its many uses. The berries could be dried in the sun and stored or preserved in crocks full of cold water. Their high acid content enabled them to be kept for long periods.

In addition to eating the berries raw, the Indians stewed the fruit to make a sauce for roasted meats. John Josselyn, a seventeenth-century English writer, ex-plained that "the Indians and English use them much, boyling them with sugar for Sauce to eat with their meat, especially with Roasted Mutton." Josselyn no doubt meant maple, not cane, sugar.

They were also a vital ingredient in a dried cake of pounded meat (often veni-son) and animal fat, called *pemmican* (an Indian word that means "grease"). The cranberries enhanced the cake's flavor and staying power, and since it was easily carried on the trail during long treks, it helped to stave off hunger.

The versatile berry was indispensable to Native Americans in other ways, as well. Cranberry juice was made into a dye to color rugs and blankets. A poultice constructed of roasted and mashed cranberries mixed with cornmeal was applied to poison-arrow wounds to draw out the toxins.

The cranberry was so esteemed that the Indians made it an emblem of peace and friendship. The great chief of the Delaware tribe was known as Pakimintzen, or "cranberry eater," because he presided over feasts with rival tribes where the fruit was enjoyed.

What to name the puzzling fruit? It resembled the lingonberry, which the English knew, but had different features. Josselyn called it a "bearberry," because bears loved them. According to one tempting theory, Dutch and German settlers contributed the name from which *cranberry* derives. They called the fruit a "craneberry" because of the wading bird drawn to bogs and swamps where the "bitter berry" grew. Cranes hunted for their beloved cranberries and other food in these areas.

The colonists developed an affection for the fruit. Convinced of its marketability, New England merchants shipped fresh "Cape Cod bell cranberries" to England in the early 1700s. The first fruits to be sent from the new land to the mother country, they were sold on London's Strand for four shillings a jar.

A store of cranberries was considered essential for sea journeys. Kept in barrels of spring water, they were eaten to prevent scurvy. In Melville's *Moby-Dick*, a sailor was angered by Captain Ahab's objection to carrying them on his ship: "Go out with the crazy Captain Ahab? Never! He flat refused to take cranberries aboard. A man could get scurvy, or worse, sailing with the likes of 'im."

Early in American history, the cranberry was extolled for its health benefits. "Properties [are] refrigerant, laxative, anti-bilious, anti-putrid, diuretic, subastringent," medicinal plant expert Constantine Samuel Rafinesque wrote of the fruit in 1830. "Their juice mixed with sugar or alcohol . . . forms a fine acidulous drink with water, allaying thirst, and lessening the heat of the body." Cookbook author Mrs. N. M. K. Lee two years later praised cranberry juice as a "fine drink for people in fevers."

The Indian staple was absorbed into American cooking. As more West Indian sugar became available, cooks found a perfect foil to the bitter berry. "Add just so much sugar as shall leave a smart [the expression for tartness]," one colonial recipe put it.

Cranberry sweets caught on. Cooking writer Amelia Simmons called for "stewed, strained, and sweetened" fruit in her cranberry tart recipe. For Eng-

lish colonists already familiar with gooseberry or sour cherry tarts, this was not a great leap. Nineteenth-century cooks also produced cranberry pies and puddings. Dolly Madison served a cranberry sherbet at her husband's second inauguration. Her instructions: "Mix 1½ cups cranberry jelly with the juice and grated rind of one lemon and the juice of one orange. Freeze for ½ hour. Add ½ pint whipped cream, pour into a mold, and freeze until solid."

Cranberry sauce gained in popularity. Author Amelia Simmons encouraged readers of her 1796 cookbook to consider pairing "cramberry" sauce with turkey dinner. The American delight in this dressing enraged a French representative in the United States, who, in a report to his superior, wrote of the "most villainous of American sauces." He was repelled by the "voracious manner in which they eat it."

Although Thoreau had rhapsodized about the "refreshing, cheering, encouraging acid that literally puts the heart in you and sets you on edge for this world's experiences," the American romance with the wild cranberry gradually lost its fervor. Soon, the wild cranberry was swept aside in a tide of commercial enthusiasm. In the early nineteenth century, Yankee entrepreneurs around Cape Cod pioneered cultivation of the berry. Unlike the Indians, who had never been interested in farming cranberries, canny land developers—many of whom were former sea captains and fishermen—avidly domesticated the fruit. They selected particularly attractive berries from the wild and transformed them into commercial varieties. Swamps and marshes were cleared and drained and bogs were carved out in which to grow the crop.

Ever new technologies for harvesting cranberries led to abundant yields. Businesses stepped in to exploit the surplus. Marcus Urann, a Massachusetts grower, founded the United Cape Cod Cranberry Company in 1912 to produce canned cranberry sauce. Noticing the many piles of cranberries rotting for lack of a market, the entrepreneur saw a business opportunity.

Ocean Spray, a cooperative of farmers established in 1930, changed the industry from a seasonal to a year-round business. Its first products were a cranberry jelly aimed at the Thanksgiving market and a tart cranberry juice. To boost sales, Ocean Spray introduced the "Cranberry Juice Cocktail," a sweeter refreshment, in 1962. Ed Gelsthorpe, a company executive, explained the strategy behind the product: "We tasted the cranberry juice cocktail, and we could understand why very few people drank it. It had actually been formulated to meet the taste of cranberry growers . . . so we did the not so brilliant thing of putting more water and sugar in it. It then became a very palatable drink, and we initially marketed it across the country."

The industry continues to search for new outlets for the berries. Craisins (sweetened dried cranberries), cookies, and cereals have all proved to be profitable avenues. "The challenge has been to get people to use cranberries at other times of the year and in a variety of products," John Llewellyn, an Ocean Spray official, observed. Most of the cranberry harvest today is channeled into overly sweetened juices and other items rather than for fresh produce. At this pace, few of us will remember the tingling tartness of the "bitter berry."

THE "BILIOUS" COWCUMBER
cool as a cucumber

"Raw cucumber makes the churchyards prosperous." As this sixteenth-century English saying suggests, the cucumber once raised the specter of death. At other times, it was a symbol of fertility that brought hope and elation. As the cucumber made its way from its birthplace in the East to the West, it was sometimes considered auspicious, sometimes frightening.

Unlike its kin, the pumpkin and squash, the cucumber is a native of the Old World, not the New. This gourd descends from a wild, unappetizing plant that grew in the moist foothills of the Himalayas. The original was small—the size of a golf ball—bitter, and spiny. Most likely domesticated in northern India, this scrawny cucumber was gradually transformed into a robust fruit with a more-pleasing flavor. Varieties of different shapes, sizes, and colors were bred.

The *sakusha*, or "pleasant food," as it was known in the ancient Sanskrit language, was invested with mythic power. Indians were impressed by its "exuberance of reproductive power" and "wealth of seed," as food historian Victor Hehn put it. In one Indian tale, Sumati, the wife of King Sagara, the Sea God, gives birth to sixty thousand sons who burst forth from a cucumber shell. The first son, Ikshvaku, a cucumber, bears a son, who climbs to heaven on his own vine.

The people of the biblical Near East also had a strong attachment to the prolific fruit. During their exile in the desert, memories of the cool, thirst-quenching cucumber burned in the hearts of the Israelites. Disconsolate, Moses longed for the cucumbers, whose seeds he had forgotten to bring: "We remember the fish which we did eat in Egypt freely; the cucumbers and the melons, and the leeks. Now our throats are parched" (Numbers 11:5). (In ancient sources, "cucumber" may have actually referred to a melon that resembled its close relative.)

The cucumber was widely grown in ancient Egypt, where it sustained both the Israelites and the country's masses. The pharaohs gave the water-rich gourds to their slaves to slake their thirst, as they labored in ferociously hot temperatures. Centuries later, a traveler in Egypt found that cucumbers were still central to daily life. "They still form a great part of the food of the lower-class people . . . serving them for meat, drink, and physic," Frederic Hasselquist wrote in the 1700s.

In the hot and dry climate of the Arab world, cucumbers were also a necessity. Botanical historian Claire Houghton notes that they were carried along on desert caravan journeys to moisten the travelers' parched mouths. Ibn Ridwan, an eleventh-century Egyptian physician, recommended eating cucumbers to relieve maladies like heartburn, suffered during the summer.

By the first century AD, cucumbers were being planted in Rome, where they acquired an enthusiastic following. Like the gourds they used as wine bottles and water pitchers, cucumbers were employed by the Romans as containers for liquids. *Cucumis sativus*, its scientific name, is similar to Latin words for "covered vessel."

The cucumber proved to be a prolific plant. The Roman poet Virgil likened it to a serpent "coiling through the grass and swelling the belly." It was the cucumber's fecundity as much as its practicality that excited him. In Rome, women wore cucumbers around their waist to induce pregnancy.

The Romans soon discovered that, with the right flavoring, the cucumber could be quite appetizing. To counteract its bitterness, gardeners planted seeds that had been immersed in honeyed wine. Gastronome Apicius developed a recipe for cucumber salad that called for a dressing of honey, vinegar, and *liquamen* (a fish sauce). Early picklers, the Romans also cured cucumbers in crocks.

The unassuming cucumber was prized by patricians and royalty. After his doctor prescribed the vegetable for him, the ailing emperor Tiberius became passionate about it. The cucumber was "a delicacy for which the emperor had a remarkable partiality; in fact, there was never a day in which he was not supplied with it," the naturalist Pliny wrote. Since Tiberius demanded the gourds year-round, his attendants had to devise a method for forcing their growth. They planted cucumbers in frames on raised beds, which were wheeled and "exposed to the full heat of the sun," Pliny says. During the frigid months, they were "placed under the protection of frames glazed with mirrorstone."

The cucumber wound its way from the Mediterranean to Western Europe. In the ninth century, Charlemagne ordered that this, his favorite fruit, be planted

throughout his realm. The emperor was especially fond of cucumber tarts and custards. In England, where Roman conquerors transplanted cucumber seeds, archaeologists have found remains of the gourd.

In the British Isles, fear and superstition hindered its acceptance. A "cold" vegetable like the cucumber, many felt, could bring on sickness or death. These fears were given credence in medical opinion. Doctors contended that cold or raw foods would disrupt the body's temperature balance. "Neither is it safe when warm to eat freely of raw fruit, salads, or the like," the English physician William Buchan warned. Compared to melons and pineapples, which are "rich and cordial," the doctor John Arbuthnot declared, the "juice of cucumber is too cold for some stomachs."

Samuel Johnson, in his *Journey to the Hebrides*, commented on the prevailing view: "It has been a common saying of physicians in England that a cucumber should be well sliced and dressed with pepper and vinegar, and then thrown out, as good for nothing."

The peril of cucumbers was a frequent literary theme in England. In his diary on September 22, 1663, Samuel Pepys noted, "[T]his day Sir W. Batten tells me that Mr. Newhouse is dead of eating cowcumbers, of which the other day I heard of another, I think." Writer Landon Carter, in his diary on July 24, 1766, expressed his fears for his daughter: "She does bear ungovernable the whole summer through, eating extravagantly and late at night of cucumbers and all sorts of bilious trash." An early eighteenth-century poem warned readers to be wary of the seemingly innocent cucumber:

> Green cucumbers, however nice,
> By all who prudent are and wise
> And health prefer to choicest dainty,
> Will ne'er be eaten in great plenty:
> Their properties, so deadly cold,
> Agree not with the human mould,
> But off to dangerous sickness move,
> And sometimes actual poison prove.

English herbalists often disparaged the gourd. For example, Nicholas Culpeper wrote, "The green tumors grow fullest and fairest when planted upon fields that were once fields of pasturage, enriched by a dominion of cows droppings." The gourd did have a few redeeming qualities, Culpeper conceded. The astrologically minded writer argued that, like its sister, the moon, the cucumber was cooling and healing.

John Gerard preached the cucumber's medicinal properties. A "pottage," a soup of oatmeal and cucumber, he said, would work wonders on skin disorders, on "copper faces, red and shining fierie noses (as red as red roses)." He advised that the soup cure should be accompanied by a cucumber face wash.

Gerard was repeating ancient wisdom about the cucumber's benefits to the complexion. Cleopatra, the story goes, applied cucumber slices to her face. Medieval herbalists recommended that women eat cucumbers three times a day, in porridge and pies, and mixed with oatmeal, to help the skin.

The French were especially enthusiastic about the cucumber as a beauty aid. Writing in the late nineteenth century, the physician Dr. Daniel Garrison Brinton observed, "[T]hey attribute sovereign cosmetic virtue to the juice of the cucumber. All the shops keep a *lait de concombre* or a *pomade de concombre*."

Ignoring their dangerous reputation, status-conscious English gentry avidly cultivated cucumbers, even planting them out of season. Growing them in "hot beds" during the winter was a form of ostentation: Cucumbers had no cachet during the summer, when they were so cheap and plentiful that even the poor could afford them.

Seedsmen like John Switzer looked askance at this practice. Some gardeners, such as John Rogers, who worked for King George III, were more understanding: "In winter when the snow is deep on the ground, a cucumber either in its green or stewed state highly embellishes the table of the higher and more wealthy classes."

The arbiters of English food remained torn about the cucumber. John Evelyn declared that, although it is "very cold and moist," the vegetable was the "most approved sallet of the vinaigrets." It helped "to sharpen the Appetite, and cool the liver." Isabella Beeton, culinary advisor to the aspiring Victorian housewife, was apprehensive about the cucumber: "It is a cold food and difficult of digestion when eaten raw." She added that "delicate stomachs should avoid the plant, for it is cold and indigestible." In spite of these misgivings, Ms. Beeton allowed that the vegetable made one of the most agreeable "sweetmeats." She provided a recipe for cucumber stewed in brown gravy, leavened with sugar to reduce bitterness.

It might be "indigestible," but cucumbers were all the rage on the tables of the aristocracy. During the Edwardian age, the cucumber sandwich on buttered, crustless bread became a fashionable finger food. It was served for afternoon tea, at cricket matches, and at elegant social functions. "You are offered a piece of bread and butter that feels like a damp handkerchief, and sometimes, when cucumber is added to it, like a wet one," Sir Compton Mackenzie jested. The Pimm's Cup, a summer cocktail enjoyed by the English leisure classes, was suitably embellished with a cucumber. Created as a digestive in the mid-nineteenth century by James Pimm, owner of a London oyster bar, it was a fixture of polo matches. It is now the official drink of Wimbledon.

While the British were skittish about the cucumbers, other cultures found in-genious ways to incorporate them in their cooking. A "yogurt belt" of countries extending from Iran to the Balkans constructed cooling, creamy repasts around the adaptable gourd. *Mâst-o kheeyâr*, a popular Iranian dish, marries "Persian milk," as yogurt was once called, with cucumber. Typically garnished with wal-nuts and raisins, it can also be thinned to make a soup. The treat is relished by all the country's social classes: "You see very poor workers, sitting on street corners, bowls in front of them, and that's their meal," chef Faz Poursohi told the *San Francisco Chronicle*.

The Indians, whose food was strongly influenced by the Persians, prepare *raita*, their version of the cucumber-yogurt partnership. Chopped cucumbers, carrots, and other vegetables are blended with yogurt. *Raita* softens the spicy, pungent flavors of the Indian meal.

The Turks, who instinctively grasped the affinity between the two products, ennobled them with their preparation of *caçik*, a medley of yogurt and cucum-bers, accented with garlic, and sprinkled with mint or dill. The Turks dissemi-nated their yogurt innovations throughout their empire. *Tzatziki*, the Hellenic dip, is virtually a replica of the Turkish *caçik*, although the Greeks often claim parentage. In Bulgaria, long an Ottoman colony, a chilled yogurt-cucumber spread studded with walnuts is called *tarator*, a Turkish word.

The cucumber has a long lineage in the Slavic countries. In Poland, where the gourd was grown as early as AD 650–950, the people blend cucumber with sour cream and adorn the dish with dill. The classic Polish cucumber salad, *mizeria*, or the "miserable ones," was a mainstay of the peasant diet. It is a tangy mixture of cucumbers, sour cream, and vinegar. The Russians, too, German food scholar Victor Hehn notes, were wedded to the cucumber: "The Great and Little Russian cannot live without cucumbers; he eats them salted throughout the winter, and with their help endures the long and strict fasts of the Eastern Church." Cucumber and sour cream salad is a staple of the *zakuski*, the Russian ensemble of appetizers.

The cucumber migrated from Eastern Europe, where it was known as *agurke*, to Germany, where it became the *gurke*. The German standard *gurkensalat*, cucumbers and sour cream, has a definite Slavic imprint. The Eastern gourd continued its Western journey, arriving in the Americas with Columbus. Appar-ently at the urging of Queen Isabella, its seeds were among the earliest planted in the New World—in Haiti, in 1494. From the West Indies, cucumbers migrated north to the mainland, where Spanish adventurer Hernando de Soto discovered Indians growing them in Florida. They were "better than those of Spain," he said.

A century later, cucumbers, along with other vegetables, had taken root in New England. One English observer, Sir Francis Higginson, wrote effusively of the bountiful produce in his book, *New England's Plantation*: "The country aboundeth naturally with store[s] of roots of great varietie and good to eat. Our turnips, parsnips, and carrots are here both bigger and sweeter than is ordinarily to be found in England. Here are store[s] of pompions, cowcumbers, and other things of that nature which I know not."

Thomas Jefferson became another enthusiastic convert to the tangy cucumber. "On a hot day," he wrote, "I know nothing more comforting than a fine spiced pickle, brought up trout-like from the sparkling depths of the aromatic jar below the stairs of Aunt Sally's cellar."

American picklers recognized the cucumber's ability to absorb a wide range of flavors. In the United States, ingenious pickling recipes found a receptive audience. The American edition of British author Hannah Glasse's *Art of Cooking* taught readers how to imbue gherkins with white wine vinegar, cloves, allspice, ginger, nutmeg, and bay leaf. Although Americans enjoyed sour pickles, it was the sweet pickle, an inheritance from England, that triumphed in the new land. Sliced or ground into relish to top the hamburger, the sweet pickle, food historian Elisabeth Rozin argues, is "emblematic of American taste."

Even though culinary experts in the United States pronounced the cucumber healthful, some food writers encouraged their readers to be vigilant about them. In her work, *American Frugal Housewife* (1829), Lydia Maria Child called for slicing them thinly and soaking them in cold water to remove the "slimy matter so injurious to your health."

Widely diffused, the cucumber is inescapable in food the world over, prominent even where it is least expected. A small dish of sliced cucumber, chopped red onion, and white vinegar accompanies satays at Thai restaurants. *Achar*, this appetizer, is a perfect foil for the tiny kebabs, which are flavored with coconut milk and served with a tangy peanut sauce. This pickle, a Thai waitress once told me, provides "balance" to the satay—a fitting tribute to the well-traveled cucumber.

Chili, as in the illustrious American dish, *chili con carne*, is more redolent of cumin than chili. Look at a supermarket container of chili powder and you will see cumin listed as an ingredient. For all its importance, few of us know much about this forgotten spice.

Cumin, I learned, is a flowering plant in Umbelliferae, the same family as dill, fennel, coriander, parsley, and anise, among others. They have in common an umbrella-shaped cluster of blossoms atop a tall stalk. Cumin, which bears white or rose-colored flowers, packs its aroma in its seeds, which are actually fruits. Cumin's robust smell comes from the intense oils in the seeds.

Where did this spice originate? Most scholars agree that it is a Mediterranean native, unlike spices such as ginger, nutmeg, cloves, and cardamom, which were grown in the East. Probably first grown along the banks of the Nile, it was one of the spices used to scent the mummies of Egyptian royalty. A late Roman cookbook calls for "fairly generous cumin" to inject zip into a sauce of pepper, mint, honey, vinegar, bay leaf, and other seasonings, for cooking oysters and shellfish. The recipe came from the Egyptian city of Alexandria.

According to the Bible, cumin was more than a spice; it was a crop that sprang from the soil. After harvesting, dried plants were "beaten out with rods," says a verse in Isaiah. Presumably threshing was done to extract the seeds.

Greeks and Romans, who were actively engaged in the spice trade, were impressed with cumin. The Greek writer Theophrastus marveled at its abundant growth: "Cumin has the most fruits of any plants." But, he cautioned, "when

people are sowing it, they must curse and slander it if they want it to be healthy and prolific." One can only imagine what demon the naturalist believed lurked in its seed. The Romans looked at the plant with awe. The naturalist Pliny praised cumin for its taste: "Of all the seasonings which gratify a fastidious taste, cumin is the most agreeable." The Romans spiced up their bread by spreading it with a paste made from this aromatic. Its scent was so intense, many believed that cumin could speed up conception if smelled during sex.

It was as much a medicine and cosmetic as it was food for the ancients. The Romans regarded it as a digestive that could soothe the stomach. It could also, they believed, induce pallor in the face, a curious property that was highly valued. Students, according to Pliny, would apply a cumin-based oil to their skin to make their teachers believe they were working feverishly.

Both Greeks and Romans considered cumin a symbol of greed. A person who would "divide a cumin seed," scholar John Ayto explains, was demonstrably selfish. The Roman emperor Marcus Aurelius was nicknamed "Cumin" because of his avaricious nature.

From the Mediterranean, cumin traveled eastward. It was adopted by the Persians, who perked up their rice with it. Their warriors probably transplanted cumin to India, whose people embraced it enthusiastically. *Jeera*, the Hindi name of the spice, is related to the Persian *zeera*. Both words, botanist George Watt suggests, allude to cumin's digestive benefits.

Cumin's trek continued. Moorish invaders from North Africa, it is assumed, introduced the spice to Spain. Spain, in turn, disseminated it in its colonies in the Americas. Latin dishes like black bean soup and tamales are invigorated with cumin. Cowboys in the American Southwest picked it wild to use in chili.

It is in India that *jeera*'s gifts were most heavily exploited. In his country, Kiran Kumar B. Kamble—an Indian chef who once lived in Washington—told me, cumin is curative. "Food is medicine," explained the Bombay native, who was once chef to India's prime minister Rajiv Gandhi. Cumin is a tonic for the eyes and stomach and, curiously, for the tongue, the chef expounded: "If you're sick and have no appetite, put *jeera* powder on your tongue. Your tongue is now fresh." A mixture of garlic, onion, ginger, and *jeera* can "make you strong."

I listened raptly as the chef spun out some recipes for this, one of his favorite flavorings. For two portions of cumin potatoes, he told me, put a little oil in a pan and fry cumin seeds for five or six minutes until they reach a brown color. Meanwhile, boil three potatoes. When they are boiled, add potatoes to the frying pan. Sprinkle a little salt and turmeric on them and fry the potatoes, with the cumin seeds, for six or seven minutes. Finally, sprinkle with coriander leaves and serve.

To make *dahi jeera*, a cuminy yogurt, the chef instructed, first roast two teaspoons of cumin seeds in a very hot frying pan until they are dark brown. Then lay them on a plate. When they are cool enough, take your hand and crush the seeds into a powder. Then add the powder to a bowl of sixteen ounces of yogurt, mix well, and add a pinch of salt. Sprinkle coriander leaves on top and enjoy.

In Indian cooking, there is a plethora of cumin dishes. There is also cumin rice, a cumin-infused drink, and "cumin everything," chef Kamble pointed out. Fans of Indian food—and other zesty cuisines, such as Tex-Mex—may not notice the cumin they are consuming, but their pleasure owes much to this Mediterranean native.

A FINE FEATHERED FRIEND
the wonders of dill

It was a perfect marriage—the energetic fragrance and the earthy root vegetable. I still savor the memory of the dill that adorned the bracing beef borscht at Sir Nicholas, a Polish restaurant in Toronto. On another memorable occasion, I relished a plate of tender strips of sautéed zucchini covered with a garlicky yogurt sauce that was flecked with dill. A variety of other Balkan dishes served at Café Sofia, a Bulgarian restaurant in Washington, D.C., arrived with the same herbal flourish.

Dill, I would discover, was more than just an aromatic. The ancient herb, native to the Mediterranean and Southern Russia, was also revered as a tonic for mind and body. The herb "strengthens the brain," English herbalist Nicholas Culpeper wrote. The plant, with its distinctive green, feathery leaves is—along with anise, fennel, coriander, and carrots—a member of the parsley family. The group is known for its fragrant leaves and seeds and its umbels, parasols of yellow flowers.

Both the Greeks and the Romans praised the potent herb. The Greek word for dill, *anethon*, meant "burn," an early suggestion of its electric force. The Romans, who called it *anethum*, invested dill with additional powers. Dill, they believed, could produce feats of muscular strength. The meals of gladiators were thus infused with dill oil. The herb, which the poet Virgil praised as a "pleasant and fragrant plant," was also associated with gaiety and celebration. Romans wore feathery wreathes woven from the weed to their feasts.

Dill was seen simultaneously as invigorating and relaxing. Dioscorides, the Greek herbalist, recommended it for indigestion. The aromatic "stayeth the hickets [hiccups]," he declared. Northern Europeans would later come to value dill as a remedy for intestinal distress. "The seed . . . is used in medicines that serve to expel wind," Culpeper observed. Dill was originally put in the pickling solutions for cucumbers, a gas-producing vegetable, because of its reputation. Only later, spice expert Maggie Stuckey says, did preservers use it to impart fragrance.

In Scandinavia, dill was given a new name in recognition of its soothing effects. *Dilla*, the Norse word for the herb, meant "lull." The Saxons in Britain adopted the name, and it migrated into English. Colicky babies for centuries were given dill water to calm their stomachs and make them sleepy. Medieval churchgoers chewed on dill seeds to ward off hunger.

Dill seems to have taken hold in a swath of land stretching from Russia and Scandinavia in the north, through Eastern Europe and the Balkans, and south to Iran and Afghanistan. Despite its Mediterranean origins, it has few outposts in the region other than Greece and Turkey. It is rare, for example, in the Italian kitchen. But in the herb's heartlands, dill invigorates the cuisine. It lends a zing to Polish sautéed chicken, pickled herring, and cucumber salad. The Swedes, who are ecstatic about it, make a mustard dill sauce for salmon cured with dill and other flavorings, and scent bread with the herb. Chesnochnaya, a Russian vodka, is infused with dill, garlic, and peppercorns.

A simple Greek salad of lettuce, tomatoes, spring onions, and feta gets verve from dill. *Tzatziki* and *caçik*, the Greek and Turkish yogurt-and-cucumber dips, respectively, are often accented with the herb. Both cultures elevate grape leaves with a dill-laced filling.

Dill also plays a prominent role in the cooking of Central Asia. The Persians, who traditionally lay out a plate of fresh herbs to grace their table, adore dill. During the Persian New Year, dill contributes its aroma and vitality to a verdant frittata. The profusion of herbs symbolizes rebirth. Polows, or Persian pilafs, fragrant with dill, are both elegant and sumptuous.

America's dill heritage pales when compared to these richer traditions. The herb, however, did play a role in our country's religious life. Children were given the "meeting seed" to chew on during sermons, presumably to keep them from getting restless.

THE "MAD APPLE"
the terrifying eggplant

The "mad apple," as eggplant was known centuries ago, was transformed into a regal vegetable. A member of the terrifying nightshade family, it was long feared for the maladies imputed to it. Eggplant was also considered unappetizing. But is there another vegetable today that so often takes center stage and assumes so many incarnations—fried, baked, pureed, grilled, stewed, stuffed, pickled?

Native to India (or, as some suggest, Southeast Asia), the once-prickly shrub with spiny leaves grew wild on the hillsides. In India, the wild eggplant was domesticated. Farmers bred spineless plants with bigger, less acrid fruits. It bore little resemblance to today's familiar variety, a plump purple hybrid. The early eggplant was smaller than a baseball. Its fruit was also intensely bitter.

From its earliest days, the eggplant aroused fear. It was known as *vatingana*, belonging to the "windy class," in Sanskrit. In India, insanity was likened to volatile air currents. The eggplant could also be immensely pleasurable. It was believed to be erotically stimulating. The *Kama Sutra* claims that rubbing eggplant juice on the male organ produces a monthlong erection.

The saga of the eggplant is inextricably linked with the history of the Arabs, who gradually came to adore it and who disseminated the plant throughout their empire. They most likely stumbled on the eggplant when they conquered Persia in AD 642. It had migrated from India, which had close ties to Persia. The Arabs took the eggplant's Persian name, *badingan*, except for the "g," which they changed to "j."

As Islam expanded, its followers carried the plants to which they were devoted to new lands. Spinach, artichokes, almonds, and citrus traveled westward
from the eastern side of the realm, transplanted, historian Andrew Watson says,
by sailors, merchants, royalty, and ordinary travelers. In the process, plants sired
in tropical Asia and adopted by the Arabs reached the Mediterranean.

Spain—large parts of which the Islamic conquerors controlled for five hundred
years (from 721 to 1212)—was the portal through which the foods of the Orient
reached the West. Skilled Arab agriculturists irrigated, planted, and tilled the new
crops in Andalusia, a Muslim kingdom. Land that had once been fallow during the
summer now teemed with hot-weather crops like eggplant, rice, and sugarcane.

Andalusian agronomist Ibn al-Awwam was enchanted by the great variety of
eggplants that were now growing. He described Egyptian plants with white fruits
and purple flowers and Syrian varieties with purple fruits and violet flowers. He
observed two kinds of Spanish eggplant—one with black skin and the other with
brown skin, and both with purple flowers.

The Spaniards were not so ecstatic about the import. The *berenjena*, the eggplant's new name (and source of the later French word *aubergine*), was viewed

with suspicion. The Moorish invaders, the story went, had craftily planted the poisonous eggplant in order to kill Christians.

The plant, moreover, had an alien image. It was regarded as a "Semitic" food favored by Muslims and Spain's large colony of Sephardic Jews. Recipes for *berenjena* "Jewish style" and "Moorish style" appeared in thirteenth- and fourteenth-century Spanish cookbooks.

The *conversos*, the Jews forcibly converted after the Christians overpowered the Moors, were mocked for their eating habits. "At the Jewish wedding party," a fifteenth-century poet wrote, "a bristly pig was not consumed; not a single scale-less fish went down the gullet of the groom; instead an eggplant casserole with saffron and Swiss chard."

The Italians, who likely received the eggplant from Arab traders, were slow to embrace the "apple of the moors." Commentators saddled it with a host of ills. Castore Durante, a sixteenth-century doctor, attributed melancholy, cancer, leprosy, and headaches to eating the "unsavory" vegetable. The name Italians attached to it, *melanzane*, revealed their fears: they derived it from the Latin *mala insana*, or "mad apple."

In Italy, eggplant eaters were stigmatized. Muslims, it was thought, could enjoy eggplant without danger. Christians, however, risked psychic disorder or intoxication. Only after Armenian Christians in Venice ate the vegetable without ill effect, the story goes, did the fears abate.

Eggplant fanciers, some of its detractors argued, were of vulgar character. "Eggplants should be eaten only by people of lowly status or by Jews," the seventeenth-century writer Antonio Frugoli warned.

Considered an ornamental plant because of its pretty leaves and white and purple flowers, it was mostly relegated to the garden. In northern Italy, in the late seventeenth century, eggplants were tended to in monastery gardens and rarely eaten. When they were prepared at all, they were cooked in the most basic fashion. "Fried in oil with salt and pepper, it is eaten by the masses, in the way that mushrooms are eaten," the physician Pietro Andrea Mattioli remarked.

Away from the mainland, however, Sicilians exulted in the eggplant. In the ninth century, the Saracens, Arab warriors, marched onto the island and occupied it for two hundred years. The eggplant, which flourished in the fields the Arabs skillfully irrigated, became central to Sicilian cooking. The Sicilians put their own stamp on the *melanzane*, stuffing it with anchovies, black olives, tomatoes, and capers. Pine nuts and raisins, an Arab touch, enlivened the sauces for eggplant dishes.

Caponata, the piquant eggplant relish, is of Sicilian origin. Typically prepared during the summer, it is a blend of tomatoes, onions, celery, and eggplant suffused with olive oil. The dish is sharpened with olives, capers, and vinegar. Now a mainstay of the antipasto buffet, caponata may have started as a food for sailors. Vinegar kept it fresh and savory during a long voyage.

Like ratatouille, its Provençal cousin, caponata is mostly eaten cold or at room temperature. When Sicilians talk about the appetizer, they can be rhapsodic. "He who has not eaten a capontina [a variation of caponata] of eggplant has never reached the antechamber of the terrestrial paradise," author Gaetano Falzone writes.

When the eggplant reached Northern Europe, it was greeted warily. John Gerard, the sixteenth-century English herbalist, urged his countrymen to avoid it. Although it was eaten by Spaniards and Arabs, "I rather wish English men to content themselves with the meat and sauces of our owne country, than with fruit and sauce eaten with such peril," he cautioned. "Doubtlesse these Apples have a mischevous qualitie. . . . it is therefore better to esteem this plant and have it in the garden for your pleasure and the rarenesse thereof, than for any virtue or good qualities yet knowne."

Its leaves, Gerard noted, had a worrisome resemblance to henbane, a member of the poisonous nightshade family, which, along with eggplants, includes potatoes, tomatoes, peppers, and tobacco. The nightshades, many of which share a fleshy berry (the eggplant is botanically a berry), are part of the genus Solanum. Its Latin name, which comes from the word for quieting, is an apt one, botanist Charles Heiser points out: some of the plants in the group are indeed sedatives.

Eggplants also cause disease, English herbalist John Parkinson warned. They are suitable for Italy and "other hot countries," he conceded. "They [the people] doe eate them with more desire and pleasure than we do cowcumbers." People should only eat the vegetables after boiling them with vinegar, "for by their bitternesse and acrimony . . . they engender Melancholly, the Leprosie, Cancers, the Piles . . . the Headache, and a stinking breath, breed obstructions in the Liver and Spleene, and change the complection into a foule blacke and yellow colour." To add to its perils, Parkinson writes, the eggplant "invites to venery [sexual desire]."

Parkinson and Gerard were not speaking of the familiar purple aubergine, but of something more egg-shaped. The vegetable was named accordingly. "The fruit . . . [is] great and somewhat long, of the bignesse of a Swans egge, and sometimes much greater, of a white colour, sometimes yellow, and often brown," in Gerard's depiction.

Even in the Middle East, where it achieved its greatest fame, the eggplant had to battle fears and prejudice. Ibn Wahshiyya, an Arab toxicologist, wrote in his book on poisons that eating the raw vegetable could be fatal. In Arab lore, the *badinjan* was considered threatening and distasteful. "Its color is like the scorpion's belly and its taste is like the scorpion's sting," Middle East food scholar Charles Perry writes, quoting an eleventh-century Bedouin adage.

Its bitterness, Perry argues, may have been the most difficult handicap eggplant had to overcome. Arab cooks gradually discovered that salting slices before frying them diminished their bitterness. Meat stews that featured fried eggplant became standards of court cuisine.

The fearsome vegetable was now welcomed with delight. The tenth-century Syrian poet Kushajam was passionate about it: "The doctor makes ignorant fun of me for liking eggplant, but I will not give it up. Its flavor is like the saliva generously exchanged by lovers in kissing."

The eggplant acquired an esteemed position in Middle Eastern cuisine. Cooks devised new presentations for it, with one Arabic cookbook outlining eighteen ways to cook the vegetable. The "lord of vegetables" (*sayyid al-khudar*, in Arabic) crowned dishes served at weddings, festive parties, and royal functions. So embedded did the eggplant become in Arab culture that it was said every young girl should know a hundred ways to cook it.

The Ottoman Turks, who learned of the eggplant from the Arabs and Persians, treated it regally. The palace kitchens in Constantinople transformed the once-lowly "apple" into a luxurious food. Eggplant was prominent among the *dolma*s, the wide array of Turkish stuffed-vegetable dishes. These sumptuous plates spread from Turkey throughout the Middle East.

Oil-rich eggplant creations were a hallmark of Turkish court cuisine. The lavish dish *imam bayildi* (meaning "the priest fainted") is one example. The baked eggplant is stuffed with a bountiful filling of tomatoes and onions and is enriched with olive oil. One legend has the priest so overcome with the pleasure of the dinner that he faints—or perhaps he succumbed after discovering the lavish amount of olive oil that went into its preparation.

The eggplant and other Turkish foods followed the path of the Ottoman armies into the Balkans during the fourteenth and fifteenth centuries. The eggplant was cultivated for the first time in colonized Bulgaria, Romania, and Yugoslavia, and it was subsequently absorbed into their cuisine.

Numerous takes on *imam bayildi* emerge from Balkan kitchens. The menus of these lands also list variations on moussaka, sometimes called the "cottage pie of the Balkans." Its Turkish name comes from the Arabic *musaqqa*, or "moistened." The spellings of the dish may be different—*muska*, *musaca*—but the casseroles have common features: they either combine layers of vegetables (usually eggplant, but sometimes potatoes and other produce), as well as minced lamb or beef, or are exclusively vegetarian.

The Lebanese, the Middle East's preeminent restaurateurs, have spread the fame of a wide array of eggplant dishes that are fixtures of their *mezze*, or appetizer, tables. From Australia to the United States, the immigrant entrepreneurs have showcased the eggplant in their cafés, restaurants, and groceries.

Baba ghanouj, the classic eggplant dip, is a Lebanese specialty. Its smoky fragrance, left over from the roasting process, and rich, creamy flavor are seductive. Redolent of garlic and lemon, the *baba* gets a tang from the sesame tahini whipped into the dish. Luxuriant in olive oil, the "spoiled daddy" (the dip's Arabic name) evokes an endearing decadence. *Bethenjan makli* is a plate of crisp disks of fried eggplant with a garlicky yogurt dipping sauce. Chunks of eggplant mixed with crunchy pieces of fried pita bread, tomatoes, and parsley highlight a salad called *salatet bethenjan*. Decorated with pickled turnips, it is dressed with pomegranate molasses.

Initially, the new world was no more welcoming to the eggplant than was the old. The Spaniards, the sixteenth-century naturalist José de Acosta noted, transported the "apples of love" to the Americas. As it circulated in the United States, the eggplant made few converts. One notable exception, Thomas Jefferson, who mentions purple and white eggplant among his crops, experimented with cuttings from the plant at Monticello. For the most part, though, except in pockets like the Creole enclaves of New Orleans, it was regarded primarily as an ornamental plant until the early twentieth century.

Even then, the eggplant had an alien image. It was regarded as the fare of Southern European and Middle Eastern immigrants, and therefore it couldn't be considered truly "American." By the 1960s, however, American diners became more receptive. Greek restaurants excited patrons with moussaka. Introduced to eggplant parmigiana at Italian "red sauce" eateries, Americans warmed to the once-exotic vegetable. Today, we no longer shrink when the "mad apple" is served—we salivate.

THE TRUTH ABOUT FINOCCHIO
fragrant fennel

Roman naturalist Pliny observed that after shedding their skin, snakes instinctively rubbed against fennel plants, trying to regain their sight by getting fennel "juice" in their eyes. In addition to sharpening eyesight and preventing blindness, the herb, Pliny contended, could vanquish at least twenty-two illnesses. One of the world's oldest plants, in many civilizations fennel has been invested with awesome powers.

Native to the Mediterranean, fennel, like Queen Anne's lace, grew wild in meadows and along country roads. Feathery green fronds spill out from its stalks. A cluster of brilliant yellow flowers forms a parasol over the plant. Fennel shares this floral umbrella with other members of the parsley, or Umbelliferae, family. Like its cousins, coriander, dill, and anise, fennel's seeds, actually fruits, are infused with aromatic oil.

Another variety with a quite similar appearance but not as tall is known as Florence fennel. It develops a distinctive white bulb that makes the plant look like a "pregnant celery," to use writer Maggie Stuckey's image. This fennel is treated very much like a vegetable (more about that later).

Fennel is attractive because so much of the plant is appetizing. Its leaves, stems, seeds, bulbs, and even pollen are tasty, and they have a sweet anise, or licorice, fragrance.

The Romans named fennel *foeniculum*, or "little hay," possibly because of its refreshing aroma. Its pungent flavor, Pliny said, was invaluable for "seasoning a

great many dishes." Seeds were sprinkled on cakes and bread. The flavor of stalks and shoots was enhanced by marinating them in brine and vinegar.

In Greece, fennel developed a mythic reputation. In the most celebrated tale, the Greek god Prometheus breaks off a lump of charcoal from the torch at the chariot of the sun and absconds with it. "For I am he who hunted out the source of fire and stole it, pitched in a pith of a dry fennel stalk," Prometheus exclaims in Aeschylus's play, *Prometheus Bound*. Defying Zeus, Prometheus offers his fennel-hidden gift to mankind.

Other legends sprang from the association between the plant and the battle of Marathon in 495 BC, in which the Greeks fought the Persians. Since the armies clashed on fields covered with fennel, it was natural to name the herb *marathon* (the Greek spelling) after the battle site.

In another story, *marathon* is derived from the word *maraino*, "to grow thin." Connotations of strength, valor, and physical fitness are thus linked to the herb.

Ancient warriors, English poet William Wordsworth wrote, treasured these virtues:

Above the lowly plants it towers,
The fennel with its yellow flowers,
And in an earlier age than ours,
Was gifted with the wondrous powers
Lost vision to restore.

It gave new strength, and fearless mood;
And gladiators, fierce and rude,
Mingled it in their daily food;
And he who battled and subdued,
A wreath of fennel wore.

Fennel not only made you lean and fit, the Greeks believed, but also soothed your stomach. For stomach upset, Socrates recommended a stalk of fennel and a drink of water. Centuries later, in the mid-nineteenth century, mothers prepared *gripe water*, a sort of honeyed tea made with fennel and other herbs, to relieve stomach upset in their colicky children. A bag of fennel seeds applied to a child's temples, it was thought, induced sound sleep.

In Western Europe, where fennel was most probably transplanted by the Romans, people were delighted with the aromatic. The English poet Milton wrote rapturously about its scent in *Paradise Lost*:

When from the boughs a savory odor blown,
Grateful to appetite, more pleas'd my sense
Than smell of sweetest fennel.

Fennel retained its aura of power and vitality in medieval times. Leaves were hung over doorways to ward off witches and evil spirits. Cows' udders were smeared with fennel paste to frighten off witches.

Echoing Greek lore, health advocates promoted the herb. "Both the seeds, roots, and leaves of our Garden Fennel are much used in drinks and broths for those that are grown fat," the seventeenth-century English naturalist William Cole wrote. Fennel, he added, helped "to abate their unwieldiness and cause them to grow more gaunt and lank."

Just like the Greeks and Romans, Western Europeans savored fennel in their cooking. It was "eaten as a condiment to accompany salt fish during Lent," the herbal scholar Maude Grieve notes. Seventeenth-century botanist John Parkinson, who lauded fennel for its value to both "meate and medicine," remarked on its "sweet and hot flavor." It "helpeth to digest the crude quality of fish and other viscous meats."

Culinary writers continued to stress the inseparability of the herb's tasty and healthful qualities. The seventeenth-century English gastronome John Evelyn, who recommended that his readers eat fennel peeled like celery, also emphasized its restorative value. It "expels wind, sharpens the sight, and recreates the brain."

Fennel seeds were a godsend to the poor, English gardening historian Alicia Amherst points out. They worked "to relieve the pangs of hunger." On fasting days, the destitute, she says, partook of fennel as "a relish to unpalatable food." In the medieval work, *Piers Plowman*, a priest asks a poor woman if she has any "hote spices" in her purse. She responds that she has a "ferthingworth of fennel seed for fastying days."

Fennel was also a plaything of the rich. At the end of luxurious banquets, nobles were offered sugar-coated fennel seeds and other sweetened aromatics. The herb was popular as a *digestif* and mouth sweetener.

Among Europeans, Italians were the most passionate about fennel. They developed a fennel variety whose leaf stalks swelled to form a bulb. Covered in earth to protect it from the sun, the bulb emerges a soft white when harvested. Florence fennel, as it is frequently called, was embraced as a fragrant vegetable in the Italian kitchen.

Giacomo Castelvetro, the seventeenth-century Italian commentator, was enthusiastic about it as a condiment: "We preserve quantities of fresh fennel in good white wine vinegar and eat in summer and in winter when offering drinks to friends between meals. We also serve this pickle with fruit on special occasions, when fresh fennel is not to be had."

The Italians called the vegetable *finocchio*. Literally meaning "fine eye," the name evoked the plant's vision-improving quality. Over time, it gradually came to suggest flattery and dissembling. The expression *dare finocchio* meant to "give fennel," or flatter.

It acquired this connotation, some suggest, because its potent fragrance could mask something unsavory. The word *infinocchiare*, food writer Faith Willinger notes, derives from a sales practice of Tuscan wine sellers. In order to hide any problems with their product, they gave customers slices of *finocchiona*, a fennel-laced salami, to sample first.

Intriguingly, in Shakespearean England fennel took on a similar allusion. Fennel implied falsity or flattery. In Ben Jonson's play, *The Case Altered*, Christopher has the following exchange with the count:

Christopher: No, my good lord.

Count: Your good lord! Oh! how this smells of fennel!

Finocchio developed into a slang word for "homosexual" in Italy. Trading on the term, a nightclub in San Francisco famous for its female impersonator acts called itself Finocchio's.

The Italian aromatic captured the attention of Thomas Jefferson, who planted its seeds at Monticello. Thomas Appleton, an American consul in Italy, sent him the seeds in 1824, along with a letter extolling the vegetable: "[T]he fennel is, beyond every other vegetable, delicious. It greatly resembles in appearance the largest size celery, perfectly white, and there is no vegetable equals it in flavor. It is eaten at dessert, crude, and with, or without, dry salt, indeed, I preferred it to every other vegetable, or to any fruit."

In colonial days, American settlers were fond of coriander, caraway, fennel, and other spices, mixtures of which they baked in cakes. To stay alert and possibly stifle hunger during services, Puritan congregants chewed fennel and other "meeting seeds." They also used fennel to suppress their appetite during fasts.

Once the stuff of myth and lore, fennel has been discovered by modern cooks and diners. Slices of the bulb sautéed in olive oil make a mildly sweet dish. Fennel wedges salted or dipped in olive oil, *pinzimonio*, is a refreshing relish. A salad of fennel and orange slices is a pleasant repast. As we indulge, however, let's not forget that the herb is also good for our eyes, minds, and bodies.

THE "STINKING ROSE"
the glories of garlic

"Stinking rose." "Camphor of the poor." "Truffle of Provence." Garlic has simultaneously been admired and reviled through the centuries. At times it has been perceived as a sinister force; at other times, as life-giving and protective.

The "stinking rose" is actually a member of the lily family. Most likely native to Central Asia, from whence it traveled to the Mediterranean, garlic belongs to the Allium genus, which includes onions, chives, and leeks. Its English name derives from the joining of two Anglo-Saxon words: *gar*, the word for "spear" (an allusion to the shape of its leaves), and *leac*, the word for "herb." *Allium sativum*, garlic's scientific name, comes from the Celtic word for "hot."

The ancient plant, which bears whitish-lavender flowers and whose bulb grows entirely underground, must have captivated early civilizations. Propagating garlic required conscious human choice and effort. To cultivate the warm-weather crop, farmers had to plant individual cloves in the soil.

The builders of the pyramids, according to Herodotus, subsisted on a diet of radishes, garlic, leeks, and onions. When their bosses cut their rations, the workers walked off the job, precipitating what garlic aficionado Lloyd Harris thinks may have been the earliest recorded strike. Ardent garlic eaters today, the Egyptians inherited their infatuation. The "garlic and onion" eaters, as the Romans called them, may have fancied a garlic and oil sauce that is the ancestor of the aioli of Provence.

Garlic remains have been unearthed from the tomb of Pharaoh Tutankhamun. The Egyptians treated garlic as a holy object, swearing oaths on it and offering the bulb to the gods. However, the country's priests banned all who smelled of garlic from their temples.

The herb was also prized for its medicinal and restorative properties. In preparing their mummies, Egyptians used garlic to prevent bodies from decaying, early proof of its effectiveness as an antifungal agent. Garlic fortified remedies for headaches, bites, and heart ailments. The Egyptians even employed it as a diagnostic tool. To test for pregnancy, a clove of garlic was placed in a woman's womb and left overnight. If she had a garlicky taste in her mouth the next day, she was assumed to be pregnant.

During their exile from Egypt, the Israelites fondly recalled the taste of the alliums: "We remember the fish, which we did eat in Egypt freely; the cucumbers, and the melons, and the leeks, and the onions, and garlic."

The Jews, who referred to themselves affectionately as "garlic eaters," had contradictory feelings about it. Believing the spice to be erotically stimulating, an ancient Hebrew decree proscribed the eating of garlic during the Friday Sabbath evening. A bite of garlic, it was believed, promoted marital union.

Garlic was both elixir and taboo to the Greeks and Romans. "Now bolt down those cloves. Well primed with garlic you will have better mettle for the fight," Aristophanes urged in his play, *The Knights*. Garlic, the Hellenes believed, invigorated the body and rejuvenated the spirit. Lethargy was a condition for which many ancient physicians prescribed the smelling of garlic.

Rooted in the lower depths of darkness, garlic was reputed to be a guardian against diabolical forces. In *The Odyssey*, the god Hermes advised Odysseus to eat garlic to protect himself against the spells cast by the wily sorceress Circe. In more recent times, Greeks have employed garlic as a lucky charm. Midwives tied a clove of garlic around the necks of newborns to ward off danger.

The Romans had similar ideas. Garlic was hung on doors to frighten away witches. Laborers and galley rowers ate it to make themselves stronger and more energetic. Gladiators took the herb to inspire boldness in the ring. Because of its sharp fragrance, the Romans also adopted garlic as an antiseptic. The "physic of the peasantry" cleansed the city's fetid air.

Like the Greek and Roman nobles, to whom garlic was repellent, the upper castes in India shunned garlic. Intent on achieving purity, the Brahmins feared that garlic, a popular taste among the lower classes, was polluting. Moreover, the smell of garlic was thought to be offensive to the gods. Therefore, Hindu priests and devout believers were expected to renounce it.

Garlic's association with the body reinforced the taboo against its consumption, food scholar Frederick Simoons argues. Since its color resembled flesh and blood, garlic offended committed vegetarians among orthodox Hindus. In addition, the similarity of a head of garlic to a human head made for a distasteful image.

In the new religion of Islam, garlic's potency reflected its sinister origins. When Satan stepped out of the Garden of the Eden, the story goes, garlic sprang up from where he placed his left foot, onions from where he placed his right. The Prophet Muhammad recommended garlic as an antidote for snake and scorpion bites: "Applied to the spot bitten by the viper or sting of scorpion, it produces successful results."

Still alluring and dangerous, garlic arrived in Europe with the Roman armies who occupied England. In the medieval age, the herb, denigrated by the nobility as peasant grub, was excluded from the diet of knights. The supposed aphrodisiac was forbidden to the celibate clergy. Its fragrance made Shakespeare squeamish: "[D]ear actors, eat no onions nor garlic, for we are to utter sweet breath," Bottom says in *A Midsummer Night's Dream*.

If garlic could vanquish evil, why not sickness and disease? Garlic's medicinal powers became the stuff of European folktales. In one story about the plague of 1726, four thieves robbing rotten corpses in Marseilles miraculously escaped unscathed. They were protected, the thieves said, because they breathed in a concoction of garlic steeped in vinegar. The solution became a popular home remedy. Such myths were transformed into medical practice. During World War I, the British army treated wounds with garlic juice.

The diabolical herb also retained its charm-like status. In Central and Eastern Europe, people hung garlands of garlic on their doors to keep vampires away.

Garlic found a more receptive home in southern European than in Anglo-Saxon kitchens. Garlic is "eaten with almost everything . . . by both Spaniards and Italians and the more Southern people," the seventeenth-century English gourmet John Evelyn wrote. "We absolutely forbid its entrance into our salleting [salads] by reason of its intolerable rankness."

The Mediterraneans created entrancing blends of garlic and olive oil, from which mayonnaise, food writer Paula Wolfert suggests, was derived. Aioli, the "butter of Provence," is a festive sauce of garlic, olive oil, and eggs, often enjoyed on New Year's Eve. Greece's *skordalia* is a pungent sauce traditionally made by pounding bread and garlic into a paste with a mortar and pestle. Olive oil is then drizzled in and beaten until the *skordalia* thickens. This traditional peasant dish is a wonderful accompaniment to slices of fried eggplant and zucchini.

We now know that garlic's mystique had a certain scientific basis. A strong sulfur compound, the amino acid *alliin* is contained in the bulb. When the bulb is crushed or broken, scientists have learned, *alliin* becomes *allicin*, the source of garlic's smell, and also an antibacterial and cholesterol-reduction agent.

Old prejudices against the pungent spice have largely evaporated. Greeks, Italians, and other immigrants in the United States were once accused of being "garlic eaters." Early Mediterranean restaurateurs muted the garlic in their dishes to avoid offending squeamish customers. Yet today, many diners insist, the more garlic, the better.

"POOR MAN'S MEAT"
the lentil

The chopped onions were sizzling in olive oil, ready to be added to the pot of lentils simmering on the stove. I measured out a cup of rice, which I mixed in with the lentils. I seasoned the blend with a couple of teaspoons of black pepper. While waiting for the dish to finish, I cut up onion wedges, which I fried until they browned. I took them out and put them aside. In a saucepan, I began heating Italian whole tomatoes dosed with red pepper. After about twenty minutes, when the rice was cooked and the lentils were still nutty and tender, I took the pot off the flames and ladled out helpings for my wife, Peggy, and myself. I crowned each plate with several spoonfuls of tomato sauce and garnished them with the fried onions.

I was experimenting, trying to make a variation on *koshary*, the famed Egyptian street food, which was traditionally vended from hand-painted donkey carts. "You have hot dog stand, we have *koshary*," an Egyptian cab driver once told me. Unlike mine, the Egyptians fortify their dish with macaroni. The hawkers, who used to concentrate on poor neighborhoods, now also station themselves in commercial districts. They arrange the lentil specialty on china dishes, which, when finished, are "dumped into a bucket of hot water," restaurant owner Abdullah Hashid observed. During the recent protests at Cairo's Tahrir Square, demonstrators lined up for helpings of *koshary* prepared in communal kitchens.

The origins of the staple remain murky. It began as an Indian meal of rice and lentils called *kitchari*, some speculate, which English colonials introduced to Egypt in the late nineteenth century. The Egyptians borrowed the idea and adapted it to their tastes.

Lentils, often dubbed the "poor man's meat," are a simple food that, with a little effort, can be made into a zesty meal. But where did these seeds come from? To appreciate them, one has to journey back thousands of years to a time when pioneering Neolithic agriculturists tended one of the world's earliest cultivated plants. The one-foot-tall shrub with violet-striped white flowers is native to the Near East. Planted in the winter, the lentil grows pods with one or two seeds (the commonly eaten part of the plant), which are harvested in the spring and early summer. They thrive in a semi-arid Mediterranean climate and can spring up in rugged, inhospitable soil. The lentil also replenishes the soil with needed nitrogen.

They were probably first gathered wild, botanists say, in what is now Turkey, Syria, Iraq, and Iran. The remains of lentils have been found in the ruins of early farming villages that archaeologists trace to 7000 BC. Early farmers likely seized on lentils to complement the wheat and barley they were growing. They passed over pods that easily burst and husbanded firmer plants. An agricultural revolution was definitely occurring in the Fertile Crescent. Without realizing it, the villagers had found a combination of foods—grains and lentils—that provided complete protein. In cultures short of meat, lentils, peas, and beans were indispensable.

The lentil, which arrived in Egypt around 4000 BC, has long been a touchstone of that country's civilization. Lentils have been uncovered in tombs and in the underground stores of the pyramids. Lentils were presented as offerings to the gods and as gifts to feed the dead. To many observers, Egypt and lentils were synonymous. The "lentils of the Nile . . . cheaper than spelt, dearer than beans," the Roman poet Martial wrote. "You men of Alexandria have been brought up on lentil food and your entire city is full of lentil dishes," Greek writer Athenaeus noted. Bread made from lentils and barley was a basic foodstuff.

Extolled in the Koran, the legume was also vital to Egypt's Christian community. Along with *ful* (the fava-bean repast) and other meals made from beans and peas, lentil dishes were heavily consumed by the Copts and other Christian sects during fasting times. A simple dinner of boiled lentils and bread often sufficed.

In addition, lentils produced material rewards. Egypt became the largest trader of the commodity in the ancient world. One ship left the banks of the Nile for Italy, its hold filled with 2,800,000 pounds of lentils, the Roman writer Pliny reports.

The Semitic neighbors of the Egyptians were also fond of the lentil. To the Hebrew tiller, the seeds were the ultimate nourishment. In one biblical tale, lentils were a godsend to the famished Esau. He was so desperately hungry that he offered his brother Jacob his inheritance in exchange for "red pottage," a lentil porridge: "And Jacob said, Sell me this day thy birthright. And Esau said, Behold, I am at the point to die: and what profit shall this birthright do to me?" (Genesis 25:29–34).

The lentil porridge of the Bible is the ancestor of *mujadara*, the Arabic dish known affectionately in the Middle East as the "favorite of Esau." It is typically a plate of grains (rice or bulgur) mixed with lentils and seasoned with cumin, allspice, and other flavorings. Although food scholar Charles Perry points out that the original medieval creation was not made this way, *mujadara* today comes topped with caramelized onions. Its evocative Arabic name summons up a vivid image, a dish of grains "pockmarked" with legumes.

Egyptian-raised food writer Claudia Roden remembers her aunt regularly offering guests a plate of specially made *megadarra* (a version of the lentil dish), pleading, "Excuse the food of the poor!" Her friends ritualistically responded, "Keep your food of kings and give us *megadarra* every day."

In ancient Greece the common legume had a lowly reputation. "When you cook lentil soup, don't add perfume," Jocasta says in the play *Phoenician Women*. When a Greek acquired wealth and status, he was expected to give up legumes for more refined fare. "Now that he is rich he will no longer eat lentils; formerly when he was poor, he ate what he could get," Aristophanes wrote.

Although lentils were considered plebeian fare, Roman aristocrats esteemed them nonetheless. Guests at funeral banquets were served plates of lentils and salt. To achieve a moderate temper, a lentil diet was necessary, the writer Pliny insisted. Even its preparation required an accomplished hand. "A wise man acts always with reason, and prepares his own lentils himself," Zeno, Rome's Eastern emperor, stated. To the early Roman Republicans, such basic foods symbolized the plain, frugal virtues they wanted to be associated with. The leading Roman families took their names from the common legumes: Lentulus (lentil), Fabius (fava), Piso (pea), and Cicero (chickpea).

The lentil's Roman name, *lens*, migrated from Latin into English by a curious route. Apparently one sharp-eyed observer named the optical instrument after this legume because of their similar shape. Edmond Halley (the comet investigator), food historian Ken Albala points out, was the first writer to use the new term in 1693.

The image of the lentil as an unsavory food fit only for the poor was hard to shed. During the Middle Ages, it was believed the fearsome bean could bring on nightmares and inflame the stomach. As recently as the late nineteenth century, American cookery writer Ella Kellogg (who married into the cereal family) could pronounce it as "of little value except for soups, purees, toasts, and other dishes as require the ejection of the skin. Lentils have a stronger flavor than any of the other legumes, and their taste is not so generally liked until one has become accustomed to it."

Modern culinary experts, food historian Waverley Root observes, have been making a vigorous effort to "rehabilitate" the lentil. Robert Courtine, food editor of French newspaper *Le Monde*, was one such missionary. The lentil "merits the consideration of the gourmet," he wrote. "It is called vulgar. It brings with it a whiff of the boarding school and the barracks, not to say the prison. . . . Nevertheless the true gourmet revels in it . . . at every moment of the meal, from lentil soup to lentil salad."

The ennobling of the lentil continues. "The Lentil Moves Uptown" announced a headline from the January 26, 2005, *Los Angeles Times* food section. Featured in the piece were recipes for lentil and duck salad with hazelnut dressing, and sole with beluga lentils and rosemary cream.

Recently, Koshari Street, a new restaurant, opened in London. The dining room features the Egyptian dish from a recipe conceived by Middle Eastern food writer, Anissa Helou. Soon smart diners everywhere will be able to tuck into a spicy plate of lentils and pasta.

VIGOR AND VENERY
the story of mint

"The savor or smell of water minte rejoyceth the heart of man," the seventeenth-century herbalist John Gerard wrote. "The smell of minte does stir up the minde." Mint, it was long thought, invigorated the spirits and stimulated the appetite. Native to the Mediterranean and a member of an aromatic family that includes basil, marjoram, and oregano, it was beloved in ancient cultures.

A minty fragrance suffused Hebrew synagogues as parishioners stepped on the leaves and stems scattered on the floor. To the Greeks, mint was an exhilarating tonic for the body. They scented their bathwater with the aromatic, and Athenians rubbed their arms with it to strengthen them. In Greece, the herb added a festive touch to celebratory occasions. Guests often arrived wearing crowns made from the leaves. Sprays of mint decorated dining tables. When guests visited, families rubbed crushed mint leaves on their tabletops.

Mint, however, could be fearsome as well as exhilarating. It could chill the body in addition to reviving it. The Greeks captured their conflicting feelings about the herb in a myth about its origins. In one version of the tale, the water nymph Minthe, charmed by his golden chariot and four black horses, became the mistress of Hades, god of the underworld. When Hades instead married Persephone, the thwarted nymph threatened to drive her rival from the palace. Enraged at this seductress, Persephone "tore her limb from limb," as French scholar Marcel Detienne puts it. Hades transformed the remains of his lover into a plant called *menthe*, or "sweet-smelling." The herb flourished in the shade of the lower depths. In honor of Minthe, young Greek women wore bridal wreaths adorned with sprigs of mint.

A second recounting of the myth is more hostile to the nymph. In this story, Demeter, Persephone's mother and the goddess of agriculture and fertility, tramples on Minthe. A common grass springs up in her place.

As represented in the myth, mint is simultaneously hot and cold. In the first story, Minthe, a woman of seductive powers, is turned into a fragrant plant. In the other, the nymph metamorphoses into a cold, wet herb emblematic of death and darkness. To the Greeks, scholar Detienne contends, mint arouses men but also destroys sexuality by melting sperm or making women sterile.

Compared to the Greeks, the Romans welcomed mint effusively. It inspired intellectual excitement, naturalist Pliny believed. He urged students to wear crowns of spearmint to "exhilarate" their minds.

It also sharpened the taste buds. "The very smell of mint reanimates the spirits and its flavor gives a remarkable zest for food," Pliny wrote. The Romans pickled mint in vinegar and scented wine with it. Recipes from the gastronome Apicius called for a mint sauce with cumin seeds and pine nuts to enhance roast pork, and for one flavored with almonds, oregano, and honey for cold fish.

To the Romans, mint was a potent curative. When someone fainted, they used its leaves like smelling salts. The same restorative powers, Pliny thought, made the "juice of mint gathered, inhaled . . . a remedy for afflictions of the nostrils." It also worked like a general decongestant. "Taken in honied wine," Pliny advised, "it carries off purulent phlegm."

There was also a rich mint tradition in the Middle East. The court cuisine of Baghdad and other capitals of the medieval Islamic empire capitalized on the flavors of mint, anise, parsley, thyme, and other herbs. The thirteenth-century *Baghdad Cookery Book*, a manual written at the height of Arab power, gives tantalizing instructions for a mint and vinegar dressing: "Take fresh large-leafed mint, and strip the leaf from the stalk, wash and dry in the shade: sprinkle with aromatic herbs. If desired, add celery leaves and quarters of peeled garlic. Put into a glass bottle and cover with good vinegar, coloured with a little saffron. Leave until the mint has absorbed the sourness of the vinegar so that the latter has lost its sharpness: then serve."

In the Arab world, mint is an indispensable aromatic. Mint was "always on the table," my friend, Lebanese cook Nawal Rababy, reminisced. "Every supper you put out a plate of radishes, tomatoes, watercress, and mint." Gathering the herb, she said, was a seasonal ritual in her homeland. "At the end of the spring, we start drying for wintertime."

Village dishes in the region were perked up with mint. The herb-laden *tab-bouleh*, the rural salad that was incorporated in the restaurant *mezze*, an array of appetizers, is one such delight. The tingle of mint refreshes this mixture of tomatoes, spring onions, parsley, and bulgur.

Persians, who strongly influenced Arab cooking, were infatuated with mint and other herbs. The *sabzi khordan*, a welcoming bowl of mint, marjoram, and tarragon, commonly opens an Iranian meal. The herbs are accompanied by flat bread and *panir*, a cheese similar to feta. The cheese is commonly spread on the bread, a mint leaf is laid on, and the "sandwich" is rolled up. The mint addition was "like using lettuce in sandwiches," Esmail "Sam" Dehi, an Iranian chef, explained to me.

Persian cooks play on the affinity of yogurt for mint. The herb they call *na'na* gave verve to their cucumber and yogurt dip. Mint is also sprinkled on *doogh*, the classic Iranian drink made from "Persian milk," as yogurt was once known in the Middle East.

Mint traveled west. Most probably, it arrived in Britain with the invading Roman armies. In fact, some speculate that the occupiers introduced the English, who loved the combination of lamb and mint, to the herbal sauce. Herbalist Gerard invokes Pliny, who was convinced that "the smell of mint . . . doth stir up the mind, and the taste to a greedy desire for meat."

In medieval England, monks and nuns cultivated mint in their gardens. From their plants, they concocted herbal remedies for a receptive public. During this era, people applied powdered mint leaves to alleviate sores in their mouths and to whiten their teeth.

Writers in England celebrated the herb. Chaucer was enthralled by the sight of a "a little path full of mints and fennill green." "Here's flowers for you; Hot lavender, mints, savory, marjoram," says Perdita, a character in Shakespeare's *The Winter's Tale*. In order to make footpaths fragrant, the Elizabethans planted "those which perfume the outdoors most delightfully being trodded upon and crushed," Francis Bacon observed.

English herbalists also revived ancient beliefs about the plant. Like the Greeks and Romans, John Parkinson applauded its ability to energize both body and soul. "Put into baths with balm and other herbs," he wrote, adding, "[Mints] are a help to comfort and strengthen the nerves." The herb "could also strengthen and comfort weak stomackes."

Many years later, Mrs. Beeton, the British dispenser of kitchen wisdom, passed on similar advice to her audience of housewives. Mint, she said, is "a stomachic and antispasmodic, on which account it is generally served at table with pea soup." But not all commentators were so lyrical. The herbalist Nicholas Culpeper warned that mint "stirreth venery or bodily lust."

Mints traveled with the Puritan settlers to New England. Originally picked wild or grown in family gardens, mint soon blossomed into a commercial crop. By the middle of the nineteenth century, Yankee peddlers throughout New England were vending medicinal essences, spirits, and cordials produced from distilled spearmint and peppermint oils.

As mint gradually lost its allure as an herbal, manufacturers found more profitable uses for its oils. It captured the attention of makers of chewing gum, candy, toothpaste, and other products. Spearmint gum, manufactured by William Wrigley, who got his start as a Philadelphia soap dealer, was by 1910 the nation's most popular flavor.

Consumers began looking on mint more and more as a confection to sweeten the mouth, the air, even rugs and carpets. Once exotic, mint had become commonplace—although still appreciated.

THE "HAREM TREE"
nutmeg

A yellowish-orange fruit resembling an apricot hung from the spreading branches of a tropical evergreen. Underneath the fleshy, outer skin of the fruit was a red, lacy membrane that enclosed a dark brown shell. This covering, known as mace, was a spice in its own right. Ludovico di Vartherna, one of the first Europeans to see the fruit, described it with a floral image: "Before the nut arrives at perfection, the mace stands around [it] like an open rose, and when the nut is ripe the mace clasps it." When the shell was dried, the nutmeg (actually a seed) rattled inside. It got its name from a Latin phrase meaning "musky (or aromatic) nut." The scientific name for the spice, *Myristica fragrans,* translates as "smelling of myrrh." The fruit of the nutmeg tree, then, contains two spicy treasures. It is truly, as food writer Elisabeth Ortiz observed, "one of nature's great packaging jobs."

The spice was native to the Banda islands, a small chain of tiny, volcanic coral islands at the eastern extreme of Indonesia. The Bandas were the most remote and least accessible of the fabled Spice Islands, more formally known as the Moluccas. A finicky plant, the nutmeg required the islands' rich volcanic oil and tropical climate in order to flourish. It also needed the shade of forests, which cover the Bandas. Thick with nutmegs, the islands caught the eye of one English visitor: "There is not a tree but the nutmeg, so that the whole country seems like a contrived orchard."

The tree grows slowly, only reaching its full height after fifteen or twenty years. Thirty or forty years later, after its pink flowers blossoms, the nutmeg bears its colorful fruit. Nutmeg breeding is a complex art. Since male and female flowers blossom on separate trees, a single male can pollinate ten or twelve females. Hence, a cluster of female seedlings is planted around a male. Food writer Waverley Root aptly dubbed the nutmeg the "harem tree."

The nutmeg has an ally—a pigeon that spreads its seeds. The "very handsome fruit-pigeon," naturalist Alfred Russel Wallace wrote, announces its presence with a "loud booming note." The relationship between pigeon and fruit made the sixteenth-century Portuguese poet Luis de Camões rhapsodic: "Look at the isles of Banda, enameled with the bright color of their russet fruit; the brightly colored birds . . . take a tribute of the green unripe nuts."

Before the arrival of the Europeans, the Bandanese engaged in a lively trade in nutmegs. After carefully picking the fruits from the trees using a long pole called a *gai gai*, to which a basket was lashed, they dried the spices and prepared them for sale. They bartered the product for rice and *sago* (a palm starch) with mariners, like the Bugis, intrepid navigators who sailed the surrounding seas. Nutmeg buyers brought them to market in Java, Indonesia's largest island.

By the first century AD, Hindus from India, who had conquered Java, began transporting nutmeg to their homeland. Many of the names for nutmeg, which came from Sanskrit, derived from Indian languages. The *mada shaunda*, or "narcotic fruit," as it was called in the medical texts known as the *Ayurvedas*, became a staple of Indian medicine. To quiet irritable children, parents gave them small amounts of nutmeg. English nannies later gave their charges the grated spice to make them sleepy. The Vedas, sacred writings, extolled the spice for its warm and stimulating effects and recommended the nuts as a soother of stomachs.

In Indian culture, nutmeg also functioned as a perfume. It was expected to eliminate body odor and bad breath. Kings rubbed the oil on their bodies before bathing.

Chinese merchants were also eager to reap gains from the nutmeg trade. Junks carried loads of nutmegs and cloves from the Indonesian archipelago to China and Southeast Asia. Nutmeg never became a central ingredient in Chinese cooking but was appreciated as a medicine. It perked up a broth, food scholar Frederick Simoons discovered, which the Chinese sipped to alleviate intestinal disorders.

Arab and Persian seafarers also purchased nutmeg and other items in India and took them in their *dhows*, small seafaring vessels, west to the Mediterranean. In Middle Eastern lore, the "aromatic nut" was valued as a splendid perfume.

Women scented themselves with nutmeg oil. To make themselves even more fragrant, they also wore the nuts as necklaces.

Arab physicians treated their patients with nutmeg. The spice, one medical authority said, healed the "digestive organs," adding that it also remedied "freckles and skin blemishes."

Europe's maritime powers were also avid about nutmeg. Portuguese spice traders were eager to exploit the Spice Islands, the "lands below the winds," as the Malays called them. The islands promised a wealth of the more expensive "fine spices," cloves and nutmeg. In 1511, their caravels were the first European vessels to reach the nutmeg-rich Bandas.

The ever-curious Portuguese, who held sway over the islands for the next hundred years, picked up some nutmeg lore. Garcia de Orta, a sixteenth-century physician who lived in the Portuguese colony of Goa, described the delight of the tangy outer fruit. The "thick outside rind" is "made into a conserve with sugar. . . . It comes from Banda in jars of vinegar, and some people eat it as a salad."

The conserve, de Orta pointed out, was also mentally invigorating. It was "very good for the brain and nervous complaints."

Nutmeg became a major lure for the Netherlanders. Dutch traveler Jan Huygen van Linschoten, who went on the first expedition to the Bandas, was excited by the spice: "The nutmeg comforts the brain, sharpens the memory." The fruit, he added, "warms and strengthens the maw [stomach], drives wind out of the body, makes a sweet breath."

Portuguese trading power waned and the Dutch seized control of the spice trade from them in the early seventeenth century. "No lover is as jealous of his mistress as the Dutch are of their trade in spices," a Frenchman remarked in 1697. Compared to the Portuguese, who were content to be traders, the Dutch pursued a ruthless economic policy. They employed every conceivable method to maintain a stranglehold over the spice. The trees were cut down to prevent smuggling, and nutmegs were coated with lime to keep them from being grown elsewhere. To keep prices high when there was a spice glut, the Dutch sometimes burned their product. In 1735, 1,250,000 pounds of nutmeg were destroyed in a bonfire in Amsterdam. A bystander watching the fire, who tried to grab some of spoils, was hanged for his transgression.

In Europe, the newly arrived spice became a luxurious plaything in high society. Eighteenth-century gentlemen in England carried silver nutmeg graters, which had handy compartments to hold the spice, to parties. Candied nutmeg and other spices, called *confits*, were served to guests at festive occasions. Nutmeg perked up punches and mulled wine served at such affairs. "Take a gallon of wine, three ounces of cinnamon, two ounces of slic't ginger, a quarter of an ounce of cloves, an ounce of mace, twenty corns of pepper, an ounce of nutmegs, three pounds of sugar, and two quarts of cream," the Tudor cook Robert May recommended in his recipe for *ipocras*, a spiced wine. An English custom was also "to put [nutmeg] in ale no matter whether fresh or stale," Chaucer wrote. The spice helped to preserve the drink and gave it a pleasing tang. Equally important, nutmeg enhanced its potency.

In noble kitchens, nutmeg was used profusely to flavor both savory and sweet dishes. A fifteenth-century cookbook called for nutmeg in rabbit stew. In addition to doses of black pepper, ginger, and cloves, a recipe for a sixteenth-century meat pie included two and a half teaspoons of nutmeg. Nutmeg was also indispensable for desserts. It infused Christmas puddings and spice cakes with an earthy warmth. The clown talks of "nutmegs, seven" to accompany spiced pears in Shakespeare's *The Winter's Tale*.

Soon the spice was a hallmark of the fashionable meal. "Do you like nutmeg?" an aspiring host asked his dinner guests in a sketch written by Nicholas Boileau, an eighteenth-century French writer. "It's in everything."

The hedonistic spice also paid virtuous dividends. Elizabethan nutritionists urged students to consume candied nutmeg as a dietary supplement. Doctors often urged their patients to drink mulled wine to remedy chest coughs. Monks on fast days in ninth-century Constantinople sprinkled nutmeg on their pease pudding (savory pudding made of boiled legumes). Others took nutmeg to alleviate the excesses of drinking and dining. Lacing alcohol with the spice helped to "reduce the flatulence and dyspepsia resulting from such stimulating liquids," English folklorist L. F. Newman observed.

Nutmeg, it was thought, did wonders for the digestion. English women, Newman notes, used to regularly carry a nutmeg in "the large bag pockets" worn "under their voluminous skirts and petticoats" as an aid for intestinal ailments. They grated it over food and drink "as a carminative to relieve flatulence and dyspepsia."

The spice also served as a common sedative, with apothecaries dispensing nutmeg oil for this purpose. In the sixteenth century, some applied a paste made from violet petals and nutmeg to their foreheads to make themselves drowsy.

During the plague years, nutmeg and other spices were said to prevent the fatal disease. Europeans carried pomanders, perforated metal balls filled with aromatics, as they walked around the streets, to ward off toxins. In seventeenth-century London the price of spices rose as the demand for these lifesavers increased.

Larger amounts of nutmeg, however, could produce dangerous, sometimes fatal results. *Myristicin*, the component of nutmeg responsible for its "warm" taste and intoxicating fragrance, also had hallucinogenic power. A pregnant English woman, the Flemish doctor Lobelius reported in 1576, "became deliriously inebriated" after eating ten to twelve nutmegs. She was apparently trying to induce an abortion, a consequence widely ascribed to taking the drug. Many of the instances of nutmeg poisoning were, in fact, the result of attempts to stimulate menstruation or an abortion.

Commentators worried about nutmeg's narcotic potential. Victorian food writer Isabella Beeton warned that the spice "be used with caution by those who are of paralytic or apoplectic habits." As recently as 1907, *The Dispensatory of the United States of America* sounded the alarm. Excessive amounts, it said, could "produce stupor and delirium."

In recent years, nutmeg has maintained its psychoactive appeal. During the 1950s, outsiders and rebels, bohemians, sailors, and musicians were attracted to the spice. A musician who played with jazz great Charlie "Yardbird" Parker remembers his leader's nutmeg enthusiasm: "Bird introduced this nutmeg to the guys. It was a cheap and legal high. You can take it in milk or Coca-Cola. The grocer across the street came over to the club owner and said, 'I know you do all this baking because I sell from eight to ten nutmegs a day.'" On the group's bandstand, the owner noticed, were a pile of nutmeg boxes.

Nutmeg caught on among the prison population. In his autobiography, Malcolm X recalls his experiences with nutmeg in his prison days: "I first got high in Charlestown [Prison] on nutmeg. My cellmate was among at least a hundred nutmeg men who, for money or cigarettes, bought from kitchen worker inmates penny matchboxes full of stolen nutmeg. I grabbed a box as though it were a pound of heavy drugs. Stirred into a glass of cold water, a penny matchbox full of nutmeg had the kick of three or four reefers."

Inmates in New Jersey were infatuated with the spice. They typically stirred two to three tablespoons of nutmeg into hot liquids to achieve a high. They likened its effect to that of marijuana, according to a 1960 report on the New Jersey State Prison. Prisoners ingested nutmeg "to escape from one's self and depressing, immediate surroundings." The drug "tended to narcotize the subjects against the unpleasant experiences of incarceration." In response, the New Jersey prison system banned the use of the spice.

Makers of today's consumer products have tried to harness the power of the ancient spice. The fragrances of nutmeg and clove permeate Obsession, the Calvin Klein perfume. The manufacturer of Vicks VapoRub puts nutmeg in its inhalant.

Even Coca-Cola may have been improved with nutmeg. In *For God, Country, and Coca-Cola*, his history of the drink, Mark Pendergrast lists nutmeg, along with cinnamon and coriander, as ingredients in its original formula. Another reason why the drink has been so addictive?

"A TASTE AS OLD AS COLD WATER"
the story of the olive

The olive tree is not a majestic one. But the striking evergreen, with its twisted trunk and gnarled roots, has inspired loyalty and affection throughout the ages. Its silvery-green leaves have their own special beauty.

The Mediterranean was its birthplace. To many, the sea and the fruit were synonymous. "The Mediterranean ends where the olive ceases to grow," as French writer Georges Duhamel puts it.

Early societies happened upon the wild olive, a spiny shrub with small, extremely acrid, inedible fruit, lacking the heavy, rich oil that permeates the domesticated one. Farmers in the Near East, in Syria and Palestine, botanists generally agree, had cultivated the olive by 6000 BC.

At about the same time, farmers on the island of Crete were farming the crop. Since the cultivated olive could also not be eaten raw, ingenious people in these cultures had to figure out techniques of treating them (curing with salt, for example) so that the glycosides, the substances responsible for the bitter flavor, were leached out. Experimenters developed tangy marinades in which olives were soaked to make them more appetizing.

Archaeological remains on Crete provide a glimpse of an early and energetic olive oil industry. The Palace of Knossos housed a plant in which pipes carried oil into large storage vats. Jars of olive oil, called *amphorae*, stored the olive oil before it was shipped out to Greece, North Africa, and other locations. Records of supplies and their costs were kept rigorously.

Cuttings from the olive trees in Crete likely reached Greece in the tenth century BC. In time, groves bearing fruit would cover the limestone hills of Attica, the area surrounding Athens.

The olive's needs were simple. Long, hot summers and a period of winter chill nurtured it. The tree was able to thrive in arid, rocky soil and could withstand strong winds and storms. Its taproots penetrated deep into the soil, drinking up whatever moisture was to be found. The evergreen's leaves were also an asset because water did not evaporate from them.

Olive farming demanded patience because the tree took a long time to rise up, and then to bloom. After harvesting the fruit, maintaining the tree was not taxing. "Olives have no use for the sickle knife or the stiff-tooth rake," the Roman poet Virgil writes.

The trees survived for hundreds of years. Even when a tree was cut down, its root network lived on to send out new shoots. After the Persians burned the Acropolis in their war with the Greeks, the story goes, an olive stump remained from which a single branch grew. The Greeks transplanted pieces of the branch to new ground. Ten olive trees rose up in those spots.

Before they turned to it for food, the Greeks relied on the olive tree for many other needs. It furnished fuel for lamps, provided building material, and offered shade. For those who could afford the luxury, olive oil was also medicinal and cosmetic. Wrestlers rubbed it on their shoulders. After work or exercise, classical scholar John Boardman points out, men and women rubbed perfumed olive oil on their bodies and then scraped off the oil, dirt, and sweat with an iron tool called a *strigil*. So revered was this cleansing instrument that it was placed in tombs.

The perfumed oil, sometimes scented with iris or other flowers, could be sexually inviting. Hera, Zeus's wife, set out to seduce him by "anointing herself with the delicious olive oil she uses," Homer writes in *The Iliad*. "It was perfumed and had only to be stirred in the Palace of the Brazen Floor for its scent to spread through heaven and earth."

Since they had few sources of animal fat, the Greeks seized on the olive as a tasty and inexpensive substitute. For a snack, they ate bread moistened with olive oil. Butter, they felt, was reserved for "barbarians."

They frequently ate their olives immersed in brine, as the playwright Aristophanes observes in a vivid passage: "Old man, do you like the girls who are fully ripe or the almost-virgins, like firm olives dripping with brine?" The Greeks also

enjoyed the fruits crushed and seasoned as a kind of "cheese," food historian Andrew Dalby says.

Olives and oil were inextricably linked in the Hellenic mind. The Greeks called the fruit *elaia*, from which the Latin name, *oliva*, the root of our own word, derives.

Because of its unique features, the olive also exerted a powerful hold on the ancient imagination. The tree, its fruit, and its oil symbolized values prized by these civilizations.

The olive tree embodied all the elements on which settled societies were founded—peace, wisdom, skill, order. The Greek goddess Athena, who presented a gift of the tree to the Athenians, was extolled for these virtues. In a contest between her and Poseidon over who could provide the city with the most valuable present, the goddess won. Poseidon had offered the horse, whereas Athena struck the ground with her spear and caused an olive tree to spring up.

The venerable olive tree was admired for its hard wood and polish. "An olive's cloudy grain the handle made," Homer writes of Pisander's ax in *The Iliad*. But much more important than these features were the tree's mythic qualities. It stood for longevity and immortality. Homer used it to convey fidelity and constancy. Odysseus's marriage bed was immovable because its post was the trunk of an olive tree deeply rooted in the ground.

So beneficent was the olive that it symbolized good fortune and the promise of abundance. In the Old Testament, a dove brings a green leaf to Noah on the ark, and "in her mouth was an olive leaf pluckt off." This was a sign that God's wrath had ended and that the earth would soon turn green and lush.

The olive also stood for purity. In Greece, harvesters of the fruit were required to take a vow of chastity. The Greeks anointed the faces of the dead with olive oil.

In the Old Testament world, olive oil was a sacrament. "Take thou also unto these principal spices . . . and . . . olive oil," God commands Moses in Exodus. "And thou shall make it an oil of holy ointment, an ointment compound after the art of the apothecary: it shall be a holy anointing oil. And thou shalt anoint the tabernacle of the congregation therewith."

Regal and spiritual authorities were blessed with anointments of oil. *Chrism*, a Semitic word for oil, was applied to the bodies of the priests and kings of Israel. *Chrism* is the origin of the Greek *kristos*, or "the anointed one." Christ, in turn, comes from *kristos*.

The spiritual fruit generated material wealth. Trade in oil developed into a booming business in the fifth century BC, Greece's classical age. The export of olives spread wealth throughout the economy of Athens. The ceramics industry prospered because of the demand for amphorae, the vase-like containers in which olives were stored and shipped. Shipbuilding became a profitable business.

Cargoes of olives and of wine, another major commodity, helped in building Magna Graecia, the greater Greek empire. The Greeks traded their products for the wheat, metals, and timber from the "barbarian" lands in the Mediterranean and Asia Minor.

The town of Massalia, the site of today's French Mediterranean port of Marseille, was a stepping-stone in Greek expansion. A Greek tribe, the Phocaeans, established an outpost there between 690 and 900 BC. The Greeks also took control of Sicily. From these early bases, the Greeks pushed further into France and Italy. While colonizing these territories, they taught their subjects the arts of olive and vine cultivation.

Beneficiaries of the Greek olive, the Romans became the world's largest olive oil producer by the first century AD. The Romans spread the fruit throughout their empire. But the olive's sphere remained the Mediterranean. How would it ever reach the New World?

The Romans were enthusiastic olive eaters. To give the fruit a sprightly flavor, they steeped it in oil, garlic, and salt, a marinade we have inherited. Street vendors hawked olives in cones made of papyrus and sold olive cakes accented with cumin, anise, and fennel.

"There are two liquids especially appealing to the human body, wine inside and oil outside," Pliny, the Roman naturalist, wrote. His society gloried in both the olive and the grape on festive occasions. A shop in Pompeii, unearthed by archaeologists, provided partygoers with olive wreaths to wear and oils to beautify their bodies.

A practical people, the Romans improved techniques for processing olive oil and exploited it as a commercial product. Donkeys pulled wheels made of millstones that pulped the fruit. A screw press, a Roman invention, extracted oil from the paste. The mills produced a spectrum of oil, from the most luxurious to the ordinary. Even its wastes had value. The black residue was used as a weed killer and as an insecticide.

Since the olive crop in Rome and its colonies was uneven, plentiful one year and meager the next, the empire faced an ongoing dilemma. The answer was trade. To fill in the gaps, Rome especially depended on imports of the commodity.

The colony of Tunisia was by the fourth century AD Rome's largest provisioner of olive oil. The Romans wrung a bountiful crop from the barren soil in the country's interior. They invested large sums in olive mills and large presses that could turn out oil in bulk.

The oil business enriched African traders, who showed off their wealth in expensive villas. Magnates parlayed their financial gains into political influence. African businessmen held seats in the Roman Senate.

Spain, the largest exporter of olive oil today, grew into an oil bastion during Roman rule. The Phoenicians, mariners who sailed out from what is now Lebanon, planted the land's first olive groves. By the second century AD, the Roman occupiers had built an extensive system of orchards and oil mills in the southern region of Andalusia. Along the banks of rivers, kilns manufactured amphorae, the vessels in which oil was transported to market. Classical scholar D. J. Mattingly points out that hundreds of thousands of these vases were crafted each year to meet the insatiable demand in the capital. Vessels plied the rivers loaded with stores. Visit Rome today and you can gaze at Monte Testaccio, a hill near the wharves of the old city, formed from discarded or smashed amphorae.

Fortunes were also made from Spanish oil. Although Italian-born, illustrious families like those of Trajan and Hadrian reaped huge profits in the Iberian colony.

The Moors, who invaded Spain in the seventh century AD and who controlled large parts of the country for several centuries, revitalized olive culture. Keen agriculturists, the Muslims laid out new fields and tended them religiously. The center of cultivation continued to be Andalusia, which today produces 80 percent of Spain's olives. The familiar pimento-stuffed green olives, the manzanillas (or "little apples"), are grown in this region.

Olive oil was only slowly accepted by the Spanish Christians, who stuck to lard in their cooking. Because olive oil was associated with Muslims and Jews, Catholics shunned it. After the Reconquista, the vanquishing of the Islamists by the Christians, pork was extolled. In time, though, olive oil became the country's flavoring of choice. The Spanish names for olive and olive oil, *aceite* and *aceituna*, respectively, are Arabic in origin.

The olive was incorporated in church rituals. Priests were ordained with anointments of oil, a symbol of constancy. On holy days, worshippers were blessed with olive fronds often cut from trees grown on church land. During the Lenten fast, many Catholics abstained from butter in favor of olive oil.

Spain was eager to adorn its colonies with the olive tree. Since the fruit only flourished in a Mediterranean climate, the crown's ambitions went largely unfulfilled. The tropical climate of the Spanish possessions in the Caribbean, Cuba and Hispaniola, was hostile to the olive. In Latin America, only along the desert coast of Peru was there fertile ground for the Spanish import.

In North America, Thomas Jefferson—who called the olive "the worthiest plant to be introduced into America"—found the South inhospitable to large-scale cultivation. The continent's West Coast was friendlier. The Franciscan friars, who pioneered the Spanish settlement of California, carried olive cuttings there from Mexico in the 1700s. In addition to pears, pomegranates, figs, dates, and almonds, the padres filled their mission gardens with olive trees, which they planted primarily for their oil. The variety was naturally called a "mission" olive.

The West Coast olive industry didn't take off until the late nineteenth century, when the number of orchards had expanded and the product, shipped in railcars, arrived in the East and Midwest. The California olive was a characteristically American invention, a creation of technology and mass production.

Freda Ehmann, whose son owned an olive ranch in the state, devised a way to chemically ripen green fruit. On the back porch of her daughter's home in Oakland, culinary historian Raymond Sokolov recounts, she tinkered with curing methods. She discovered that a lye bath would produce a "black ripe" olive.

This olive was perfect for canning. Techniques for pitting, sizing, and stuffing the fruit were also developed. The mass-produced, bland olive appealed to a public fearful of any exotic item with a sharp, pungent taste.

Since then, we have grown more conversant with olives, but they are still not part of our daily routine. How many of us grace our dinner tables with a plate of olives before a meal? We are still a long way from being Mediterranean, from fully savoring "a taste as old as cold water," as author Lawrence Durrell described it.

KNOWING YOUR ONIONS

"I will not move my army without onions," General Ulysses S. Grant wrote in a message to the War Department. Three trainloads of this necessity arrived the next day. Grant was just one of many throughout history who have placed their faith in onions. So ubiquitous that it often goes unnoticed, the common bulb has quenched the hunger and added zest and bite to otherwise-ordinary diets of countless cultures.

Honored as a provider of health and vitality, it was, curiously enough, also a source of disgust and dread. Relished by the multitudes, it was often scorned by members of the elect.

The onion belongs to the vast Allium genus, a group of eight hundred species, which also includes garlic, leeks, and chives. The *alliums*, whose name comes from the Greek word for "to avoid," were most probably first domesticated in the mountainous regions of Central Asia near Tajikistan and Uzbekistan. The seeds and bulbs reached the Middle East with travelers and caravans who plied the Silk Road and other trade routes.

Their birthplace, *allium* authority Eric Block argues, helps explain the plants' distinctive flavor and fragrance. "These plants originated in a very tough neighborhood, in Central Asia north of Afghanistan, and they evolved some serious chemical weapons to defend themselves." Mostly odorless, they release sulfur chemicals when their tissues are disturbed by cutting, crushing, or other injury. The molecules easily disperse to excite our senses and even to attach themselves to our hair and clothing.

The chemical reaction that produces their appealing pungency is a survival mechanism. "They're not there for our pleasure," Dr. Block points out. "They're there to allow the plant to survive in a very hardscrabble world, a world where there are lots of worms in the ground and animals that would devour something that exists in a bulb and has to survive in the ground."

It is these same irritating chemicals that account for the onion's medicinal properties. The onion helps to fight bacteria, stops blood clotting, and remedies inflammation, among other things.

The chemical explosion ignited by peeling or slicing, Dr. Block observes, is also responsible for our eyes tearing and our noses running. The sulfuric burst is known as the lachrymatory factor. The potent chemical dissolves in the eye's fluid, making a weak sulfuric acid.

Cooking enables the onion to redeem itself. With heating, its harshness soon vanishes. From an onion base, an endearing sweetness and an earthy fragrance suffuses stews, curries, and soups.

The earliest civilizations sustained themselves on onions and other basic foodstuffs. Five-thousand-year-old clay tablets from Mesopotamia (modern-day Iraq), the earliest recorded recipes, show that onions, leeks, and garlic were mainstays of cooking. Instructions for braised turnips highlight these vegetables: "Meat is not needed. Boil water. Throw fat in. [Add] onion . . . coriander, cumin.

. . . Squeeze leek and garlic and spread [juice] on dish. Add onion and mint." Onions were sacred in these cultures. Onion patches, a Babylonian official wrote, were "God's best fields."

In Egypt, peasants subsisted on bread, onions, and beer. When other foods were scarce, onions that had been dried and plaited in strings came to the rescue. Their masters knew what they needed to fuel their bodies. The cost of these spicy daily rations was inscribed by bookkeepers on the Great Pyramid: the workers were provided sixteen hundred talents' worth of onions, garlic, and radishes.

Onions remain essential to today's Egyptians. "We don't have any dish without onions," Abdallah Hashish, the Egyptian-born owner of Washington's Astor Mediterranean restaurant, once told me. "Farmers eat raw onion and bread and salt and pepper." Abdallah himself enjoys a simple snack of a raw onion sprinkled with salt and cumin.

Tomb carvings depict onions being planted and watered. Grown in the rich soil along the banks of the Nile, onions are still a prominent feature of the Egyptian landscape. Drawn by donkeys or water buffalos, wagons piled with bulbs leave the fields for market.

So fond were the Israelites of the onions of the Nile Valley that they pined for them in their exile: "We remember the fish, which we did eat in Egypt freely; the cucumbers, the melons, and the leeks, and the onions and the garlick" (Numbers 11:5).

The onion, wooden models of which were found in the Egyptian tombs, assumed cosmic meaning. Emblematic of the universe, the layers of the onion represented the concentric circles of heaven, earth, and hell. (In Latin, the word for onion means "one" or "unity.") Leaders, it is said, swore with their right hand on the onion when making oaths. The Roman poet Juvenal poked fun at this peculiar Egyptian devotion: "It is sacrilege to bite the leek or onion. O holy nation in whose gardens divinities spring up."

In ancient Egypt, onions were blessed by the clergy. Frequent tomb motifs featured priests laying a bundle of onion leaves or roots on the altar. Mourners carried baskets of onions to funerals. Bulbs were inserted in the bandages of mummies, probably to awaken the senses of the dead. The mummy of King Ramses the IV, the twelfth-century BC monarch, was found with onions bulging from his eye sockets.

An honored antiseptic, the onion accompanied the dead on their journey to the afterlife, probably to cleanse the body of poisons. Onions in Egypt were grated for dressings and ointments for cuts and wounds, and even acne.

The revered vegetable could also arouse contradictory feelings in Egypt's religious leaders. Some feared that the bulb might awaken lascivious impulses. Others renounced it, the Greek historian Plutarch notes, because of other spiritual considerations: "The priests keep themselves clear of the onion and detest it and are careful to avoid it, because it is the only plant that naturally thrives and flourishes in the waning of the moon. It is suitable for neither fasting nor festival, because in the one case it causes thirst and in the other tears for those who partake of it."

Impressed by Egypt's bountiful and invigorating onion harvest, Alexander the Great ordered Greek farmers to grow the crop. Onions, Alexander believed, would energize and fortify his soldiers. To prime themselves for Olympic competitions, athletes drank onion juice and massaged their bodies with the bulb. Hellenic doctors applied onion salves to wounds.

Favored by commoners, who often supped on raw onion and bread for breakfast, the onion was a basic plebeian food in ancient Rome. Vendors in Pompeii, who hawked the staple, were shunned by the sellers of more prestigious produce.

In Rome the upper classes felt the onion should be reserved for piquant sauces and marinades. Onions pickled in honey and vinegar was a popular condiment. Roman gourmet Apicius conceived a sauce of onion, pepper, coriander, vinegar, and oil to flavor grilled fish.

For all their contempt for the vegetable, the cultivated classes occasionally indulged. Excavators turned up a basket of onions in a Pompeii brothel.

The Romans maintained the age-old faith in the onion's curative powers. Roman naturalist Pliny offered twenty-seven remedies in which the bulb could work its wonders: "The cultivated onion is employed for the cure of dimness of sight, the patient being made to smell it till tears come into the eyes; it is still better even if the eyes are rubbed with the juice."

In the East the onion met strong resistance from the high religious orders. The onion offended those committed to leading a holy and pure life. Orthodox believers associated the plant, whose bulb grew underground, with sinister and unclean spirits from the lower depths. Onions and garlic, according to an early school of Hindu philosophy, embodied "darkness." In some Hindu myths, onions are beloved by demons, who also lust after meat, blood, alcohol, and other strong foods. The pungent vegetable, it was feared, might arouse forbidden passions and lewd thoughts.

In Islam the alliums were also equated with evil. In Muslim legend, when Satan left the Garden of Eden, garlic shot up from where he placed his left foot, and onions, his right.

Many devout Hindus renounced the onion because its strong aroma, they felt, offended the gods. Onions therefore had no place in the temple. Their fears were in stark contrast to the feelings of ancient Egyptians, who made holy offerings of the vegetable.

Hindus who followed a strict vegetarian regimen also tended to abstain from onions. Their resemblance to meat, food scholar Frederick Simoons suggests, helps explain the repugnance. Because they looked like meat when cut or looked like a head, onions could be categorized as "flesh food."

To higher Indian castes like the Brahmins, the onion was especially taboo. Priests, who were typically Brahmin, were expected to avoid the impure food. Partaking of the vegetable threatened the Hindu aristocracy with the loss of their exalted status.

Intriguingly, the same belief that led the orthodox to renounce onions led soldiers to embrace them. Warrior castes in India were permitted to eat the "very hot" vegetable. Onions would apparently provide them with martial strength.

In China, where the spring onion has been enjoyed since ancient days, the onion has been simultaneously inviting and threatening. Kumarajiva, a Buddhist scholar who came to China from India, pronounced the onion one of "five vegetables of strong odor" banned for the clergy.

As in India, the onion was linked to the demonic underworld in China. Hence, its powers could be harnessed to repel hostile invaders. For many centuries, the Chinese hung onions and garlic above their gates and doors from red cords to ward off evil. They were also supposed to scare away insects.

The Chinese also turned to onions for protection against illness. Onion tea has long been sipped to combat fever, headaches, and digestive woes. Savored in its own right, the spring onion was appreciated as a tonic that could keep one warm when it was cold outside.

Onions traveled west, feeding the Roman soldiers on their imperial marches. As Roman rule spread to Britain, Spain, and other lands, the new plant sprouted.

In the Middle Ages, friars planted onions in their gardens. The sturdy crop, easy and inexpensive to grow, was a medieval staple. The nobility, who once might have sneered at the bulb, lost some of their wariness. Charlemagne, for example, ordered his staff to grow onions in the royal gardens. Lords accepted onions from their tenants as payment for the use of their fields.

Onions were invested with supernatural and medicinal powers. During the plague years in Eastern Europe, people strung onions and garlic in their doorways to keep away vampires. The magic charm, others believed, could also repel germs. Medieval physicians prescribed onions for hearing loss, headaches, and even snakebites.

Early herbalists, who were investigating the intricacies of the vegetable kingdom, were impressed by the onion. The English commentator John Gerard worried about the plant and spread his fears to his fervent following: "The onion being eaten, yea though it be boyled, causeth head-ache, hurteth the eyes, and maketh a man dimme sighted, dulleth the senses, ingendreth windinesse, and provoketh overmuch sleep, especially being eaten raw." Surprisingly, though, Gerard believed that the bulb had hidden benefits: "The juice of an onion anointed upon a bald head in the sun bringeth the hair again very speedily."

The English developed a fondness for the onion and its cousin, the leek. Among the Elizabethans, they overshadowed all other vegetables in popularity. Shakespeare wrote poetically about the onion and gave voice to persistent anxieties about the plant. In *Antony and Cleopatra*, Enobarbus the eunuch says, "The tears live in an onion that should water this sorrow." Bottom from *A Midsummer Night's Dream* tells his acting troupe "to eat no onions nor garlic, for we are to utter sweet breath."

The more cooks learned about onions, the more enthusiastic they became about what culinary writer Brillat-Savarin called the "truffle of the poor." Onions enhanced cabbage and potato dishes and elevated a basic stew. French chefs, in particular, enlivened bourguignon, soubise, and other classic sauces with the vegetable.

A recent study bears out the popular wisdom about the onion's utility. Onions and leeks, the investigators concluded, were the strongest element in the gravy aroma of stews they studied.

The venerable bulb from the Old World was swiftly adopted by America's earliest settlers. "Onyon seed" was one of the items ordered in 1631 by John Winthrop, governor of Massachusetts. "The onion is the most favored food that grows," George Washington enthused. The president was not picky; he liked the vegetable cored, baked, or "stuffed with mincemeat like an apple." He was a man who truly "knew his onions."

SWEET FOR SOUR ORANGES

Its scent imbues Earl Grey tea, and its peel is essential for British marmalade. Born in the East, the scarlet-skinned sour orange captivated the West several hundred years before the arrival of its sweet cousin in early sixteenth-century Europe. Native to China and domesticated in India, the orange was beloved for the intoxicating fragrance of its skin and flowers. It was generally not coveted for eating and juicing. The tree, which had dark green foliage and whose flowers bloomed in beautiful white colors, was planted to ornament the landscape.

Hindus called the fruit *naranga*, a word whose first syllable means "fragrance." The Persians, who adopted it from India, named the orange *narang*. The versatile fruit, which grew wild along the Caspian Sea, brought its aroma to Persian cooking. Blossoms were used for jam, and the skin perfumed rice dishes and stews.

The Arabs, who transported it to the Mediterranean, discovered the fruit during their reign in Persia in the seventh century AD. Like so many other elements of Persian culture, the fruit seduced the invaders. They soon made the sour orange their own, changing its name to *narandj* because they couldn't pronounce the "g."

The Islamic warriors built an empire that stretched from the Middle East to the Mediterranean. During their rule, from the seventh through the twelfth centuries, the colonizers brought the orange—along with the pomegranate, sugarcane, spinach, and a host of other new plants—into their possessions. Accomplished agriculturists, they planted citrus seeds first in Iraq, Syria, Egypt, and Palestine. They went on to grow sour oranges in their colonies in Spain and Sicily.

The orange tree was displayed lavishly in Spain. The Moors created gardens with luxuriant citrus and with tulips, jasmine, lilacs, and other flowering plants from the East. The brilliant evergreen adorned the courtyards of mosques, palaces, and royal residences. Orange and lemon trees graced the Alhambra, the palace complex in Granada. The mosque in the Spanish city of Cordova boasted the Patio de los Naranjos, a courtyard resplendent with nineteen rows of orange trees, each leading up to one of the building's arched openings. The grandeur of many of these settings was enhanced with pools and fountains. The magnificence, some suggest, was meant to represent an earthly paradise complete with the sensuous pleasures and beauty of the Islamic afterlife.

Arabic poets wrote lyrically of settings beautified by citrus. Abd ur-Rahman Ibn Mohammed Ibn Omar marveled at an island on the lake of a Sicilian villa: "The oranges of the island are like blazing fire amongst the emerald boughs."

The Arabs also drew intense pleasure from the fragrant fruit itself. They preserved bitter oranges and their skins in sugar, fashioning a forerunner of marmalade. Cooks enlivened dishes with their aromatic juice. (One variety of the bitter orange, the Seville, came to be used especially for marmalade.) From the flowers they distilled orange blossom water (*mazaher*), a fragrant liquid akin to rose water. In Morocco, another Moorish society, where many families made their own orange blossom water, a carrot salad is dressed with the aromatic. Sliced oranges redolent of cinnamon and the citric perfume are a favorite Moroccan dessert.

Orange blossom water often lends its aroma to baklava and other Arab sweets. Adding a few drops to boiling water yields a treat called *white coffee*. A little sugar and the aromatic in warm milk will put you to sleep at bedtime.

Mazaher invested domestic life with sensual pleasure. After washing their hands, Arabs often perfumed them with a dash of flower water. In fourteenth-century Sicily, the *Oxford Companion to Food* notes, bed linen was frequently scented with orange blossom water, an Arabic habit.

The orange also acquired a sacred and ceremonial role. The Moors introduced the custom of brides wearing orange blossoms. The flowers continue to be part of the Spanish marriage bouquet. To the Muslims, the white flowers were an emblem of chastity, and the orange fruit, a symbol of fecundity.

Citrus confections from the Islamic world would soon reach Europe. The Arabs, who made sugarcane a cash crop in Egypt, Persia, Sicily, and southern Spain, sweetened citrus to make tempting delicacies. *Suckets*, or candied orange and lemon peels, caught the fancy of the English. At the coronation of Pope Clement VI, diners indulged in "candied fruit of many colors," which were served in two courses of the feast.

Europe's upper classes reveled in the fragrance of the exotic fruit. Italian novelist Giovanni Boccaccio writes of a Sicilian courtesan who wooed her clients with tantalizing aromas: "Her own chamber . . . was perfumed with roses, orange-flowers, and other costly scents." Noble women bathed in orange-scented water. "The perfumers and hairdressers . . . every morning supply the ladies' rooms with rose water, citrus-blossom water, and myrtle water," the sixteenth-century French writer Rabelais observed of a manor house.

In France, to satisfy the cravings of the aristocracy, merchants shipped oranges from Provence in southern France, where they were grown, to northern cities. Paper-wrapped sour oranges were sent from the French and Italian Riviera. Barrels of orange blossom flowers were shipped north in the spring.

Naturally, perfume makers were tantalized by the commercial potential of the sour orange. Its fragrance invigorated eau de cologne, a new "water" manufactured in the early eighteenth century in the German city of that name. John Maria Farina, its inventor, explained the secrets behind its aroma: "I have created a perfume which is reminiscent of a spring morning following a soft shower where fragrance of wild narcissi combine to that of sweet orange flowers. The perfume refreshes me and stimulates both my senses and imagination."

Oil from the Bergamot orange, a bitter variety, was an essential component of the product. The cologne was also marketed as a health aid, as a preventive for tooth decay and bad breath, as well as for infectious diseases. Europe's nobles and royals were thrilled by the fragrance. Napoleon Bonaparte, it was said, finished a bottle of the "water" every day and enjoyed sugar cubes dipped in it. The same rapturous fragrance permeates many of today's colognes.

As the Islamic empire ebbed, a new imperial power, the Portuguese, rose up. They introduced the West to the glories of a new citrus flavor—the sweet orange. These mariners, navigating the route to India and trading with the East during the fifteenth and sixteenth centuries, sighted the luscious fruit. The Portuguese poet Luis de Camões wrote of a citrus forest seen by mariner Vasco da Gama: "A thousand trees are seen towards heaven rising, with beautiful and sweetly scented apples. . . . The orange, wearing on its lovely fruit the colour Daphne carried in her hair."

The Portuguese returned from Ceylon and India with seeds and trees. Groves of oranges were planted in the Iberian nation. "The whole country is so well provided with them that in springtime, no matter where a person may happen to find himself, the orange blossoms will envelop him with their scent," historian Duarte Nunez de Leao wrote in 1610. The *portugal*, as it came to be known, was transported to Italy, England, France, and other European nations. The delicacy edged ahead of the sour orange in popularity.

An even more succulent sweet orange would soon take center stage. Jesuit missionaries, who had followed Portuguese traders to South China in the early 1500s, wrote back with glowing reports of superlative fruit: "[T]he oranges of Canton might well be queens over our own, in fact, some people hold that they are not so much oranges as muscat grapes disguised," Padre Alvaro Semedo exulted. The Portuguese cultivated and exported the "China orange." The scientific name of the sweet orange, *Citrus sinensis*, points to its lineage.

In the social world of Europe's leisure classes, the orange was transformed into a symbol of status. To show off their wealth and lofty position, French kings and nobles constructed "orangeries" to display the impressive evergreen. Sheltered from the cold, these elegant enclosures were forerunners of greenhouses. In most of them, the trees were planted in huge boxes, which sometimes could even be rolled outside in warmer weather. For a monarch like Louis XIV, who placed orange trees in his palaces, apartments, and garden, they were synonymous with royalty and opulence.

Profligate Europeans demanded the fruit for their tables. Lavish spreads of orange-based dishes were offered to guests at fancy dinners. At one such affair in 1529, the archbishop of Milan fed his friends fried caviar with cinnamon- and sugar-dusted oranges, fried sardines with oranges, sturgeons scented with orange juice, and sparrows fried with oranges.

The rich also incorporated citrus into their drinking customs. The juice and fragrance of orange rind perked up wine and other alcoholic drinks. The Dutch, who revered the fruit, steeped orange and lemon peels in spirits. Curaçao, the liqueur made from bitter green oranges from the Caribbean island of the same name, was first produced in Holland by this process.

Lowly peddlers in the cities labored to provide the upper classes with this indulgence. Nell Gwynn, the mistress of England's King Charles II, started out as one of the "orange girls," hawking baskets of fruit in the theaters of seventeenth-century London. Members of high society often sneered at the common vendors. "Anybody may know she has been an orange wench by her swearing," the Duchess of Portsmouth said of Nell.

Some traditionalists, however, were apprehensive about citrus refreshments. The seventeenth-century English writer Samuel Pepys was skittish about drinking an orangeade, then in vogue, at his cousin's home: "[H]ere, which I never did before, I drank a glass . . . of the juice of oranges, of whose peel they make confits; and here they drink the juice as wine with sugar . . . but it being new, I was doubtful whether it might not do me hurt."

For all their grandeur, oranges retained an aura of sacramental simplicity. Scientist Pierre Laszlo points out that citrus, revered by Islam, was Christianized: "Because orange trees came to fruition during winter, they became part of rituals celebrating renewal, and the hoped-for return of spring in pagan times; later they were involved in Christian activities." In Christian art, the Virgin Mary was associated with white orange blossoms.

As Europeans expanded into the Americas, they brought the fruit along. Bequeathed the orange by their Islamic conquerors, the Spaniards were intent on making citrus a cash crop in their tropical empire. During his second expedition, Columbus, the agent of the Spanish monarchy, gathered "pips and seeds of oranges, lemons and citrons" from one of the Canary Islands and sowed them on a plantation on the Caribbean island of Hispaniola.

Ultimately, the barriers to enjoyment of the orange crumbled in the New World. No longer a plaything of the wealthy, the orange became widely affordable, and its juice a breakfast staple. In the twentieth century, the orange became a fruit for the masses.

THE "FRUIT OF ANGELS"
the papaya

Papaya and hot dogs? An unlikely marriage. But not in New York, where the combination has been a winning formula for many small eateries. Hot dogs and papaya juice are "a New York institution," Larry Feierstein, vice president for Nathan's Famous, a frankfurter chain that doesn't sell the drink, told the *New York Times* in 1991.

Credit for the idea goes to Constantine ("Gus") Poulos, a young Greek immigrant from Athens, who settled in New York during the 1920s. Poulos, who owned a deli in the Yorkville section of Manhattan, became a fan of the tropical fruits he encountered on his first vacation, to Miami. He launched his first juice shop, Hawaiian Tropical Drinks, in 1931. Since his business initially attracted few customers, Poulos tried some imaginative promotion. Waitresses wearing Hawaiian shirts offered passersby on the street slices of papaya and free drinks.

The entrepreneur got his first break when Birdie, a young German woman, initiated him into the food of her country. Pairing the hot dog, loved by the residents of this German enclave, with papaya juice, he decided, could be a winner. He married Birdie, and soon the shop was booming. Poulos, who changed the name of his business to Papaya King, opened more outlets. Imitators—Papaya Heaven, Papaya Jack, Original Papaya—proliferated. Since the name *papaya* could not be copyrighted, the businessman had no way of stopping the competitive frenzy.

Few patrons of these shops knew the story of the papaya. Many people today still associate it with Hawaii, when, in fact, the papaya is a child of the Americas. Native to Mexico and Central America, this fruit captured Columbus's attention in the Caribbean. The Carib Indians "[are] very strong and live largely on a tree melon called the 'fruit of angels,'" Columbus wrote in his journal. J. H. van Linschoten, a Dutch explorer, remarked on a "fruit that came out of the Spanish Indies . . . and is very like a Melon, as big as a man's fist."

The tropical tree shoots up rapidly, producing fruit from seed in a year's time. A crest of giant leaves crowns its woody stalk, which can grow as high as twenty feet. Fruit that might be as light as half a pound or as mammoth as twenty pounds clusters under the canopy. The prolific papaya bears twelve to thirty fruits a year, and it grows in the most ordinary circumstances. A few seeds from kitchen garbage might sprout into fruit in backyards or alleyways.

The Indians taught their conquerors to use the melon as a tenderizer. Wilson Popenoe, a self-styled "agricultural explorer" for the US Department of Agriculture, explained the technique in a 1920 fruit primer: "Its digestive action has long been recognized in the tropics, as is evidenced by the common practice of the natives, who rub the juice over meat to make it tender, or in preparing a food, wrap it in papaya leaves and let it remain overnight before cooking it." The Indians had grasped a scientific truth. Researchers found that inside the leaves and skin of the green fruit was a milky sap containing a valuable enzyme called *papain*. When used in commercial meat tenderizers, the enzyme promotes digestion.

The Spanish called the fruit *papaya*, probably from the Carib Indian word, *ababai*. In other countries, it evoked a host of images. It became *fruta bomba* ("small hand grenade") in Cuba, *lechosa* ("milky") in Puerto Rico, and *mamão* ("large breast") in Brazil. The English called it the *pawpaw*. Whatever its name, the papaya became a traditional breakfast fruit in the tropics.

Iberian voyagers carried the papaya to new lands. The Philippines received papaya seeds from the Spaniards. The Portuguese brought the fruit to Malacca, their entrepôt in Southeast Asia. The papaya soon became common in Asia and ultimately throughout the tropics.

Once exotic, the papaya has become less of a novelty in the United States. These days, during the warm months, a Hispanic vendor in Columbia Heights—a Washington, D.C., neighborhood with a mix of Latinos and young professionals—sells slices of the fruit. I have fond memories of Paul Petit, a Washington chef who made inventive use of the papaya: he dreamed up a mango-papaya salad with fiery Scotch bonnet peppers, and papaya juice flavored one of his salad dressings.

Thai restaurants around the country have been introducing diners to the green, unripe papaya. *Som tam*, a staple of their menu, is a dish of julienned sticks of white papaya dressed in a tart and spicy blend of fish sauce, lime juice, chili, and garlic. It is typically garnished with peanuts, a Thai favorite. The salad's

name comes from *som*, the word for "sour," and *tam*, which refers to the sound coming from pounding ingredients in a pestle. Papaya salad, a popular street-corner food in the Southeast Asian country, is thought to calm the stomach.

At Jolt 'N Bolt, a coffee shop in my Washington, D.C., neighborhood, Pakistani owner Farooq Munir displayed the hefty fruit in a straw basket on the counter. I watched the skin turn a yellowish, slightly brown color. The delectable fruit was ripening. It was ready to be converted into a smoothie, the coffee shop's drawing card. One afternoon, Farooq passed me a frothy, light pink refreshment that married the papaya's delicate sweetness with the creamy flavor of milk. I savored the drink, relishing the pleasure of the "fruit of the angels."

FOUND A PEANUT

"The Fruit, which are called by Seamen Earth-Nuts, are brought from Guinea in the Negroes' Ships, to feed the Negroes withal in their Voyage from Guinea to Jamaica," the English physician Hans Sloane observed in the early eighteenth century. Many commentators assumed that the peculiar nuts carried in the holds of slave ships were African foods. The peanuts were, in fact, a basic staple of the West African diet, but they were of American origin. Born in the New World before being transported to Africa, the "earth-nuts" were making a return voyage. In the hands of African slaves, the peanut would be transformed once again.

The plant was probably first cultivated in the foothills of the Bolivian Andes. From there it was disseminated through Brazil, Paraguay, and neighboring lands. The Indians who tilled it would carry the peanut as far as the Caribbean. The legume and its bounty of underground nut-filled pods were highly esteemed in the ancient civilizations of Peru. Archaeologists have unearthed funeral vases decorated with likenesses of the pods. A necklace found in coastal Peru that dated back to between AD 200 and 800 had ten gold and ten silver peanut-shaped beads. Scientists have even found the ground on their sites strewn with peanut shells.

In the peanut's American heartland, cooks capitalized on its culinary assets. A creamy peanut sauce spiced with chilies is spread over chicken in the Peruvian classic, *aji de gallina*. Potatoes are draped with peanut dressing in *papas a la arequipeña*, another Peruvian dish. The people of the Bolivian highlands fashioned a bracing peanut soup, *sopa de mani*, to fortify them in this chilly region.

Westerners who first encountered the plants were often dismissive. The sixteenth-century Spanish writer Fernandez de Oviedo noticed the Arawak Indians in the Caribbean growing peanuts: "They sow and harvest it. It is a very common crop about the size of a pine nut in the shell." Although they enjoyed raw and roasted peanuts and considered them a healthy food, de Oviedo was not persuaded. The nut had a "very mediocre taste and little substance." Most Christians, he wrote, shunned the vulgar legume. Heaping more scorn, de Oviedo called the peanut a food for people "who would eat anything." Bernabé Cobo, a Spanish missionary, blamed the peanut for a variety of maladies. Raw peanuts, he said, could cause headaches, migraines, and giddiness.

Another observer, the Portuguese naturalist Soares de Souza, who visited Brazil in the late sixteenth century, was struck by an unusual quality of peanut farming. It was essentially the province of women: "The plants are grown in a loose humid soil the preparation of which has not involved any male human being; only the female Indians plant them, and their husbands know nothing about these labours. If the husbands of their male slaves were to plant them they would not sprout; the females also harvest them."

The plant's peculiar appearance made the peanut even more difficult to embrace. Unlike the familiar cashew and almond, it did not grow on trees. The confounding peanut bears its flowers aboveground and its fruits below. Jean de Flores, a sixteenth-century French missionary, struggled to describe the baffling plants: "They grow in the soil like truffles connected to one another by fine filaments." After the peanut's yellow flowers wither, the stem bends and burrows into the ground. A shell, an ingenious protection against predators, soon forms. The pod encloses what looks like nuts but are actually edible seeds. This makes the peanut a legume, not a nut. The plant's scientific name, *Arachis hypogaea*, Greek for "the weed whose fruit grows underground," is most fitting.

If the peanut had any value to the colonials, it was for sweets. Like the almond of which they were fond, it could be made into marzipan-like treats. Naturalist Soares de Souza notes that peanuts were "cut and covered with sugar as confections" by Portuguese women in Brazil.

As they built their overseas empires, the Spaniards and the Portuguese carried the peanut along their shipping routes. The seeds were stored in Spanish galleons that sailed across the Pacific from Peru in the sixteenth century. In the Philippines, a Spanish colony where the ships unloaded cargo, the peanut was given its original Indian name, *mani*.

The legume ultimately arrived in China, where citizens were fascinated by the import. They called them *lo-hua-sheng*, seeds "born from flowers fallen to the ground." After this happens, the plant develops seeds that resemble "silkworm cocoons," a Chinese historian observed. The legume proved to be a valuable crop in its new home. The peanut flourished in sandy soil and injected nitrogen into the earth, which kept it fertile. Chinese royalty, who ate the "longevity" nut at banquets, were early adopters. In time peanuts were taken up by commoners, who boiled and roasted them.

The Chinese took the peanut to Southeast Asia, where it was often known as *kachang* (the Chinese bean). In Indonesia, a salad of bean sprouts, green beans, fried bean curd, cucumbers, and other vegetables is enriched with a piquant peanut sauce. *Gado-gado* ("mixture"), the dish's intriguing name, was a fixture of the country's *waroengs*, or snack houses. Satés, skewers of grilled meat, a street food in Indonesia and other Southeast Asian lands, is offered with a peanut sauce for dipping. Asian food scholar Bruce Cost points out that in order to make the sauce, peanuts in Indonesia were traditionally first roasted in a wok filled with river sand. The Thais, who share the affection for the legume, make *penang gai*, a silky smooth chicken curry that combines the nutty flavor of ground peanuts with the creaminess of coconut milk. Chopped peanuts also provide a pleasant crunch to *pad thai*, the Thai noodle standard.

Portuguese mariners also carried peanuts on their voyages. The Iberians, historian A. J. R. Russell Wood reports, spread the plants of the Americas to new locations. Peanuts—as well as pineapples, sweet potatoes, maize, and manioc (also known as *cassava*)—were brought to West Africa in the early sixteenth century.

The new arrival did not startle the Africans, as it had the Europeans. They were already acquainted with a similar legume, the *Bambara* groundnut, which grows underground. Traveling in Mali, the West African state, in the early fourteenth century, Muslim writer Ibn Battuta was struck by a "grain" that the Africans were harvesting. It reminded him of the fava bean, a staple in Arab cooking. "They roast and eat it, the taste being like that of roast chickpeas." The Malians were also making peanut fritters: "Sometimes they grind this grain to make a kind of round spongy dough which they fry."

The peanut supplanted the *Bambara* as field plant and foodstuff. Compared to the oil-rich peanut, the woody seeded legume yielded a meager product. Grown more easily, the peanut also had a more abundant harvest. Even as it lost favor among the Africans, the traditional nut's name lived on. In different countries, people attached their language's word for the *Bambara* to the peanut. *Nguba*, for example—the Zairian word for both nuts—was the origin of the peanut's nickname in the United States: "goober."

The peanut immeasurably strengthened the African diet. It was hungrily appropriated in cultures desperate for protein. Roasted nuts were converted into pastes for soups or stews or hawked by street vendors. The staple was processed into cooking oil. Peanut soup remains an essential part of the West African cook's repertoire. A bowl of the thick reddish-brown puree redolent of ground peanuts, tomatoes, and onions has the zing of chili pepper. (It can be served with or without meat.) The stew-like soup is typically accompanied by *fufu*, a starchy mass of plantains, cassava, maize, or other carbohydrate which has been relentlessly pounded and mashed. A sort of African mashed potatoes, the *fufu* sops up the tasty gravy.

When slave ships hauled African captives to the Americas, peanuts and other foods loved by the captives were taken on as provisions. The peanut's hard shell made the legume a top choice for captains stocking items for a long voyage. In the United States, where the peanut reached the East Coast in the seventeenth century, slaves planted peanuts, watermelon, okra, black-eyed peas, watermelon, and other crops of African origin.

"Sometimes Massa let [slaves] have a little patch," a former slave quoted by food historian Andrew Smith recalled. "They'd raise taters or goobers." African cooking customs were also re-created. Slaves prepared peanut pie and peanut soup. They gathered for festive peanut boilings, historian Joseph Holloway points out.

The transplant was, however, saddled with a lowly reputation. It was considered suitable only for feeding the destitute and for "hogging off"—fattening up pigs. Because of its connection to slavery, the peanut carried a certain stigma. In Brazil, peanut brittle was dubbed *pé de moleque*, or "foot of the street urchin." During slavery, black children were given the name *moleque*, a demeaning term. To gain broader appeal, the peanut needed a more attractive image.

Peanuts lacked respectability generally because they were considered poor people's food. The nuts were associated with cheap entertainment, as a snack eaten in the lowly theater seats called the "peanut gallery" or at circuses. Their appeal was strongest in the South, where they were enjoyed boiled or fried.

The maligned bean gradually gained wider acceptance. During the Civil War, Union and Confederate soldiers staved off hunger by eating peanuts. The chorus of a popular song paid homage to the goober: "Peas! Peas! Peas! Peas! Eating goober peas / Goodness, how delicious / Eating goober peas!"

Promoters of health food and vegetarianism gave the peanut a boost. John Harvey Kellogg, an enterprising innovator who developed both cornflakes and granola, was a leader in popularizing peanut butter. Kellogg ran the Western Health Reform Institute (later renamed the Battle Creek Sanitarium), a Seventh-day Adventist clinic in Battle Creek, Michigan, devoted to vegetarianism and hydrotherapy. Experimenting with grinding peanuts, Kellogg produced a paste that he described as "moist, pasty, adhesive, and brown. . . . For distinction," he added, it is "termed 'butter,' or 'paste.'"

Kellogg's health views strengthened his commitment to the product. The doctor was a firm believer in thorough mastication. Kellogg, many of whose patients had difficulty chewing, stressed that peanut butter was "perfectly digestible." In 1897, Kellogg founded the Sanitas Food Company, which marketed "nut butters." The peanut proselytizer also gave thousands of lectures, many of which praised the benefits of his product. In a talk to the Tuskegee Institute in Alabama, Kellogg advocated the peanut as a valuable meat substitute.

Peanut butter developed a strong following among vegetarians. Health-conscious eaters learned how to make mock versions of veal cutlet, meat loaf, and steak from cookbook recipes. The new fashion also won converts among upper-class diners in the early twentieth century. Ye Olde English Coffee House in New York City offered a "Peanut Butter and Pimento Sandwich." "Dainty tea rooms and high-class restaurants proudly announced that their salads, sandwiches, and soups were made with peanut butter," food historian Andrew F. Smith observed. As the popularity of sandwiches spread to the mainstream, peanut butter became a natural choice.

Large manufacturers equipped with more efficient machinery transformed peanut butter from a health food and luxury item into a large-scale product. In the early 1900s, the Beech-Nut Packing Co. and H. J. Heinz Company began selling peanut butter to retail outlets. In an early ad, Heinz reaffirmed its product's nutritional value, especially for children: "Food scientists will tell you that Heinz Peanut Butter peculiarly supplies the solid nutriment that makes their legs grow plump—that builds firm flesh—gives them rosy color."

In America, then, the peanut was becoming more and more synonymous with peanut butter. Where other nations use peanuts primarily for its oil, half of our output goes into making the spread.

The peanut blossomed into a major commercial crop. In order to fortify the soil that "King Cotton" had depleted, many Southern farmers replaced it with peanuts. The plant injected nitrogen into the soil. George Washington Carver, the African American scientist at Tuskegee University, encouraged this trend. Lauding the goober as a culinary and commercial godsend, the peanut champion spread the gospel. The promoter once served a group of Alabama businessmen a lunch—chicken, bread, ice cream, coffee—made entirely from the versatile legume. Carter invented paints, linoleum, and cosmetics, a few of his three hundred creations, from the peanut.

Street vendors also helped to popularize the peanut. In northern cities during the pre–Civil War era, Italians were groundbreakers in this trade. One of the hawkers, Amedeo Obici, the son of an Italian saddle maker, had arrived in Scranton, Pennsylvania, in 1886 to live with an uncle. After working at a cigar factory in the city, the twelve-year-old moved to Wilkes-Barre, where he had a short stint as a fruit vendor. A natural salesman, who sold peanuts along with fruit, he decided to concentrate on the legume.

"He was interested in peanuts because they have a better shelf life than produce," Mary Ruth Burke, curator of the Luzerne County Historical Society museum, told the *Wilkes-Barre Times-Tribune*. He began driving a horse-drawn cart through the city, vending roasted peanuts. The steam from the roasting peanuts set off a whistle that announced Obici's presence.

The Italian soon embarked on a larger enterprise, opening in 1906 a two-story factory in Wilkes-Barre marketing blanched, salted peanuts. The company, the Planters Nut and Chocolate Company, was the forerunner of Planters Peanuts, which became a household name. The firm, which promoted its brand with the top-hatted figure of Mr. Peanut, was a pioneer in radio and print advertising. The *Saturday Evening Post* ran an ad for the product in 1918, the first notice for a salted nut ever to appear in the magazine.

What a remarkable journey for the "humble goober"—from the Americas to West Africa and back again, through many incarnations, the peanut has become both a nutritional staple and a popular snack food.

GIFT OF THE GODS
the pear

"There is only ten minutes in the life of the pear, when it is perfect to eat." Nine-teenth-century American writer Ralph Waldo Emerson captured the ephemeral quality of the pear, which endeared it to elites through the ages. In contrast to its cousin, the commonplace apple (also a member of the rose family), the pear became the special favorite of the upper orders.

Probably native to Central Asia, the pear migrated to the Mediterranean, arriving in Greece in 1000 BC. The wild pear—small, gritty, and sour—was slowly domesticated. One of the "gifts of the gods," as the poet Homer called it, the pear tree rose in a garden he depicted in *The Odyssey*: "[T]here grow tall trees blossoming, pear trees and pomegranates, and apple trees with bright fruit, and sweet figs, and olives in their bloom. The fruit of these trees never perisheth, neither faileth winter or summer, enduring through all the year. Evermore the West Wind blowing brings some fruits to birth and ripens others. Pear upon pear waxes old."

The Romans, adept gardeners, were consummate cultivators of fruit. Pears, adored by the nobility, were planted in villa gardens, often lining the sides of a marble watercourse. The Romans bred a remarkably diverse crop; Roman naturalist Pliny refers to thirty-five varieties. The descendants of these trees filled the orchards of medieval Europe.

The distinctive names of the Roman pears reflect a culture exquisitely attuned to subtle differences in their produce. Color—*Onychina* (onyx), *Purpurea* (purple)—was the hallmark of some. Aroma set the *Myrappia* (myrrh) and the

Laurea (laurel) apart. One, the *Bromus hordeaceus* (barley), got its name from the season in which both fruit and grain were harvested.

Pears graced the tables of the city's patricians, and Roman cooks developed ingenious ways of exploiting the fruit. They were dried, cooked in wine, and conserved in grape syrup. Less palatable fruit was saved for making pear cider and wine vinegar.

Pliny advised against eating the raw pear: "All kinds of pears, as an aliment, are indigestible, to persons in robust health, even; but to invalids they are forbidden as rigidly as wine." When cooked, he noted, they were quite pleasurable: "Boiled, however, they are remarkably agreeable and wholesome. . . . All kinds of pears, too, boiled with honey, are wholesome to the stomach."

The pear also had a curative role. The wild pear, Pliny commented, "cut in slices and hung in the air to dry . . . arrests looseness of the bowels, an effect which is equally produced by a decoction of it taken in drink."

The Roman imprint followed the pear on its journey through Europe. Its Latin name, *pirum*, was adapted in other languages. The descendants of the Roman trees filled the orchards of medieval Europe. In this age, as in the ancient, the pear enjoyed an exalted status. To the aristocracy, fruit borne on lofty trees was superior to earthy vegetables like cabbage and turnips, which were best left to commoners. In a brilliant book, *Cheese, Pears, and History in a Proverb*, food historian Massimo Montanari argues that the perishable pear epitomized the elegant fruit esteemed by the upper strata: "The pear is a symbol of the ephemeral, of unessential tastes and pleasures, and thus, once again, symbolic of social difference."

Its prestigious position made the pear an ideal gift to be exchanged among the nobility. Rurizio, the bishop of Limoges, France, in the sixth century, expressed his gratitude to another gentleman with a present of a hundred pears, hoping that "they do not offend his taste." He gave another hundred to his friend's wife.

The pear strengthened erotic bonds between lovers, Montanari points out. The poet Tommaso Campanella penned a sonnet "on the occasion of a gift of pears sent to the author by his lady which were nibbled by her teeth." The pear itself conveyed a sexual energy, Campanella suggests. The fruit is a "cherished gift between lustful lovers."

The image of the "partridge in a pear tree" from the carol "The Twelve Days of Christmas," some think, is erotically charged. It summons up medieval associations—the partridge as a representation of lust and the pear as a symbol of the phallus.

Unlike the leisure classes, the peasantry typically did not have the luxury of growing and tending to pears. When they did plant them, Montanari observes, the poor treated the pear as an economic necessity, not as a delicacy to fondle and savor. The famine of 1338 in Italy forced farmers to convert their pears to flour. To the nobleman, drying the pear to preserve it, a peasant device, defeated the fruit's purpose. The perishable pear no longer was a precious pleasure when it had to be saved for the future.

The fruit that was so vital to social standing, however, came with considerable peril. Medical authorities had long warned of the dangers of eating raw fruit. The Greek physician Galen, whose pronouncements influenced medieval opinion, was dismissive of fruit's culinary rewards: "We never eat them for food, but only as a medication." People worried that fruit might bring on headaches, indigestion, and fever. Pears were categorized as "cold" and "dry," a mixture of earth and water, as Galen put it.

The aristocracy thus faced a dilemma: If they were to enjoy the prized pear, they had to take precautions. To counter its coldness, the pear, it was believed, must be cooked. In addition, for the best digestive benefit, the pear should conclude the meal.

An accompaniment of wine, experts claimed, could reduce the ill effects of the pear. Castore Durante asserted that pears are "less harmful eaten with a lot of sugar on top, along with a flavorful full-bodied wine, or actually cooked in wine, with sugar, cinnamon." The Salerno School of Medicine, a powerful institution, went even further: "Without wine, pears are poison."

The stewardship of court and church elevated the pear during medieval times. Cultivated in castles, villas, and monastery gardens, pears proliferated and new varieties multiplied. In France, where pears had most likely traveled with the Roman conquerors, planting the fruit was vigorously promoted. Charlemagne, the ruler of the Franks in the ninth century, ordered that a wide spectrum of pears be planted on the royal estates: "Plant pear trees, whose products because of pleasant flavor could be eaten, those which will furnish fruits for cooking, and, finally, those which mature late to serve for use in winter."

Monks devotedly tended to their fruit trees and cultured varieties which would be named for their monasteries. English fathers bred the Warden pear, the preeminent pear for pies and pastries. Its name may have come from the Anglo Saxon "to keep and preserve." Guests at King Henry IV's wedding feasted on Warden pears in syrup. The dish was served along with quail, venison, sturgeon, and other elegant foods.

The wealth of flavors, colors, aromas, and shapes the pear was capable of producing made it the darling of the aristocracy. Olivier de Serres, the seventeenth-century French horticulturist, urged that orchards be planted to display these assets: "Pears are found round, long . . . blunt, small, and large. Gold, silver, vermillion, and satin green are found among the pears. Sugar, honey, cinnamon, clove, flavor them. They smell of musk, amber, and chive."

Royal sponsorship gave the pear luster. King Louis XI, a passionate fruit enthusiast, hoped that the fruit would save him from eczema and other ailments. The king, the story goes, summoned Francis of Paola, a holy Italian hermit, to work a medical miracle. Francis's cure was a small pear tree, which he asked the monarch to care for until it fruited. Tending to the tree, the holy man thought, would soothe the king's fevered mind, the root of his sickness. The king hoped that if pears sprang up by St. Martin's Day (November 11), he could be treated to a pear compote, a sweet flavored with honey and rose water that was reputed to alleviate digestive disorders.

The monarch waited impatiently but died before he could sample any pears. The tree Francis bequeathed bore a variety known as the *Bon Chrétien*, or "Good Christian," a famous type said to be the ancestor of the American Bartlett.

Eating an occasional pear, each of which tasted more or less alike, was not enough to satisfy the aristocracy. Lengthening the pear season and producing more distinctive varieties would meet these needs. Horticulturists set out to achieve this objective. Jean-Baptiste de la Quintinie, master gardener for King Louis XIV, was able to marshal five hundred species of pears for the monarch, enough for his patron to delight in a different one each day.

Especially juicy pears were reserved for the king. One that Louis XIV was enamored of was named *Ah! Mon Dieu*, after the words the king supposedly uttered after eating one.

For all their passion for the fruit, Europe's upper strata still lacked a truly succulent pear. By the middle of the nineteenth century, cultivators in France and Belgium were breeding *beurre* (buttery) pears that gradually supplanted the more common dry, solid-fleshed varieties. The groundbreaker was a Belgian priest, Nicolas Hardenpont, who was determined to develop a superior pear. His followers, apothecaries, attorneys, businessmen, and other amateur gardeners, were swept up in a frenzy that historian U. P. Hedrick compared to Holland's tulip craze.

The most influential of the horticulturists, Jean-Baptiste van Mons, a Hardenpont disciple, led the way in producing luscious pears with "melting" tastes. A gentleman of wide-ranging interests, he had worked at various times as a pharmacist, physician, and physicist, and had been engaged in liberal politics. Van Mons searched out wild or roadside trees, selecting those that promised the juiciest offspring. He plucked seeds from tough and woody fruit growing on the thorny trees, then seeded and reseeded in an unrelenting push to grow new varieties. "To sow, to re-sow, to sow again, to sow perpetually, in short to do nothing but sow, is the practice to be pursued," he insisted.

Rearing many in the hospitable soil of the old Belgian convent in Louvain, van Mons developed more than four hundred varieties between the 1780s and 1830. Among them were the renowned Beurre Bosc and the Beurre D'Anjou. His single-minded focus on the pear tree as first and foremost a fruit creator paid off. "In the right garden environment ordinary pears would turn their energy from the vulgar growth of wood and leaves to the higher goal of fruit production," said historian Philip Pauly of the van Mons method.

Esteemed by the well-to-do, the noble pear was also embraced by Europe's *philosophes* and men of letters. In Diderot's *Encyclopédie*, the eighteenth-century naturalist Louis Daubenton writes that "the pear is the most . . . commonly cultured fruit tree in the fruit and kitchen gardens of the wealthy, while apples abound in the orchards of common people." Apples, he added, "keep longer and may be eaten before they are ripe, whereas pears are edible only when they are more or less ripe. But good pears, by their variety, different ripening seasons, and the rich and refined flavor of the majority, are infinitely superior to the finest apples."

America had its own version of the aristocratic pear culture. Since the United States lacked a native pear tradition (most of our fruit have descended from European varieties), American agriculturists looked to Europe for models. Gentlemen farmers wanted to emulate the Belgian horticulturists who raised pears that have been compared to "wine skins filled with juice." The early American pears, in contrast, were hard and bitter. They were suitable only for cooking, or for hard cider.

Apples, however, did not appeal to the well-bred growers. While apples grew rapidly and almost effortlessly, pears took longer to fruit and required close attention. The perishable pear, which had to be picked before it was ripe, could easily deteriorate without vigilant supervision. If it was not to lose its exquisitely delicate flavor, the pear must be served quickly. Unlike pears, apples, with their "honest, ruddy faces," as one nineteenth-century horticulturist described them, were an everyman's fruit.

In the Northeast during the early nineteenth century, a feverish craze—sort of a pear mania—gripped the upper classes. Merchants or lawyers by day, they aimed to grow the most fashionable pears on their suburban farms. European gardeners helped out by sending over pear cuttings. Van Mons contributed several hundred from his own collection.

Boston was the center of this mania. Pear devotees flocked to tasting parties. "They savored the fruit in the library as an occasion for male bonding and connoisseurship, much as they played golf and smoked cigars together in later periods," fruit expert David Karp wrote. The aspiring farmers formed the Massachusetts Horticultural Society, where the amateurs socialized and exchanged gossip on farming techniques and the latest varieties of fruit.

The society staged an annual exhibition at which farmers displayed their most prized pears. In 1852, the event boasted 310 varieties. The exhibitors competed for accolades and curious visitors stared in puzzlement at the novelties. Horticulturist Andrew Downing observed the spectacle: "Every year the tables at the Horticultural Hall groan under vast contributions of pears; but the thousands of uninitiated visitors are, besides what may be gained by feasting the eyes, not much the wiser."

Awards went to the most aesthetically pleasing fruit. "Size and color counted far less in awarding prizes than quality," historian Hedrick observed. "The 'commercial pack' cut no figure."

The obsession with pears was contagious. It spread from the gentry to smaller growers. "It is the ambition of every fruit-grower in the circle of ten miles about Boston, to possess all the newest pears," horticulturist Downing commented. "Every little cottage has its Bartlett, and its Beurres; and many amateurs annually import from France, Belgium, and England, the last novelty of the nurseryman's catalogues, at prices where *guineas* count as freely as *shillings*."

Horticultural pursuits were also morally satisfying. Fruit culture, the gentlemen farmers felt, demonstrated their ability to rise above grubby, material concerns. "He who cultivates a garden, and brings to perfection flowers and fruits, cultivates and advances his own nature," Ezra Weston, one of their leaders, declared in a speech in 1837 to the Massachusetts Horticultural Society. Growing pears, historian Tamara Thornton suggests, was an apt vocation for the New England elite: "They felt they had something in common with their pears. Both were the choice product of cultivation."

Not everyone joined in the pear adulation. One commentator dissented. "They [pears] are a more aristocratic fruit," Henry David Thoreau wrote. "How much more attention they get from the proprietor! The hired man gathers the apples and barrels them. The proprietor plucks the pears at odd hours for a pastime, and his daughter wraps them each in its paper. . . . They are named after emperors and kings and queens and dukes and duchesses. I fear I shall have to wait till we get to pears with American names, which a republican can swallow."

HOT COMMODITY
a pepper story

So ordinary today, black pepper was long ago renowned as an exotic and luxurious spice. The "king of spices" was at once exquisite condiment, "drug," and preservative. Since the pungent berry grew in the mysterious Indies and few had ever seen the plant, it carried a powerful mystique. Because of its appeal, states, both ancient and modern, embarked on a feverish quest to capture the spice at its source and then monopolize trade in the commodity. During the battle, trading empires rose and fell.

Pepper is the fruit of a tropical vine with dark green leaves that, in the wild, grasps onto a supporting tree. Its ancient homeland was the steamy rain forests in the Western Ghats, mountains parallel to the Malabar Coast of southwestern India (near the present state of Kerala). When Peter Mundy, a seventeenth-century English writer, spotted a young pepper shoot in an orchard there, he described it "clasping, twyning and fast'ning itselff theron round about as the ivy doth the oake or other trees with us."

The monsoon rains nourished the pepper plant. The first torrents of late May and early June started the early budding. Later, the dry heat of November caused the berries to cluster and swell on the vine. "There grow five, six, and eight clusters, a little longer than a man's finger, and they are like small raisins, but more regularly arranged, and are as green as unripe grapes," Ludovico di Varthema, a sixteenth-century Italian writer, marveled. In the ancient Indian language Sanskrit, *pippali* meant "berry." From this root, the Greek *peperi* and the Latin *piper*, the foundation of our name for the spice, originated.

These first berries, green and unripe, are the parents of our black pepper-corns. Workers today pick them by hand and lay them out on palm-leaf mats to dry in the sun. In the steady heat, the berries shrivel and gradually turn black. If the green fruit remains on the vine, they become "ruby and transparent cleare," Peter Mundy writes. The outer skin of this ripe fruit is removed to leave an inner core, which is dried to make the milder white pepper.

Pepper was "hot" and "dry," Sanskrit writers emphasized. Indian physicians recommended it as a remedy for fever, hernia, and dyspepsia. Pepper, one medi-cal text stated, perked up the stomach and cleansed the sinuses: "[I]t is light and adds relish to food. It dislodges or dries up phlegm." Because of the action of *piperade*, an alkaloid that stimulates the saliva and gastric juices, pepper does, in fact, help digestion.

Greek sailors who traveled to the Malabar Coast were enthralled with the pepper berry, which locals nicknamed *yavanesta*, Sanskrit for the "passion of the Greeks." It was the Romans, however, who became the supreme traffickers in the spice. By the first century AD, large Roman trading ships were sailing to India's Malabar Coast to reap the spoils of the pepper country. Harnessing the monsoon winds, the fleets headed east from Alexandria, the Roman outpost in Egypt, each summer and returned with their cargo of spices in the winter. The five-thousand-mile passage was the longest trade route of the time.

Gold and silver coins, central to the pepper transaction, were a vital part of the cargo. "They arrive with gold and depart with pepper," Indian poet Tayan-Kannanar wrote of the Roman traders on the Malabar Coast. Back in Rome, the pepper was unloaded and stored in mammoth warehouses. In the "perfume quarter," vendors sold paper packets of pepper, the wrapping made from the papyrus taken from old books.

The enticing spice was also the equivalent of capital. Reserves of pepper were stored in the Roman treasury, and the spice quickly became a medium of exchange. The Romans often demanded pepper as tribute from their subjects. Their enemies took heed. Alaric, the king of the Visigoths, threatened to destroy Rome with his army unless he received a ransom of three thousand kilos of pep-per. The Romans agreed, but the city was sacked nonetheless.

Pepper pleased the Roman palate. It laced many of the rich sauces of impe-rial cooking. Historian Jack Turner notes that black pepper, cardamom, cumin, mint, honey, and other seasonings infused a "digestive sauce" that accompanied meat dishes. Sweets were also enhanced with pepper. Apicius, the Roman gastro-nome, offers a recipe for a honeyed white-flour fritter spiced with black pepper.

Pepper even added its punch to alcoholic refreshments. "[P]ut ground pepper with skimmed honey in a small container for spiced wine," instructed Apicius. "When it is the time for drinking, mix some of the honey with the wine."

The "choice delicacy," as Apuleius, the Roman author dubbed it, was most common on the tables of the wealthy and rarer in the homes of plebeians. A form of display, pepper was dispensed from *piperatoria*, silver pepper pots. Nobles gave gifts of pepper to show off their status. A lawyer, historian Turner notes, distributed three half-pounds of incense and pepper, Libyan figs, and Tuscan sausages at the annual festival of Saturnalia.

There were, however, naysayers who carped about the Roman infatuation with pepper. "Some foods attract by sweetness, some by their appearance, but neither the pod nor the berry of pepper has anything to be said for it," the writer Pliny complained. "We only want it for its bite—and we will go to India to get it! Who was the first to try it with food? Who was so anxious to develop an appetite that hunger would not do the trick? Pepper and ginger both grow wild in their native countries, and yet we value them in terms of gold and silver."

During the Middle Ages, the heyday of European consumption of spices, tenants paid rent to their masters in black pepper, the spice enriched wills and dowries, and it was accepted as payment for taxes. Pepper entered the language as a symbol of wealth. To "lack pepper" was to be poor.

The Venetians, who dominated the spice trade from the twelfth through the fifteenth centuries, bought their goods from Muslim merchants in Alexandria and Beirut and marked them up for sale in Europe. The cooks of the medieval gentry were lavish with pepper. The Venetian upper classes dined on bear, game, and other dark meat doused with *peverada*, a pepper-based sauce. A celebratory dinner was not complete without the hot spice. A troubadour rhapsodized about one such feast: "For dinner they gave me capons, more than a brace of them . . . the bread was white, and the wine was good, and the pepper was thick."

Pepper started to lose it distinction as its price declined and it became more widely available. When a Tudor warship that had sunk in 1545 was raised, the body of nearly every sailor, historian M. N. Pearson points out, was found with a small bag of peppercorns. As pepper lost its cachet, the educated and well-bred sneered at the lowly spice. A fifteenth-century medical treatise referred to pepper as the "seasoning of the rustics."

Other powers resented the Venetian and Muslim stranglehold over pepper and other spices. Especially vexed were the Portuguese, who were determined to find a direct passage to the spice wealth of the East. They had a special distaste for the Muslims, who had ruled their country and now stood in the way of their ambition. Prince Henry the Navigator, who sent the Portuguese mariners on their missions, said that if only "a way could be found to obtain pepper at its source, a double blow would be dealt to both Venice and Islam," adding, "It would also be good business."

Vasco da Gama, who landed with his ships in 1498 on India's Malabar Coast after rounding the Cape of Good Hope at the tip of Africa, reportedly exclaimed, "We have come looking for Christians and spices." Having carved out an alternative route to India that joined the trade routes of the Atlantic and the Indian oceans, the Portuguese were ready to dethrone their trading rivals. Flexing his muscles, King Manuel of Portugal advised the Venetian envoy, "From now on, you should send your ships to carry spices from here."

Fifteen years later, the humbled city-state was buying spices in Lisbon. Four or five carracks (large merchant ships) a year left Goa, the seat of the empire, for Lisbon, loaded "with pepper and drugs and with all other oriental merchandise and riches," a Portuguese commentator wrote.

By the end of the seventeenth century, two trading giants, Holland and England, were mounting a sharp challenge to the Portuguese monopoly. The Dutch built highly efficient pepper plantations in Indonesia. Especially ruthless competitors, they sometimes burned their pepper crop to maintain high market prices.

The Americans also entered the pepper fray. Captain Jonathan Carnes, who gained a profit of 700 percent on a cargo of pepper brought from Sumatra in 1797, pioneered the spice trade from Salem, Massachusetts. Over the next ninety years, nearly one thousand spice-laden vessels returned to the United States from Indonesia.

Yale University, I discovered, owes a debt to the pepper trade. Boston-born Elihu Yale, who started out in Madras, India, as a clerk for the British East India Company, went on to make a fortune in the spice business. In the early 1800s, Yale made a large contribution to a Connecticut college that took his name. This revelation gave me a fresh insight into the history of my alma mater.

YES, WE HAVE NO ANANAS
the pineapple

Its succulent flesh is really a mass of small fruits (up to two hundred of them) fused together. The pineapple's fruits, which come from purplish to lavender flowers, grow on the stalk. Its "eyes" are the remnants of the flowers. Tissues that store water enable the plant to weather hot temperatures and dry periods. The fruit, which aids digestion, contains a potent enzyme—bromelain—that literally devours protein.

Brazil is the birthplace of this intricate fruit. The Indians called it *nanas*, meaning "excellent fruit or fragrance." The pineapple, which sprouted wild in the Amazon rain forest, was probably domesticated in 2500 BC. It did not reach Hawaii, which many mistakenly consider the source of the fruit, until thousands of years later. The islands' people called the fruit *hala kahiki*, or "foreign plant."

Brazil's Tupi-Guarani Indians took a seedy, very sour fruit, no larger than an apple, from the wild, and they transformed it. In their gardens, they gradually propagated a heftier, sweeter, and seedless fruit that was the precursor of today's pineapple.

The pineapple was eaten fresh and in jam, and was the basis of a potent wine. It also was a practical tool. From its fibers, historian Fran Beauman notes, strings for bows and arrows were constructed. Tribes forced their young men to prove their manhood by racing through rows of the prickly plant.

When Columbus came ashore on the Caribbean island of Guadeloupe in 1493, he found the gardens of the Carib Indians burgeoning with pineapples. They had been taken there by the nomadic Tupi-Guarani, who had carried plants north from Brazil to the Caribbean. The Carib tribe pounded the fruit into a paste laced with chilies. The pineapple also came in handy as a poultice to salve bruises and wounds.

The pineapple also played a symbolic role in Indian life. Tokens of hospitality, crowns of its leaves festooned village doorways and gates.

Spaniards visiting the Americas were enthralled with the fruit's beauty: "When a man looks upon the beauty of this fruit he enjoys seeing its composition, the adornment with which nature painted it and made it so pleasant to the sight, rejoicing the other sense by a fragrance, mixed with quinces, peaches, and very fine melons," the sixteenth-century writer Fernandez de Oviedo wrote. The Spaniard also admired its health-giving powers: "It restores a healthy appetite and stimulates [those who are ill] to endeavor to eat, restoring enjoyment."

The pineapple started the next leg of its journey with Columbus on his return trip to Spain. His crew loaded their vessels with fruit. Unfortunately, all except one, which was presented as a gift to King Ferdinand, rotted. As the writer Peter Martyr tells it, the king was enamored of the fruit, "which is like a pine-nut in form and colour, covered with scales, and firmer than a melon." The Spanish seized on its resemblance to the pinecone and named the fruit *pinas*. Columbus called it the "pine of the Indies."

Europe's fleets transported the fruit to new realms. Mariners carried the pineapple, which generally held up well on long voyages (Columbus's experience notwithstanding), as protection against scurvy. When they anchored, sailors often planted its crowns to provide nourishment for future crews.

During the sixteenth and seventeenth centuries, the empire-building Portuguese transported the fruit, which they called the *ananas*, after its Indian name, to new lands. These societies frequently borrowed or modified the Portuguese word for the fruit. In West Africa, for example, the people called the pineapple *manasi*, *anasi*, and other similar-sounding names.

In India, another outpost of its empire, both the fruit and its Portuguese name were adopted. In his 1590 account, the Muslim chronicler Abu al-Fazl sketched the "traveling jack fruit": "In color and shape they resemble an oblong orange: The leaves have the shape of a hand. The edges of the leaves are like a saw."

The pineapple was revered because it conveyed majesty. In Goa, the seat of Portugal's "Indies" empire, a sculptor carved a pineapple as the capital of the column of a Catholic church. Moghul emperor Jahangir elevated the fruit by planting it in his palace gardens. During his reign, several thousand pineapples, whose "great fragrance and excellent flavor" the emperor loved, were harvested each year.

In pursuit of spices, the Portuguese advanced into Southeast Asia. The pineapple went with them. From Malacca, their entrepôt on the Malaysian peninsula, the fruit was taken to Macao, another Portuguese trading post on the coast of China. By the early seventeenth century, the Chinese were embracing the "royal pear."

Grown by British planters in the West Indies, the fruit received a royal reception in England. King Charles II welcomed it enthusiastically. Dubbed the "Patron of Pineapple," he is portrayed in a 1672 painting accepting the first fruit ripened in England from his gardener.

The English aristocracy made the pineapple an emblem of wealth and status. Landowners built *pineries* (hothouses) in order to grow the fruit in an inhospitable climate. They competed feverishly to produce the most luxurious fruit.

In stately homes, the pineapple or its likeness was displayed. At fancy dinners, the pineapple was often featured as a centerpiece. The fruit was depicted on Wedgwood china, sugar dishes, bowls, and teapots. Carvings of the pineapple decorated entrance halls and stone representations ornamented gateposts.

In early America, the well-to-do emulated English aristocrats in their zeal for pineapple display. As in England, pineapple motifs decorated doorways, roofs, and gateposts. The fruit adorned tea sets, cups, saucers, and other dining wares. It was also depicted on doilies, tablecloths, carpets, and quilts. So eager were hostesses to grace their tables with a pedestal of pineapples that they often rented the fruit from confectioners.

The pineapple also became a way of expressing hospitality. Returning from the tropics, sea captains welcomed friends by affixing a fresh pineapple to a fencepost.

So long as pineapples were scarce, the fruit remained a luxury for most people. In the early twentieth century, a larger market developed due to the efforts of James Dole, a Yankee entrepreneur who pioneered the large-scale planting and industrial production of the fruit. Dole, the founder of the Hawaii Pineapple Company (which later became part of the Dole Food Company), launched his first cannery in 1902. Soon large shipments of the canned fruit were streaming out of Hawaii for the mainland.

A shrewd marketer, Dole capitalized on the pineapple's Hawaiian connection, with the company's ads proclaiming, "Don't ask for pineapple alone; insist on Hawaiian pineapple."

Shoppers, Dole recognized, would be more likely to buy his wares if they knew how to eat them. In another early ad, the company offered advice on handling the mysterious fruit: "It cuts with a spoon like a peach." Targeting his audience, Dole ran ads in women's magazines that included pineapple recipes.

The modern pineapple was bred for canning, not fresh eating. The Champaka, the most popular variety, was attractive to manufacturers but was otherwise acidic and fibrous. As customers began to demand fresh fruit, companies had to develop a more attractive pineapple. Del Monte unveiled a hybrid, the Gold, in the mid-1990s. In contrast to the Champaka's green exterior, the new breed's skin was a brilliant gold. Moreover, the hybrid was sweeter and more succulent than its predecessor.

Battling Del Monte for the market, other companies—such as Dole and Chiquita—started selling their own versions of the Gold. The race to create an ever more tempting pineapple still rages on today.

THE PRINCELY PISTACHIO

Young couples, the story goes, strolled through pistachio gardens in Persia and stood under a tree in the moonlight, hoping to hear the nut's shell crack open. This was an auspicious sign, a promise of future happiness. The distinctive split-open shell of the pistachios suggested a laughing (*khandan*) face to the poetic Persians.

When the tree's nuts are ripe, the shells open to reveal a rosy skin covering a pale green seed. This is the consummation of what can be a four- to five-year period from first planting to fruiting. Reproduction requires careful orchestration. A single male must be strategically located in order to pollinate six female nut-bearing trees. The nuts hang in grape-like clusters on the branches.

The pistachio, a bushy evergreen with fragrant leaves, flourished in the dry, barren terrain of Iran, Turkey, and neighboring lands. Long, hot, dry summers and cold winters suited the ancient tree, which today adapts to a similar climate in the Central Valley of California.

The member of a curious family, the pistachio's kin include the cashew, mango, poison ivy, and poison oak. One variety of pistachio, the turpentine tree, was tapped for this resin. Interestingly enough, the fruit of unripe mango and these wild pistachios both emit a turpentiney aroma.

The terebinth, or turpentine tree, was coveted by the nomadic tribes of northern Afghanistan and Iran. They were fond of its aromatic oils and often sought refuge under its spreading branches. They also buried their dead in its shade.

Persia's young warriors, the scholar Berthold Laufer relates, were trained to survive in the wild on acorns, pears, and terebinth nuts. The soldiers acquired a fearsome reputation. "Woe, how brave are these pistachio-eating Persians," the king of the Medes is supposed to have said from his throne after his forces had been vanquished by the Persians. Persian kings treasured the pistachio, whose oils were presented daily to the royals.

The history of the pistachio is steeped in myth and legend. The sons of Jacob, according to the Book of Genesis, carried the nuts to Egypt as gifts for their brother, Joseph. Jacob tells them, "Take in your luggage, as a gift for the man, some of the produce for which our country is famous: a little balsam, a little honey . . . myrrh, pistachio nuts."

The pistachio was a fabled aphrodisiac. The Queen of Sheba, according to legend, commanded that all of her country's pistachios be reserved for her and her retainers.

Pistachios, archaeologists say, were growing wild in the Near East as early as 7000 BC. The pistachio tradition runs deepest in Iran, where the nuts grow prolifically and where families greet friends and visitors with bowls of them. Our name for the nut comes from the Persian *pesteh*, their word for both "pistachio" and "nut."

One of the country's largest sources of foreign exchange today, the pistachio had long been a profitable article of Persian commerce. Caravans carried them along the Silk Road to China, where they were known as the "hazelnut of the Westerners." They could "cure catarrh of the bowels, remove cold feeling, and make people stout and robust," one Chinese commentator said.

The Persians domesticated the ancestors of today's familiar nut-bearing trees. Pistachios were a feature of the luxurious cooking style that blossomed in the Persian court. An expensive good, they ornamented pilafs, enriched sweets, and infused sauces. These extravagant dishes marked dinner parties, weddings, ceremonies, and other festive occasions.

The Arabs, who conquered Persia in AD 620, transplanted the regal cuisine of the Iranians throughout their empire. In Baghdad, their capital between the ninth and the thirteenth centuries, the caliph's cooks prepared lavish dishes that imitated Persian specialties. Pistachios, almonds, and walnuts were slivered, crushed, and powdered to add flavor and panache to a myriad of sweets. The Arabs avidly appropriated sugar, which the Persians had been cultivating a hundred years before their defeat by the invaders. Sweets and nuts became inseparable in their culinary repertoire.

An ordinary standard of the Middle Eastern menu to us, the pistachio-studded baklava has a royal flair in the Arab world. George Rababy, the Lebanese businessman who founded Washington, D.C.'s King of Falafel eatery, is proud of his pistachio desserts. Others may stint on ingredients for baklava, but not this shop. "If they want to save money, they use walnuts," George said. In Beirut, "first-class patisseries do it [baklava] with pistachios."

Pistachios also glorified meat dishes. A Baghdad recipe book instructed:

Take a tinned copper dish and spray with a little rose water. Spread a thin cake therein, and cover with newly gathered dates. Sprinkle with fine-ground pistachios and almonds . . . to form a layer. Add another layer of dates, and so continue until the dish is half-filled, making the top layer of almonds and pistachios. Cover with a thin cake. Hang over a fat chicken stuffed with sugar, almonds, and pistachio kneaded with scented rose water, and smeared with saffron inside and out.

Foods in the Persian mold later migrated to the Indian subcontinent. The Moghuls—Turkic-speaking tribes from the steppes of Central Asia who overran North India and ruled the region from 1526 to 1858—introduced exotic flavors absorbed from the Persians. Babar, the first Moghul emperor, recruited gardeners from Persia and Afghanistan to grow pistachios, almonds, and walnuts in India. Jahangir, another king, revered the pistachio, which he called "the nut of paradise," and believed in its aphrodisiac powers. Chickens prepared for Emperor Akbar's banquets were fed pistachio nuts for six to eight weeks beforehand.

The imperial kitchens produced nutty confections reminiscent of the Persian originals. *Kheer*, a creamy rice pudding familiar to Indian restaurant diners, is incomplete without crushed or ground pistachios.

In the United States, ethnic businessmen pioneered the early American pistachio trade. Syrian immigrant Joseph Zaloom, who arrived at the turn of the twentieth century, started selling his country's renowned nuts in Brooklyn. More salesmen entered the market, and soon the pistachio was dyed red to make it more attractive to consumers and to hide any flaws or blemishes on the shells. Sold in vending machines in the 1930s, the nut had been stripped of much of its Oriental glory.

Commercial pistachio farming in California did not take off until 1976, although the seeds had been transported from Iran more than forty years earlier. William Whitehouse, a USDA agronomist, had scoured the land, searching for the best variety. He gathered twenty pounds from the Persian city of Kerman and carried them home in a burlap bag. Seeds from Kerman were the foundation of California's pistachio industry.

The more common pistachios have become, the more we take them for granted. Search out one of Persia's famous ice creams, however—studded with pistachios and infused with flavors like cardamom, saffron, and rose water—and experience a taste that is exquisite, unique, and regal.

PERSEPHONE'S TEMPTATION
the seductive pomegranate

The ancient pomegranate was always more than a luscious fruit. It was a mythic vessel into which countless civilizations poured their hopes, dreams, and fears.

The Promised Land, Moses assured his followers, had a plentitude of "wheat and barley, and vines, and fig trees, and pomegranates." Wandering in exile through the desert, the Jews pined for the fruits they had loved in Egypt. They especially treasured the pomegranate, which grew prolifically in the Holy Land. A thirst-quenching fruit in the hot, dry climate, it also represented holiness, fertility, and abundance. Bursting with seeds, the pomegranate enchanted the Jews. They associated it with the commandment of the Torah—their scripture—to be fruitful and multiply.

The Jews incorporated the fruit into their rituals. Honored as one of the *shivat haminim*, the seven foods the Bible ties to Israel, it is savored on the second day of Rosh Hashanah, the Jewish New Year. An auspicious fruit, it was a harbinger of prosperity and good fortune.

Bells signifying the fruit and its flowers were embroidered on the robes of priests. The fruit also conveyed a regal splendor. King Solomon's crown was supposed to have been inspired by the pomegranate's turreted top. Two hundred brass images of the fruit graced the pillars of the monarch's temple.

The pomegranate also conjured up erotic associations. In the Old Testament, Sheba invited King Solomon to join her in the garden: "Let us get up early to the vineyards; let us see if the vines flourish, whether the tender grapes appear, and the pomegranates bud forth; there I will give thee my love." Sheba is as alluring to Solomon as the crimson fruit. "As a piece of a pomegranate are thy temples within thy locks." Sheba asks him to drink "the spiced wine of my pomegranate."

The early Christians also appropriated the fruit. A mosaic with the head of Jesus flanked by two pomegranates was unearthed in 1963 in a Roman villa. The fruit was depicted on Christian coins, lamps, and vessels. Typically split open to reveal its abundant seeds, the pomegranate later served as a religious motif in Renaissance art, symbolizing fertility and resurrection. Often shown in the hands of the Christ child, or being offered to him, it also exemplified fidelity and devotion.

The pomegranate cast its spell on the oldest civilizations of the Middle East. It grew in the Hanging Gardens of Babylon. The Phoenicians were so devoted to it that they gave the pomegranate the same name—*rimmon*—as their sun god. Fragments of rind and seeds were found in the tomb of Egypt's Tutankhamun (1343–1325 BC). Scholars surmise that these offerings symbolized the pharaoh's immortality. Another relic, an Egyptian papyrus more than three thousand years old, likened the pomegranate to a woman's breast.

Its admirers carried the fruit to new lands. The Phoenicians, a trading people, took the pomegranate to Carthage, their colony in North Africa. The pomegranate then reached Rome from Carthage, likely with returning soldiers. So fond were the Romans of the fruit that they dubbed it *mala Punica* (the Punic apple). This fruit was unequaled, they felt, in redness and succulence. At the end of the fourth century BC, Rufus Festus Avienus, a Roman, asked a friend in Africa to send him a pomegranate: "Not that my garden is without that fruit, but it is hard and sour, and not to be compared with the nectar produced in the warm sun of Africa."

Romans planted the fruit, which the naturalist Pliny compared to an apple with "special structures resembling the cells in a honeycomb," in villa gardens. Pliny praised it as a curative, an ingredient in twenty-six different remedies.

The Greeks spun myths about the pomegranate. They associated the fruit with Hera, the goddess of marriage and childbirth. It was grown near her temples and worshipped in rituals honoring her. A statute of Hera, holding a scepter engraved with an image of a cuckoo in one hand and a pomegranate in another, stood at one temple. The figure symbolized fertility and procreation, the German historian Victor Heyn suggests: "It signified the earth-goddess fructified by heaven and bearing fruit, as the cuckoo the rainy spring-time during which the fructification takes place."

The pomegranate also had a darker side, or so the Greeks believed: it was a portent of death and destruction. In the most celebrated myth, Persephone is lured to her destiny by the fruit's entrancing seeds. Picking flowers in the meadow, she is abducted by Hades, the god of the dead. Persephone is then whisked away to his underground lair in a chariot driven by black horses.

Demeter, the mother of Persephone and the goddess of agriculture, feels such rage about the crime that she leaves her home on Mount Olympus to conduct a scorched-earth campaign. The goddess, who has lost "her gaiety forever," curses the land and condemns it to infertility.

In an effort to free Persephone, Zeus finally intercedes with Hades. Hades agrees to release her, but not before offering her a "honey sweet" pomegranate seed. She eats it and is thus exiled to the underworld for the three wintry months of the year. Persephone is only allowed to rise from the lower depths in the spring.

The gloominess of the story is balanced by the promise of renewal. The pomegranate, the scholar Frederick Simoons points out, represents the cycle of death and rebirth. The kernel germinates underground and pushes through the earth to sprout, only later to wither away.

The pomegranate still has a powerful hold on the Greek imagination. Traveling through the country in the 1990s, writer Patricia Storace observed people exchanging gift packages "fastened with a tiny ceramic pomegranate." Silver pomegranates that opened to reveal their abundant seeds were a popular jewelry item. The country's New Year celebrations were not complete without the symbolic fruit. Flower merchants sold pomegranates wrapped in silver for the festivity. Hoping for a propitious new year, Greeks smashed the fruit against the thresholds of their houses.

The Greeks also mark other special occasions with the pomegranate. The Orthodox faithful offer up *koliva*, a wheat porridge, in church during funerals and Lent. Made with boiled wheat berries flavored with nuts and honey and decorated with pomegranate seeds and pieces of silver, the dish is a gift to the departed. A fruit that is emblematic of death and resurrection is perfectly suited to these rites.

When the Persian army invaded Greece in 480 BC, the troops carried spears adorned with gold and silver pomegranates. The majestic fruit stood for both martial and regal virtues in Persian culture. A pomegranate topped the king's scepter and was depicted on the robes of monarchs and priests. The Persian king Cyrus the Great, it was said, wished he had as many good generals as there are seeds in a pomegranate.

Native to Persia, where it has been cultivated for more than two thousand years, the fruit was central to Zoroastrianism, the land's oldest religion. Trees grew in the courtyards of its temples. Their leaves, which remained green for most of the year, were a vivid symbol of immortality. The fruit itself was part of Persian folkways. In Zoroastrian rites, children chewed a pomegranate seed after a purification bath. Following an age-old tradition, Persian brides still squash a pomegranate in hopes of fertility and successful childbirth.

The Persians endowed the pomegranate with healing powers. Thought to cleanse the blood, the iron-rich fruit does actually help circulation. A tea made from the powdered skin of the fruit was a common Persian remedy for nausea.

The Persians were equally enthusiastic about the fruit's succulent juices and the exquisite color it imparted to food. They reveled in pomegranate wine and other drinks made from the fruit. A *sharbat*, pomegranate juice cooled with snow, was an early delight.

The juice of the sour pomegranate was also boiled to form a thick, dark brown paste that infused dishes with its tartness. *Fesenjan*, a classic Persian *khoresh*, or stew, was enriched with this pomegranate molasses and ground walnuts. An aristocratic favorite, traditionally made with duck or game birds, it is now frequently made with chicken. A winter meal, the *fesenjan* is thought to benefit from the "hotness" of the pomegranate.

The pomegranate beautified the dishes of the dining table. "Sometimes they boyl the juice of these Pomegranates, and keep it to give a colour to the rice, which they serve up at entertainments," a seventeenth-century traveler to the country observed. Chefs often decorated their platters with its ruby-like seeds.

The Persians traded the fruit to the Chinese, on whom it exerted a strong fascination. A Chinese traveler in the thirteenth century marveled at the pomegranates that were "as large as two fists and of a sweet-sour taste." A fixture of the wedding feast and a popular wedding gift, the pomegranate was expected to bring the bride many sons and grandsons.

After the forces of Islam conquered Persia, the Arabs were introduced to the pomegranate. The desert people glorified the fruit as a present from paradise. "Eat the pomegranate, for it purges the system of envy and hatred," Muhammad enjoined his followers.

In Baghdad, the capital and cultural center of the burgeoning Islamic empire, the caliphs filled their court kitchens with the diverse foodstuffs of their realm. From Iran came an annual shipment of one hundred thousand pomegranates. With these and other ingredients, the palace chefs of the Muslim world fashioned a sophisticated and varied cuisine. A recipe from a fourteenth-century cookbook translated by Middle East food scholar Charles Perry called for a chicken suffused in a tart pomegranate sauce: "They [the pomegranate seeds] are pounded fine and sieved and [the juice] is thickened with [ground] almond meats, and sugar and a bunch of mint [is] put in it and on top of it. It [is cooked until it] binds on the fire. Chickens which have been boiled and then fried are thrown in and boiled."

As they marched west, the Muslim armies carried pomegranate, spinach, artichokes, saffron, and other foods to Mediterranean lands. They planted the heavenly fruit in Spain, which the Moors overtook in the eighth century AD. The bountiful pomegranate ripened and its crimson flowers bloomed in court gardens designed to be replicas of paradise.

The new rulers named the city of Granada after the fruit. Depicted on the city's coat of arms is an opened pomegranate and a branch of the tree. In the

Alhambra, the city's magnificent palace, the pomegranate motif appears in the designs of the doorways.

After they won back their colony in 1492, the Spaniards carried on the pomegranate tradition. The fruit was featured on King Ferdinand's coat of arms. During the military campaign against the Moors, his wife, Queen Isabella, reportedly said, "Just like the pomegranate I will take over Andalusia seed by seed." Catherine of Aragon, the Spanish aristocrat who married Henry VIII, took the pomegranate to England, where it was featured on her coat of arms.

Pomegranate symbolism runs through English letters. In Shakespeare's *Romeo and Juliet*, Juliet calls out, "Wilt thou be gone? It is not yet near day: / It was the nightingale, and not the lark, / That pierc'd the fearful hollow of thine ear; / Nightly she sings on yon pomegranate tree: / Believe me, love, it was the nightingale." Elizabeth Barrett Browning, in her poem "Lady Geraldine's Courtship," likewise pays homage to the fruit: "[I]f cut deep down the middle, / Shows a heart within blood-tinctured, of a veined humanity."

Transported by the Spanish conquerors to the Americas, the pomegranate arrived in the New World freighted with the symbolism of the old. "Fruit trees of every kind prosper extremely well, especially pomegranates," Spanish writer Motolinia wrote in the 1530s of growing conditions in Puebla, Mexico. In northern Mexico, people brewed *aguardiente*, an intoxicating drink, from the fruit. Today the pomegranate is a centerpiece of one of Mexico's national dishes—*chiles en nogada*. The creation honors the three colors of the Mexican flag: green (chilies), white (walnut sauce), and red (a topping of pomegranate seeds).

Jesuit missionaries took the pomegranate to Spanish settlements in Arizona, New Mexico, and Texas. The flower and fruit adorned mission pulpits and choir lofts in New Mexico. The emblem of fertility decorated dowry chests in the region.

The pomegranate, along with other legacies from the Moors, reached California in the late eighteenth century. The Spanish friars planted the fruit in their mission gardens. Regarded more as a festive ornament than as a delicious fruit, the pomegranate only began to be farmed commercially in California during the last century. Even then, growers depended heavily on ethnic customers. "Jews, and Italians, and Middle Eastern people were the major buyers," Victor Slayman, a pioneering grower, told writer David Karp.

Farmers who hail from its Central Asian birthplace have cultivated the pomegranate in their new homes. Hossein Khodadad, a Persian grower, has been marketing the Saveh pomegranate, a choice variety from an Iranian city of the same name. "It's big as a baby's head, has shiny purple skin, and [is] so sweet," he told Karp.

No one had yet figured out how to sell the pomegranate to a mass market. In the last twenty years, Stewart and Lynda Resnick, owners of California's Paramount Farms, have succeeded in creating a chic and healthy image for the fruit. The son of a Highland Park, New Jersey, bar owner, Stewart Resnick first planted pomegranates in 1986 when he bought a pistachio orchard in which some pomegranate trees also grew. An instinctive gambler, the entrepreneur jumped into an unfamiliar business.

"When I decided to plant that first 640 acres of pomegranates, about half of the pomegranates at the time, there was zero market," Resnick told journalist Mark Arax. "My farm manager thought I was nuts. 'At worst,' I told him, 'we can make some juice out of it.'"

Resnick's hunch was right. The couple concentrated on growing Wonderful, an especially sweet variety that does not easily crack. Since the pomegranate season is short, they looked for a way to utilize the fruit year-round. Juice was the answer.

The Resnicks decided to lure consumers by promoting the pomegranate as a healthy fruit. They spent $15 million to fund research into its medicinal benefits. The research results bore out its reputation. The pomegranate, investigators found, contained powerful antioxidants and other curative properties.

Hourglass-shaped bottles of Pom Wonderful juice began appearing in supermarkets in 2002. A sales campaign was launched. An ad in *Rolling Stone*, headlined "Cheat Death," featured a juice container with a broken noose around its neck. It read, "Dying is so dead," and extolled the juice's ability to help prevent "premature aging, heart disease, stroke, Alzheimer's, even cancer."

Lynda Resnick, the marketing genius of the two, set out to give Pom cachet. Parlaying her Hollywood connections, she arranged to make the "Pomtini" the featured drink at the Academy Awards from 2003 to 2005. Guests at the event were also offered Pom facials. Hollywood and media personalities began receiving free samples of the juice.

A new chapter in the history of the pomegranate had begun. Salesmanship was now required to sell a fruit that had long been an object of simple faith and devotion.

THE "WHITE TRUFFLE"
the perplexing potato

The houses [of the Indians] were all stocked with maize, beans, and truffles [potatoes], spherical roots which are sown and produce a stem with its branches and leaves . . . and are the size of an egg, some round and some elongated; they are white and purple and yellow, floury roots of good flavour, a delicacy to the Indians and a dainty dish even for the Spaniards.

Juan de Castellanos, a member of a raiding party that attacked an Indian village in the Andes in 1537, noticed this unusual tuber. The plant did not fit into any of the tidy compartments familiar to the Europeans. It grew underground and from roots, not seeds. The potato's passage from the Americas, from the highlands of Peru and Bolivia, to the larger world, is a product of the Spanish conquest of the Incas in the sixteenth century.

Although the outsiders might have briefly marveled at the *papa*, the Indian word for "potato" (which they adopted), they soon branded the tuber as fit only for feeding the downtrodden natives. The potato had none of the stature of their precious bread, and the Spaniards fed them to the gangs of workers laboring in Peru's silver mines.

The potato the invaders stumbled on was central to the ancient Indian civilizations of the Andes. It was their basic source of energy. In the sixteenth century, the Incas cultivated 150 different varieties of potatoes. They grew in a vast array of shapes, colors, and sizes, and their flavors varied from very bitter to delicate. Since there was no standard potato, each type of tuber was

named for its unique attributes. Today's *llunchy waccachi*, a bumpy variety, is so dubbed because it is difficult to peel.

Disdained by the Europeans, the *papa* was revered by the Incas. They chanted while tilling the earth with their *takllas* (spades with footrests). The dead were honored with burial urns shaped like potatoes. The Incas prayed to their "creator" that the potato multiply.

Equally important, the potato served a practical function. *Chuno*, freeze-dried tubers that had been chilled at night and then dried during the day, were easily preserved. Kept in underground storehouses, they fed the soldiers of the Incan empire and sustained the work gangs on its massive building projects. The potato, historian William McNeill observes, was the cornerstone of this ancient civilization.

Returning from the New World in the 1570s, ships arrived in Spain carrying potatoes. They were probably taken, scholars suggest, to protect their crews against scurvy. Leftovers from the voyage were used to sow new plants. By 1573, a hospital in Seville is recorded as having ordered potatoes for its patients.

From Spain, the potato leapt to Europe in the 1600s. Basque fishermen from Spain, who stocked them on trips to the Grand Banks of Newfoundland, left remnants behind on Ireland's west coast, according to historian William McNeill. The Basques stopped there to dry their fish. Spanish ships also brought them to northern Italy, from whence they traveled to the Netherlands and then to other parts of Europe. The Italians called the curiosities "white truffles."

Originally, Europeans treated the potato as an ornamental plant. It was grown in gardens, often by botanists working for wealthy patrons. But a host of fears hindered the wider acceptance of the Spanish import. An early rumor, spread in England in 1620, had the potato causing leprosy. Historian Redcliffe Salaman suggests that "the white nodular tubers, with bulbous finger-like growths, may well have recalled the deformed hands and feet of the unfortunate leper."

The potato was also threatening because it—along with tomatoes, eggplant, tobacco, and other plants—belonged to the nightshade family. Like the deadly nightshade, the tuber had small green berries and white, blue, and pink flowers. This *solanum* ("quieting") plant group was thought to be narcotic.

Since it grew underground, the potato stirred up frightening feelings. The subterranean tuber was murky, mysterious, and possibly diabolical. Root vegetables were generally thought to arouse forbidden passions; it was believed they made men produce sperm and women menstruate and lactate.

Where it became a necessity, the potato lost its terrifying power. In Ireland, *praties*, as they were called, found a perfect home. They flourished in the island's cool and damp weather. Wheat and barley, on the other hand, suffered in these conditions. By the end of the seventeenth century, the potato was the mainstay of the Irish diet.

For Irish tenant farmers eking out a bare subsistence, potatoes had many advantages. They grew quickly and prolifically on tiny plots. Few tools, other than a hoe, were needed to cultivate them. Along with milk, potatoes provided enough nourishment and calories for a poor family. Preparation was simple—a kettle for boiling or a fire for roasting. For a special treat like on All Hallow's Eve, the Irish would celebrate with *colcannon*, potatoes mashed with turnips and cabbage. Many families improved their lot by buying a pig, which was fed potato scraps and, ultimately, sold. "The pig paid the rent," the saying went.

The "mighty lovers of potatoes" were extolled by some observers. David Henry, an English writer, remarked that the potato created a "vigorous population," a people with a high birth rate. Others were more disparaging. Author Jonathan Swift sneered at those "living in filth and nastiness upon buttermilk and potatoes." Slogans like "No Potatoes, No Popery," a line used in an English election in 1765, expressed anti-Irish sentiment.

Because of the prejudice against the potato, it took at least two centuries from its arrival before most of Europe accepted it. The French philosopher Diderot's opinion was typical: "This root, no matter how you prepare it, is tasteless and floury. It cannot pass for an agreeable food; but it supplies a food sufficiently healthy for men who ask only to sustain themselves. The potato is criticized with reason for being windy, but what matters windiness for the vigorous organisms of peasants and laborers."

In France, advocates for the potato faced serious obstacles. They had to not only overcome suspicion of the tuber but also wean the people away from their all-consuming devotion to bread and grains. Pharmacist Antoine Parmentier, who as a German war prisoner had subsisted almost entirely on potatoes, took up their cause. He found allies in the palace. Marie Antoinette wore a corsage of purple potato flowers to promote the tuber. In 1786, Parmentier plotted to win the French over. He planted potatoes in an unforgiving field of fifty sandy acres outside Paris and placed soldiers with fixed bayonets around it. At night, pilferers snuck into the unguarded plot and ran off with the mysterious vegetables.

Parmentier also taught the French that potatoes could be prepared with flair. He published recipes for potato dishes made with butter, cream, cheese, and herbs. Creamed, scalloped, and *gratiné* potatoes are his legacy.

In Germany, the state coerced the population into growing potatoes. Worried about famine, Frederick the Great of Prussia ordered officials in 1744 to hand out seeds to farmers and explain how to farm them. The campaign faltered when peasants afraid of contracting leprosy began digging up the potatoes. Frederick had to send out soldiers to stop them.

By the end of the eighteenth century, the Germans were at last converted. Potatoes moved east to Poland and Russia, where they complemented rye, the once-exclusive carbohydrate. The potato's superiority was becoming obvious. Since it could provide four times as many calories as grains, it could also support four times as many people. The tuber stoked the surging population growth of the nineteenth century. Moreover, as the Continent industrialized and villagers moved to the cities, the potato also fueled the energies of the urban masses. Northern Europe's rise to "world dominion," historian William McNeill argues, was hastened by the potato.

Compared to Europeans, Americans were heavier eaters of potatoes. For example, the presence of early versions of home fries or hash browns at breakfast especially surprised visitors from across the Atlantic. An Englishman eating breakfast in Ohio in the early 1830s was stunned to be offered "fried pork steaks, boiled potatoes, toast saturated with cream, coffee," according to historian Larry Zuckerman. He adds that a British traveler in America in the 1870s was amazed that elegant hotels served five kinds of potatoes—boiled, baked, steamed, fried, and Lyonnaise—for breakfast. "The homely humble tuber could grace anyone's table without evoking class consciousness," Zuckerman argues. This quick, abundant food suited the needs of a fast-paced, unpretentious culture.

Perhaps because the United States was a young nation—and thus less hidebound and stratified than the Continent—Americans have been more receptive to the root vegetable.

HUNTING FOR GOLD
the saga of saffron

A field of saffron in bloom looks like a purple carpet. Unlike its cousin, the common spring crocus, saffron's blossoms, which burst forth in the fall, are a rich, sensuous purple, close to violet. The flower is on voluptuous display for the briefest of time, about fifteen days beginning in mid- to late October and ending the first or second week of November.

Within the petals of the flower are three reddish-orange stigmas, the female sex organs, which are the most coveted part of the plant. The stigma is made up of threads that are the raw material for commercial saffron, the most expensive of spices. Infused with hot water, the dried filaments bleed a brilliant yellowish-orange color. A large volume of flowers yields a tiny amount of the spice: thirty-five threads produce just a pinch of saffron.

To capture this prize, pickers have to work quickly and nimbly. The flowers must be plucked at dawn, just when they open, and the harvesting must be completed within the two-week lifetime of the crocus.

Most of us know saffron as a food coloring and cooking spice. In earlier epochs, however, it was used only sparingly as a cooking ingredient. It was variously considered a perfume, a drug, an elixir, and a dye. Through the ages, saffron has aroused starkly different reactions from people, ranging from joy to terror. This aromatic, the sixteenth-century English herbalist Nicholas Culpeper observed, can invigorate as well as enervate the spirits. The "herb of the sun . . . quickens the brain. . . . However, the use of it ought to be reasonable and moderate; for when the dose is too large, it produces a heaviness of the heart and sleepiness; some have fallen into an immoderate convulsive laughter, which ended in death."

In the ancient world, saffron struck powerful emotional chords. The Greeks and Romans, who strewed the blossoms in the path of kings, wove them into myth. In one Greek story, the flower is an emblem of death. Hermes, the messenger god, was said to have accidentally struck his friend, Crocus, with a discus. Saffron subsequently bloomed in the blood-soaked soil. It also figures prominently in an erotic tale: Zeus and his wife, Hera, made love on Mount Ida after an argument over the Trojan War; later, the flower sprang up on this very spot.

Saffron stimulated the Hellenic imagination. In *The Iliad*, Homer describes Aurora, the goddess of dawn, as "saffron robed." The goddesses, queens, and nymphs of mythology were commonly depicted in yellow or golden garb. Saffron similarly cast its spell on the Romans. The royal spice was the preserve of the aristocracy. Dye makers colored their togas a brilliant gold.

Saffron especially appealed to the vanity of the royals. Emperors bathed in water perfumed with the fragrance. Cleopatra reportedly used it as a cosmetic to beautify her complexion. Aromatic oil of saffron made the hair of the nobility glisten. Amorous socialites, who favored it as an aphrodisiac, sported on beds scented with saffron. However, as enchanted as the Romans were with saffron, they rarely seasoned their food with it—although revelers at festive dinners and parties did enjoy a saffron-imbued sweet wine.

In Persia, a birthplace of this crocus, saffron magnified the splendor of the court. King Cyrus, botanist Berthold Laufer points out, wore yellow shoes to set himself apart from commoners. Halls holding events for the aristocracy were made fragrant with saffron, and the kingdom's rugs and carpets were adorned with its luxurious hues.

The Persians also believed in the aromatic's power over the body. The tonic, they were convinced, strengthened the heart and banished melancholy. To make them drowsy, the royals' bedding was dyed with saffron.

From Persia, saffron spread eastward to the Indian subcontinent. Just as Buddha had once worn resplendent golden robes, so Hindu and Buddhist priests dressed in saffron-colored clothes. The luminous colors symbolized the clergy's closeness to the celestial spirits. Today, statues of the Hindu gods are anointed daily with the coloring. A golden image was meant to be auspicious. Daubing the forehead with saffron paste was thought to bring good fortune.

To meet such ceremonial needs, India required an abundant supply of the purple crocus. As early as 500 BC, farmers in the Kashmir region were cultivating

saffron. Alexander the Great's invading troops, the story goes, were so intoxicated by the spectacle of saffron fields that they raced madly into the Kashmir valley.

Many centuries later, the Moghuls, the Muslim Turks who conquered northern India, brought along a passion for saffron they had acquired in Persia. The palace chefs decorated rice pilau, biryani, and other dazzling dishes with it. Along with cardamom, pistachio, almonds, and other flavorings, saffron was sprinkled on desserts such as *kheer*, a luscious rice pudding. Today, saffron ice cream is a favorite Persian delight.

Saffron's journey was just beginning. By the twelfth century, the flowers were blooming in unlikely terrain—the damp soil of England's southeastern coast.

Saffron migrated west with the conquering Moors, who invaded Spain in the ninth century and held sway there for more than four hundred years. The Muslims had learned to appreciate the flower and its spice from their Persian subjects. They adapted the Persian word for the aromatic, naming it *za'faran*, Arabic for "yellow." The older name for the plant, the Greek word *krokus*, disappeared from common usage. The Moors had also transplanted short- and medium-grain rice, which they began growing in the lakes of Valencia. The people of this region, reputedly the birthplace of paella, fashioned this dish using two Moorish gifts, saffron and rice.

Saffron thrived in the climate of Andalusia, their kingdom in southern Spain. It was a region, food writer Pat Willard observes, "rippling with a brilliant voluptuousness. In summer, the heat is thick, the air swollen with shattering sunlight. Flowers bloom in hot colors—deep reds and yellows and oranges—growing in dense profusion."

During the brief saffron harvest for two weeks every fall, Spanish peasant families working together speedily picked the flowers and brought them home to begin the delicate task of probing the blossoms: "[O]ld folk, women, girls, and boys would begin to pluck the bright red stigmas from the violet blue flowers scattered over the tables at which they sat, slicing with their left thumb nail the throat of the blooms which they pressed against the index finger, plucking whole with the fingers of their right hand the three-branched stigma which they tossed . . . into small straw baskets or jelly boxes," author Robert Johnson writes. After gathering the fragile threads, they dried them, often in sieves over charcoal fires. The filaments were then stored in leather bags or other containers to protect them from injury from light and moisture.

Saffron's arrival in Spain brought it into the orbit of the Mediterranean. The people of Marseille, for example, were fanatical about saffron—so much so that they spun myths to prove their claim to bouillabaisse, a soup to which it is indispensable. The orange-hued fish soup is credited to the Roman goddess Venus, who put her husband Vulcan to sleep with the saffron-laced dish so that she could have a liaison with Mars. The story, food historian Waverley Root suggests, contributed to the image of saffron as a "symbol of cuckoldry."

Saffron mysteriously also appeared in Northern Europe. A souvenir from the Holy Land, the story goes, led to cultivation of the exotic crop in the soggy soil of England's southeast coast. A pilgrim returning from Palestine secreted away a saffron corm (cutting) in his staff and took it to Chipping Walden in Essex in 1339. The town, later renamed Saffron Walden, burgeoned into a major dye-making center supplied by the saffron growers in the surrounding countryside. The moist, chalky earth did not at first seem propitious terrain for the crop. Rich in calcium, however, it proved to be an ideal seedbed for the Eastern import. The crokers, as the local farmers were called, tilled the fields of a region that Reverend William Harrison lauded for its "warm nights, sweet dews, fat grounds, misty mornings."

For almost four hundred years, Essex processed the world's most expensive saffron threads. In addition to marketing it abroad, merchants sold the product to local wool merchants and apothecaries. The English court and church were also avid purchasers of the regal spice. Henry VII, a devotee of saffron, made it an offense for the Irish to color their clothing with the dye.

The English perked up their spare cuisine with the spice. Saffron buns, a specialty of Cornwall, were served with cream tea. In Shakespeare's play, *The Winter's Tale*, the clown who is planning a party for his master knows exactly what he fancies: "I must have saffron to flavor my warden's peas."

Saffron flowered in another unlikely setting—the Pennsylvania Dutch region of North America. In the early nineteenth century, German religionists, some already acquainted with the plant, began cultivating it in their adopted land. Soups, pot pies, noodle dishes, and cakes, fragrant with saffron, were prepared in this close-knit community. Strong demand for their product from abroad spurred these farmers to expand their saffron fields. German Jewish merchants in Pennsylvania trafficked in the lucrative trade. Ships carrying the spice, which was priced at the value of gold, left Philadelphia, bound for the markets of the Spanish Caribbean. The War of 1812 shut down the brisk business.

The heyday of the saffron trade in Europe was during the Middle Ages. As early as the twelfth century, Venice was the main entrepôt for commerce in saffron and other spices. Vessels docked at the Egyptian port of Alexandria to load up on the Eastern treasures and then transported them to Venice for marketing to the rest of the continent. So vital was it to Venice's wealth that the city established a separate office to handle the saffron trade.

Saffron was so precious that some importers were tempted to cheat. To prevent merchants from adulterating the good, the city of Nuremberg, Germany, a major trans-shipment point into Central Europe, made such tampering a serious crime. One offender, Jobst Findeker, a merchant, was burned at the stake in 1444 for watering down saffron. The authorities made their point by using saffron as kindling for their fire.

Saffron was in culinary vogue in medieval Europe. Europeans aped Arabic royal kitchens, which were lavish with saffron. An advice book for well-born ladies encouraged them to *a jaunir* (yellow) their dishes. Middle Eastern cookbooks with recipes from Baghdad and other cities circulated in aristocratic circles.

Wealthy European kitchens glorified their food with luminous hues. Chefs *endored* (or "colored") their dishes with saffron. Roasted meats were gilded with a saffron wash. Oriental spices transformed stews into opulent creations. A fifteenth-century recipe for partridge stew called for cloves, ginger, and saffron. Saffron also made desserts luxurious. Extravagant dishes—like the creamy custard flan made with dates, prunes, and saffron—were fashionable.

The centrality of saffron reflected the adoration of gold in the culture. Influenced by Islamic theology, philosophers believed saffron contained a golden spirit. It was thought that "[t]he scent of the philosophers" infused food with the life-giving energy of the sun and the heavens.

The qualities ascribed to saffron made it an especially alluring tonic for the melancholy and depressed. It "piercest to the heart, providing laughter and amusement," one sufferer quoted by saffron historian Pat Willard remarked. In a book aimed at *The British Housewife*, Martha Bradley recommended the saffron cure for psychic suffering:

A Course to Relieve Melancholy
2 quarts white wine
1 ounce elderflower
1 ounce ash keys [fruit of an ash tree]
1 handful each of roman wormwood, centarry, and hyssop
1 dram saffron

Add all the ingredients to the wine and let steep for two days. Then drink a small . . . glass [full of the wine] two times a day.

The stimulant, it was also said, restored energy to the body. Nuns, scholar Volker Schier argues, consumed saffron to stave off fatigue during Lenten and other religious rites. Katerina Lemmel, a sixteenth-century German nun, explained the necessity for saffron: "One does need to spice things up a bit, especially when the men and the sisters have to sing and pray so much, and otherwise they do not have much variety in their diet."

Not everyone shared the enthusiasm for the spice. To his dismay, Archbishop Eudes Rigaud discovered saffron at a Benedictine priory he visited in 1234: "They [the nuns] all wear their hair down to their chins and scent their veils with saffron." Disapproving of its sensuality, he forbade its further use in the monastery.

Some observers sounded the alarm about the excessive use of saffron. "Too much using it cutteth off sleep, through want whereof the heads and senses are out of frame," herbalist John Gerard wrote.

We no longer endow aromatics with such awesome power. The more common spices have become, the less we seem to be in their thrall.

THE "PRINCE OF LEAFY GREENS"

spinach

In one ancient civilization, few had to be prodded to "eat their spinach." The Persians venerated the plant for its nobility and sprightly taste. A member of the goosefoot family, a group of greens whose spines have a distinctive webbed shape, spinach was born and nurtured in Central Asia. Unknown to the early Greeks and Romans, it was beloved by the Persians, who first cultivated it in the fourth century AD.

The Persians called the plant *isfanakh*, or "green hand." In their kitchen, spinach occupied a lofty perch. Like coriander, parsley, mint, dill, and other lively greens known as *sabzi*, spinach was prized as an herb that added verve to a dish.

Spinach also had medicinal virtues, the Persians believed. Al Razi, a ninth-century physician, pronounced spinach "temperate, good for the throat, the lungs, the stomach, and the liver. It sweetens the belly and is a good, beneficial food."

The Chinese were early devotees of the vegetable. Three centuries after it was first cultivated, the king of Nepal presented it as an offering to the Chinese emperor, who had commanded all subject states to send him their best plants. The king had gotten the spinach from Persia. The new arrival was called *poh ts'ai*, or "Persian vegetable." The Chinese, who used it in soup, also gave spinach names like "red root vegetable" and "parrot vegetable." In China, spinach satisfied a spiritual hunger. The vegetable, food scholar Frederick Simoons points out, was adopted by Buddhist priests as a "fasting food."

The Moors, who conquered Persia in the seventh century, spread spinach throughout their empire. By the eleventh century, the invaders, who now controlled large parts of Spain, were planting it around Seville. Ingenious farmers, the Muslims had mastered the art of growing produce in hot and arid regions. They irrigated dry, inhospitable soil, turning it into *ard hulawa* ("sweet earth"), a fertile seedbed for vegetables.

Isfinah, its Arabic name, tugged at the heartstrings of Muslims. Ibn al-Awwam, an agronomist who lived in Spain, extolled spinach as the "prince of leafy greens."

Spinach was a favorite ingredient in Arab cuisine. A recipe in the twelfth-century *Baghdad Cookery Book*, a collection of dishes prepared for the Islamic elite, called for a lavishly spiced kebab and spinach plate. It was seasoned with cumin, garlic, and salt and sprinkled with coriander and cumin.

In the rest of Europe, spinach was considered more as a healthful herb than as a vegetable. The "Spanish vegetable [spinach] scorns barren areas, but grows very happily whenever planted," the sixteenth-century botanist Leonard Fuchs wrote. The plant was "cultivated by everybody like a pot herb."

It fitted neatly into medieval religious culture, food historian Waverley Root notes. In 1351, spinach was on the list of vegetables prescribed for monks on fast days.

In Italy, the appetizing green was incorporated into the Catholic regimen. Introduced by Arab traders around AD 1000, it sprouted propitiously. Sown in autumn, spinach was ready to be harvested in the spring, just in time for Lent.

Spinach, the Italians discovered, was a delectable filling and melded nicely with eggs and cheese. Vincenzo Corrado, an eighteenth-century food writer, enticed his readers with descriptions of spinach dumplings filled with eggs and grated cheese.

The French, like the Italians, admired the plant. "It has longer leaves, thinner and greener than the common *parray* [chard], and it is eaten at the beginning of Lent," the Ménagier of Paris, an anonymous fourteenth-century gastronome, wrote. He praised spinach as an ideal addition to an egg and cheese tart made with green beet leaves, parsley, and chervil.

French cooks seized on spinach's remarkable ability to absorb butter. The English food writer Jane Grigson discusses a famous French recipe in which spinach was cooked and reheated every day for five days, each day infused with butter. The object was to produce a puree of one pound of spinach containing ten ounces of butter. Grilled or roasted meats were served with the sauce.

Some French culinary experts, however, were less than enthusiastic about the green. "Spinach is not worth much essentially; it is susceptible of receiving all

imprints; it is the virgin wax of the kitchen," eighteenth-century gourmet Grimod de la Reynière declared.

English horticulturists were perplexed by the curious plant. John Gerard, the seventeenth-century herbalist, lumped spinach together with the other herbs he studied, albeit one with its own unique attributes. This "sallade herb," he said, was "evidently cold and moist, almost in the seconde degree, but rather moist. It is one of the potherbes whose substance is waterie."

John Evelyn, seventeenth-century English botanist and salad proponent, was mostly dismissive of the green: "[S]pinach: of old not us'd in sallets [salads], and the oftener kept out the better . . . but being boiled to a pult . . . is a most excellent condiment." For all this, Evelyn wrote, the herb had curative powers. It was "profitable for the aged" and beneficial in a "Sick Man's Diet."

In time, the English added the green to their culinary repertoire. So irresistible were its tender leaves that spinach gradually replaced the native, wild greens in their diet.

Influenced by the Arabs' penchant for balancing the sweet with the sour and savory, English cooks prepared many spinach dishes. In one Elizabethan recipe, boiled spinach is flavored with currants, butter, vinegar, and sugar, served on bread or toast, and strewn with sugar.

The English especially fancied spinach tarts. At a time when fruits were difficult to store, spinach often replaced them in pastry. "This is good among tarts in the winter for variety," one eighteenth-century writer put it. Recipes for spinach tarts instructed readers that the green be "spiced, sugared, and often boiled 'as thick as marmalade,'" English food historian C. Anne Wilson points out.

In later recipes, pulped spinach was suffused with eggs and cream and made fragrant with crystallized orange or lemon peel. This approach was a legacy of Arab chefs who added honey, almonds, and eggs to their greens. The traditions live on when we add a dash of nutmeg to spinach today.

The Greeks, too, were experts at marrying spinach and pastry. *Spanakopita*, the triangular pie filled with feta and greens and seasoned with dill, was a city dweller's version of a village repast. Country women filled their phyllo pastries with fennel, dandelions, sorrel, mustard, and other greens.

As in Western Europe, Greek religious custom enhanced the appeal of the leafy green. Spinach pies were a fixture of the Lenten table.

The oldest cultivators of spinach, the Persians, continue to be its keenest culinary innovators. *Borani-e esfenaj*, thick, garlicky yogurt permeating chopped spinach, is a scrumptious appetizer. It was one of a group of dishes named for the wife of a caliph who adored yogurt.

In another Persian delicacy, spinach is mixed into saffron rice, which is then baked. A regal favorite, it was cooked in the court kitchens of seventeenth-century ruler Shah Abbas.

The Persians blend spinach and eggs to make a greenish *kookoo*, a pancake-shaped snack. Wrapped in bread, it is an avidly eaten street food.

Searching for a pick-me-up on a rough day, look no further than an easily prepared Persian spinach-and-egg ensemble: *nargesi-ye esfenaj*. When my Iranian friend, Majid Parcham, came home from school, he fondly remembers his mother picking spinach from her garden, steaming it, and sautéing it with onions. She then cooked two sunny-side-up eggs on top of the bed of leaves. All to soothe a schoolboy's spirits. Simple, fresh, and flavorful, this dish—named for the narcissus, a white-petaled flower with a bright yellow heart—pays homage to the noble green.

SEX AND THE
SINGLE STRAWBERRY

The Europeans were awestruck by the wild strawberries of the New World. The berries spread their runners, taking over the forest floors and meadows. "We can not sette down foote but tred on strawberries," one English colonist remarked. A "pioneer species," to use writer Peter Hatch's phrase, this member of the rose family flourished on the soil that the Indians and the European settlers had cleared of trees and brush. "Like all wild fruits, the strawberry responded to the additional light that resulted from the disturbance of the mature forest by bearing more and larger berries on a rich carpet of leaves," Hatch noted. In time, both Europeans and Indians took the strawberries from the wild and transplanted them to their gardens.

Settlers were stunned by the untrammeled, abundant fruit. "The land is fertile in soyle to produce all manners of plants . . . here are also strawberries," an early planter wrote to King James I. "I have lien downe in one place in my corne field and in the compasse of my reach have filled my belly in the place." Roger Williams, founder of the Rhode Island colony, was amazed that "in some parts where the natives have planted, I have many times seen as many as would fill a good ship." Years later, the twentieth-century American critic, Lewis Mumford, imagined the thickets of berries: "They grew so thick that . . . horses' fetlocks . . . seemed covered with blood."

The Virginian strawberry, as the early fruit was known, became an important form of sustenance. The Narragansett Indians in Rhode Island, who called the heart-shaped fruit *wuttahimneash*, made bread from strawberries and cornmeal.

"The Indians bruise them in a mortar and mix them with meale and make 'berry bread,'" Roger Williams wrote in his journal. The Native Americans also reveled in "veritable strawberry sprees, eating the delicate berries, seasoning their meat with them, drinking strawberry soup or a tea made from the leaves," writer Virginia Scully recounted.

The Europeans cherished their own wild strawberry. The *fraise de bois* (wood strawberry) that grew in the meadows and forests was the darling of artists and writers. Eighteenth-century French philosopher Diderot observed affectionately that its tiny red berries resembled the "tips of wet nurses' breasts." The fruit's "pleasing, winey taste," as one writer put it, made it especially appetizing.

From classical times, it had been the wild, not the domesticated, strawberry that was coveted. The Romans never cultivated the fruit, which Ovid celebrated in a poem about the giant, Polyphemus, who was wooing Galatea. "With thine own hands thou shalt thyself gather the soft strawberries growing in the woodland shade," he promised the young woman. The blessed fruit, Ovid felt, originated in an idyllic Golden Age. To tamper with such pristine beauty, therefore, was to interfere with perfection. "Doubtless God could have made a better berry but doubtless God never did," the sixteenth-century English physician William Butler would gush.

Gradually, hesitatingly, European gardeners began domesticating the wild berry. As it moved from the woods to the garden, however, the nature of the fruit changed only slightly. The new plant captured the interest of botanists and horticulturists. It "sends forth many strings, which disperse themselves far abroad, whereby it greatly increaseth," seventeenth-century English herbalist John Gerard observed. The strawberry got its name, many scholars believe, from the word meaning "to strew," which evokes the way it spreads out over the ground.

Initially, gardeners had planted the strawberry less for its flavor and more for its ornamental and medical benefits. Medieval herbalists invested the fruit, the leaves, and the roots with curative properties. The strawberry, it was said, alleviated throat infections, fever, kidney stones, and headaches. Eating the fruit, a sixteenth-century French herbalist wrote, "comforteth the stomache and quench the throat." Herbalist Gerard touted strawberry water as a tonic: "The distilled water drunk with white wine is good against passion of the heart, reviving the spirits, and making the heart merrie."

Strawberries also beautified and cleansed the skin, many women believed. Herbalists lent their weight to this view. Pimples disappeared, according to the sixteenth-century commentator William Langham, after the skin was layered

with a strawberry solution. In his *Herball* of the same era, John Gerard praised strawberry leaves as a way to heal "redness and heate of the face."

A cosmetic of distilled strawberry water became popular among women of the aristocracy. Madame Tallien, one of Marie Antoinette's ladies-in-waiting, the story goes, loved to immerse herself in a bath of strawberry and raspberry juice. Her attendants then sponged her skin with milk and perfumes, making it even pinker. Each session required twenty-two pints of crushed strawberries.

The rich and well-bred had more lavish goals for the new fruit. They were ardent consumers and enthusiastic displayers of the strawberry. The ennobled fruit was planted in Europe's grand houses. So avid was Louis X about the strawberry that he had glass houses built to force early blooming of the fruit.

Strawberries and cream was an aristocratic delight. England's Cardinal Wolsey, who first tried the dessert after a banquet of porpoise, popularized the treat. France's King Louis XIV, who reveled in strawberries in wine, ate the fruit voraciously. His doctor finally ordered him to stop his indulgence, because it was causing indigestion. "Rawe crayme undecocted, eaten with strawberys . . . is a rurall mannes banket," the sixteenth-century writer Andrew Boorde observed. He cautioned, however, that "such bankettes hath put men in jeopardy of they lyves."

The nobility also appropriated the strawberry as a symbol of honor and virtue. The fruit was displayed on the coronets of English lords—six leaves for a duke, four for a marquis. The strawberry, herbalist John Parkinson felt, enhanced the stature of wealthy ladies. It was "fit for a Gentlewoman to weare upon her arm, as a raritie instead of a flower."

The strawberry, which embodied purity and righteousness, played a powerful mythic and symbolic role in medieval and Renaissance culture. In one early fifteenth-century French miniature, Joseph extends a strawberry in his hand toward the child Jesus, encouraging him to walk. In *Madonna of the Strawberries*, painter Martin Schongauer portrays the Virgin sitting on a raised bed of strawberries and wearing a garland of the fruit's leaves. Monks drew its likeness in the borders of prayer books and in "illuminated" manuscripts. These drawings and tiny illustrations were done in special honor of the Virgin Mary and the baby Jesus.

This emblem of virtue also conveyed darker forces, as well. In both the literary and the popular imagination, the strawberry's inviting allure was often seen as a form of dissembling. The Roman poet Virgil creates an atmosphere of dangerous portent around the fruit. He warns children to be vigilant when picking strawberries: "Ye who cull flowers and low-growing strawberries, / Away from her lads, a chill snake lurks in the grass."

In *Othello*, Shakespeare masterfully employs the strawberry to represent the web of falsity that ensnares his leading character. A handkerchief "spotted with strawberry" that Othello gave his beloved Desdemona disappears. The schemer Iago then convinces Othello that this offering of trust has fallen into the hands of Cassio, who, he says, has been carrying on a secret liaison with Desdemona. Successfully manipulated, Othello rages against his wife.

In the licentious scenes of Hieronymus Bosch's painting, *The Garden of Earthly Delights*, voluptuous strawberries play a prominent role. Young nude figures cavort among the oversize fruit. A short, ravenous youth tries to bite into a fruit, whose massive size dwarfs him.

Real events in the journey of the strawberry would turn out to be as extraordinary as anything dreamed up in Bosch's imagination. The accidental arrival in Europe of a new strawberry from the Americas opens a fascinating chapter in the fruit's history.

A French spy, who stumbled on a large, fruited berry in Chile, sets the story in motion. Amédée-François Frézier, a naval officer and engineer, whose family name ironically derives from the French word for "strawberry," was sent on a mission to Chile and Peru by Louis XIV in 1712. His assignment: to gather information about Spanish fortifications, supply routes, and military assets. While doing his surveys, a strawberry patch growing on a sand hollow near the Chilean town of Concepción caught his eye. The fruit, much larger than the tiny variety growing in Europe, was "big as a walnut, and sometimes, as a hen's eggs, of a whiteish red," he exclaimed.

The Chilean or Sand strawberry was native to ten thousand miles of the Pacific coast from Alaska to the southern tip of Chile. Indians domesticated the fruit, selecting the plants with the biggest berries. They dried the fruits in the sun and fermented them for wine. Chile's early Spanish settlers were overwhelmed by the size of the berries. "They grow as big as pears," the writer Alonso de Ovalle observed of the Chilean berries in 1646.

Eager to introduce his countrymen to the striking strawberries, Frézier potted runners from five plants to take on his voyage home in 1714. Although he selected those with the largest fruits, only two plants survived the trip from Chile to France. On his return, Frézier donated the strawberries to private gardens. Sadly, the much-heralded plants refused to bear fruit, and no one could explain the puzzling phenomenon. In 1740, the farmers of Brest, a town in Brittany, stumbled on a solution. They inadvertently planted rows of the Chilean and the Virginian, the American variety that had arrived in Europe earlier. The Chilean plants blossomed this time, producing large, plump fruit.

Why had the seemingly barren Chilean plant finally fruited? Frézier, in his quest for the largest berries, had brought only female plants back from Chile. They needed pollen to be fertilized, and the Virginia strawberry, which had never been able to cross with the continent's wild berry, proved to be the ideal mate for the Chilean.

The idea of cross-fertilization was only imperfectly understood at the time. Even prominent scientists like the renowned plant taxonomist Linnaeus rejected it. Crossing the two strawberry varieties numerous times, a young Frenchman replicated the Brittany result. Antoine Nicolas Duchesne, who had tended the garden at the Versailles palace, explained the phenomenon to a scientific audience in his *Natural History of Strawberries* (1766).

The resulting hybrid strawberry, nineteen-year-old Duchesne wrote, was related to the Chilean like a "son with his mother." Combining the most attractive features of its parents, it possessed the firmness, plumpness, and sweet-tart flavor of the Chilean with the scarlet hues, softness, and juiciness of the Virginia. It would be called the Pine, because of its pineapple-ish fragrance. The two wandering New World fruits had finally succeeded in mating, albeit in the Old World. Ancestors of the modern strawberry, they had given birth, as Duchesne pointed out, to a new "race of fruit."

Commercial breeders and growers built on the groundwork the young scientist had laid. The English gardener Michael Keen continued tinkering with the Chilean and Virginian strawberries and, in 1821, produced Keen's Seedling, a Pine that could be taken to market. William Cobbett, an English horticulturist, was exultant about the breed: "This strawberry, which is the only one used for forcing in the King's gardens, has nearly supplanted every other sort. It is early; it is a prodigious bearer; the fruit is large, and very large; and it surpasses in my opinion all the others in flavour." Our robust, large-fruited berries are descendants of this seedling.

Americans, incurable romantics, still long for the berry of the woods and fields, for something unprocessed and uncorrupted. In an earlier day, Emerson and Thoreau extolled the wild strawberry and denigrated its civilized kin. "Strawberries bluntly lose their flavor in garden beds," Emerson wrote. Thoreau did "not think much of strawberries in gardens, nor in market baskets, raised and sold by your excellent hard-fisted neighbor. It is those little natural beds or patches of them on the dry hillsides that interest me most."

As for me, I still eagerly await the arrival of early summer strawberries at our farmers' market. They may have been tamed, but they are still a joy.

"CANDY FROM THE FIELD"
the sweet potato

Vendors in sixteenth-century London enticed their customers with candied slices of sweet potato, a popular snack among the wealthy and titled classes. Today, by contrast, the once-luxurious root vegetable is now a basic foodstuff on which many of the Third World poor rely for sustenance and nourishment.

Not at all related to the common white potato, the sweet potato is a member of the morning glory family. The only food plant in this group, the vegetable is actually a swollen storage root, a storehouse of nutrients that lies underground. The ordinary potato, on the other hand, is technically not a root, but rather a subterranean tuber.

The sweet potato, like its twining, climbing kin, spreads its vines over the ground within a few weeks of planting. (The scientific name for the morning glory family comes from *convolvulus*, or "twine around.") They look like "spinach," Bartolomé de las Casas, an early Spanish chronicler of the Americas, remarked of the New World plants. In the Philippines and in other countries, the stems and heart-shaped leaves are eaten like greens. To the Filipino, the sweet potato vine is a godsend because it is one of the few leafy vegetables to survive during floods and monsoons.

An ancient crop, possibly the oldest in the New World, the sweet potato grew wild in what is now Peru, by 8000 BC at the latest. Remains of the root were found in a cave dating back to that time. At least five hundred years before Columbus, scholars now suggest, the sweet potato began the first of many journeys. Polynesians sailed to South America's west coast and carried sweet potatoes back home with them. Tellingly, the word for the root in many Polynesian languages is similar to one in the Andean Indian tongue.

Several centuries later, Spaniards exploring the West Indies found the *batata*, a word they borrowed from the Indians, growing far from its birthplace. During his stay in Hispaniola (today's islands of Haiti and the Dominican Republic), Columbus in 1492 mistook the curved vegetable for the *niames*, the yam he had first seen on the west coast of Africa. The potato reminded the mariner of a carrot, and its taste recalled the chestnut. Other observers likened the root to a turnip.

Another variety of sweet potato, the *aje*, was starchier and drier than the *batata*. Enjoyed by the Arawaks, the native Indians, it was much less popular with the Spaniards.

The white-fleshed vegetable, less sweet than its relative, is now the sweet potato of choice in Latin America. The *boniato* (meaning "sweet and harmless," according to food writer Elizabeth Schneider), as it is now known, can be transformed into savory and sweet dishes. A famous one in the Caribbean is the *boniatillo*, a festive sweet potato puree with a citrus and cinnamon flavor. In Latin markets in the United States, the *boniato* today is displayed in bins along with other curious-looking root vegetables, one of a plethora of "tropicals" exported for nostalgic ethnics.

The Spaniards reveled in the moister, honeyed root. Fernandez de Oviedo, a writer and adventurer, sampled it and imagined an almond treat from his country. "A *batata* well cured and prepared is just like a marzipan." Writer de las Casas remarked that a roasted sweet potato tasted as if it had been dipped in a jar of jam.

Other accounts of Columbus's voyages expressed similar elation about the *batata*. "When eaten raw as in salads they taste like parsnips; when roasted, like sugary chestnuts; when cooked with pork, you would think you were eating squash," observed a passenger on his second expedition in 1493. "You will never eat [a] more delicious [dish] . . . soaked in the milk of almonds. It is a dish which lends itself to all the culinary arts and requirements of gourmets." The passenger added, "Seeds have been sent to Spain, so that our world might not lack their beneficial plant and its great variety of gustatory sensations."

On their trips back to the mother country from the Americas, ships stocked their holds with sweet potatoes. When he returned to Spain, Columbus introduced sweet potatoes to his patrons, King Ferdinand and Queen Isabella, who may well have planted them in their court gardens. Planted in the warm climes of southern Spain, sweet potatoes prospered.

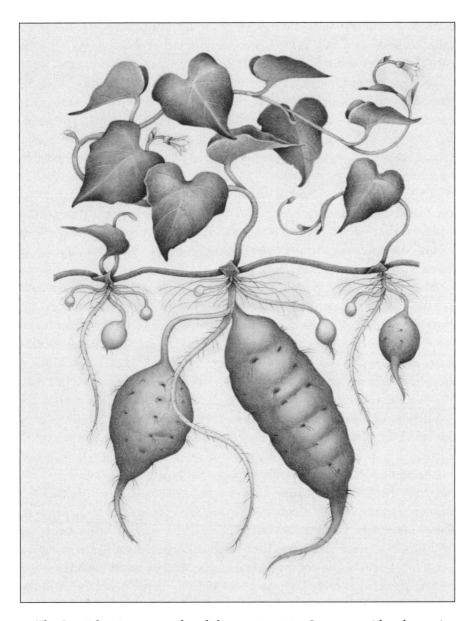

The Spanish aristocracy adored the sweet potato. It was considered superior to the *papa*, the pedestrian white potato. The common white tuber had a simple task: to satisfy the hunger of the poor and servile. The sweet root had loftier uses: it made wonderful conserves and other treats for the elite. Moreover, unlike the white potato, which grew on the *altiplano*, the frigid, unforgiving highlands of

Peru, the *batata* thrived in the tropical soil of the West Indies. Its association with the "lush" lowlands of the Caribbean gave the sweet potato a cachet the *papa* could never attain, historian Larry Zuckerman suggests.

The "Spanish potato," as the sweet potato came to be called, reached Northern Europe, arriving by 1600 at the latest. It preceded the white potato, later known as the "Irish potato," by at least fifty years. Initially shunned by the Spanish, who only took it home several decades after finding it, the white vegetable carried negative baggage. This member of the nightshade family was reputed to be poisonous and to carry disease.

Royals and aristocrats feasted on the sweet potato at festive banquets. Sweet potato puddings and pies were typical fare at these galas. Recipes instructed the well-born in the art of making these treats. Richard Bradley, Cambridge University's first professor of botany, developed a recipe for a sweet potato pudding flavored with candied orange and lemon peel.

Its reputation as an aphrodisiac made the vegetable even more fashionable. William Harrison, a sixteenth-century English writer, spoke of the "venerous roots" brought from "Spane" and "Portingale." In Shakespeare's time, when vendors sold candied slices of sweet potato at London's Royal Exchange, the dramatist played on the root's erotic magnetism. In *The Merry Wives of Windsor*, Falstaff, anticipating an amorous conquest, cries out, "Let the sky rain potatoes, let it thunder to the tune of 'Green Sleeves,' hail kissing confits."

Continuing its twisting and turning journey, the sweet potato reached China by way of the Philippines. Spanish galleons plying the route from the port of Acapulco in Mexico to Manila carried seed stock for planting. The Filipinos embraced the new crop, which they called by its Spanish name, *camote*.

Luzon, the Philippines's largest island, was "thickly settled with Fukienese," immigrants from Fukien, a southern coastal province of China, scholar I. H. Burkill notes. When famine devastated Fukien after a typhoon struck the region in 1593, China sent a mission to the Philippines to search for plants to aid the hungry. A group of settlers from Fukien, who thought sweet potatoes would help, volunteered to bring the plants back to China. Since Spain outlawed the export of vital foodstuffs from their colony, the Fukienese hatched a plot: they disguised the roots as ship cables by wrapping cordage around them and then sailed for their homeland. The returning Chinese taught local farmers how to cultivate the unfamiliar crop. The Chinese hailed the "golden tuber," which ended the famine.

By the end of the eighteenth century, the sweet potato was spreading around China. The prolific and hardy root, which thrived even in rocky and sandy soil, was also drought-resistant. A boon to the peasant farmer, the root sprang up quickly and yielded four times as much as rice. Its roots, stems, and leaves were also good fodder for livestock. Because of its reputation as a food of the poor, however, the wealthy preferred to grow wheat, rather than the lowly sweet potato.

In North America the sweet potato thrived in the South, where warm weather fostered abundant harvests. Spanish explorer Hernando de Soto discovered Indians in Louisiana growing the root in 1540. A hundred years later, English colonists, who possibly received the plants from the West Indies, were cultivating sweet potatoes in Virginia. Masters fed sweet potatoes to their slaves, who harvested them in their gardens and roasted them in the ashes of their cooking fires.

The sweet potato replaced the yam, the large tuber that had been the mainstay of their African diet. Out of habit, the slaves called the roots "yams," even though these rough and scaly tubers were drier and starchier than sweet potatoes. The name stuck, nonetheless.

African Americans in the South developed a diverse repertoire of sweet potato dishes. Pies, biscuits, breads, and pone—a treat halfway between pudding and bread—diffused from the black community into the larger population.

In his novel, *Invisible Man*, Ralph Ellison describes the "stab of swift nostalgia" brought on by the smell of Carolina sweet potatoes roasting on a Harlem pushcart: "At home we'd bake them in the hot coals of the fireplace, had carried them cold to school for lunch, munched them secretly, squeezing the sweet pulp from the soft peel as we hid from the teacher behind the largest book. . . . Yes, and we'd loved them candied, or baked in a cobbler, deep-fat fried in a pocket of dough, or roasted with pork and glazed with the well-browned fat; had chewed them raw—yams and years ago."

The vegetable's most fervent advocate was the scientist George Washington Carver of Alabama's Tuskegee Institute. He promoted sweet potatoes as a nutritious, high-yielding crop that could replenish the soil ravaged by King Cotton. In testimony before Congress, Carver said that the sweet potato and the peanut, another beneficent plant, were "twin brothers . . . two of the greatest products God has given us." Carver also preached the nutritional benefits of the vitamin A–rich root. He sent out recipes for sweet potato fries, chips, and other dishes to popularize the vegetable.

The sweet potato also benefited from shrewd marketing. Appealing to regional pride, Louisiana growers in the 1930s tried to capitalize on its traditional name. They billed their product as the "Louisiana yam." The promoters were trying to set the sweeter, moister Southern potato apart from the dry, mealy variety grown in the East. (Cajuns in Louisiana called the sweet potato *bonbon du close*, or "candy from the field.")

Fine distinctions between yams and sweet potatoes matter little to many Americans, especially those with Southern roots. At Oohh's and Aahh's, a Washington, D.C., eatery that dishes out fried chicken, greens, peach cobbler, and other Southern foods, there is no menu item called sweet potatoes; rather, they are simply "candied yams." Even my local Safeway in the District bowed to this city's Southern traditions, labeling their bin of sweet potatoes "yams." Whatever you call them, they're just as sweet.

"HOMEGROWN TOMATOES"

Luis Marroquin, the owner of Taqueria Distrito Federal, a restaurant in Washington, D.C.'s Columbia Heights neighborhood, took out a fruit enclosed in a papery husk from his refrigerator case, pulled off the covering, and sliced up the round, green tomatillo.

"They're much richer than tomatoes," Luis told me. Cooked and pureed and blended with chilies and cilantro, they are essential to his restaurant's salsa verde, the spicy green sauce, jars of which are placed on all the taqueria's tables. "If you make salsa verde, you can't use green tomatoes," Luis stressed. "You need tomatillos."

The story of the tomatillo's cousin, the tomato, begins in ancient Mexico, where, as the anthropologist Sophie Coe points out, the Aztecs were already acquainted with the tomatillo. They knew it as a type of *tomatl*, which means something "round and plump."

Later, the Indians stumbled on a plant with tiny yellow berries that resembled the cherry tomato. Its seeds were probably carried by birds from the Andean highlands. The Indians domesticated it, breeding a larger, meatier, segmented fruit. It became the *xitomatl*, "a plump thing with a navel," the ancestor of today's garden tomato.

Before the Spanish conquest of Mexico in the early sixteenth century, the Indians had already developed a dazzling variety of tomatoes in different shapes, colors, and sizes. Friar Bernardino de Sahagún marveled at the fruits a vendor was selling: "large tomatoes, small tomatoes, sweet tomatoes . . . nipple shaped tomatoes . . . yellow, very yellow, quite yellow, red, very red . . . rosy dawn colored."

The tomatoes (or tomatillos) complemented chilies, a key element in Aztec food. Francisco Hernández, a Spaniard who cataloged plants in Mexico between 1570 and 1577, discusses the combination in a section called "On Sour and Acid Plants": "One prepares a delicious dip sauce . . . from minced tomatoes, mixed with chili, which complements the flavor of almost all dishes and foods, and wakens a dull appetite."

After Spain's triumph, the first tomato seeds were likely brought in ships to Seville, food historian Rudolf Grewe suggests. The Spaniards initially did not take to the fruit, mostly growing it for ornamental purposes in royal botanical gardens. They changed its name from the Aztec *tomatl* to *tomate*. Gradually, Spanish cooks learned that tomatoes could add flavor and zest to their cooking. An early seventeenth-century recipe calls for a sauce of tomatoes, garlic, and onions for casseroles of cod, chicken, and partridge. The recipe's author, Juan Altamaras, who loved the sourness of the tomato, thought its acidity enhanced the flavor of his creations.

Before long, the classic tomato sauce, a medley of tomatoes, garlic, parsley, and olive oil, had become a standard of Spanish cuisine. For Americans coming of age in the 1950s, "Spanish rice," smothered in a bastardized version of this sauce, was their first exposure to Iberian food.

The yellow fruit arrived in Italy with the Spanish, who took control of Naples in 1522 and ruled the kingdom for more than two hundred years. In 1554, Venetian herbalist Pietro Andrea Mattioli portrayed the import as "flat and round like an apple and divided into segments like melons." The *pomi d'oro* (golden apple), Mattioli told his readers, should be prepared like the eggplant, a vegetable bequeathed to Spain by its Islamic conquerors: "When ripe of a golden color," it was "eaten in the same manner as the eggplant—fried in oil with salt and pepper like mushrooms."

The herbalist also warned of the dangers of the tomato—the *mala insana*. The "mad apple," it was believed, could derange the body and mind. Like the eggplant, the tomato belonged to the deadly nightshade family. Fearful Italians purged tomatoes of the presumed poisons by cooking them for many hours and by seasoning them heavily with vinegar and spices.

Paradoxically, the treacherous tomato was also seen as an aphrodisiac. The tomato, Mattioli points out, is kin to the mandrake, the "love plant" of the Old Testament, whose roots looked like entwined lovers. The tomato's erotic reputation led to another evocative name. The French called it *pomme d'amour*, the

"apple of love." "Love apples are marvelous and golden," the seventeenth-century French agronomist Olivier de Serres rhapsodized. "They serve commonly to cover outhouses and arbors."

The first Italian recipes for the tomato, developed in Naples, had a strong Spanish imprint. Antonio Latini, who cooked for Neapolitan nobility, was an influential chef. His recipe for "Tomato Sauce, Spanish Style" plays on the fruit's affinity with the eggplant, slow-frying tomatoes and aubergines with onions and herbs in olive oil.

When it reached Northern Europe from Spain, the tomato received a mixed welcome. In England in 1597, herbalist John Gerard scorned its "ranke and stinking savour." It was also depicted as an exotic southern product. According to John Parkinson, an apothecary to King James, "love apples" were adored in the "hot countries," where they were eaten "to coole and quench the thirst of the hot stomach."

Back in Italy, the tomato was quickly adopted by the peasant and working classes, who enthusiastically cultivated and consumed the fruit. Tomatoes sustained them when other foods were not available. Equally important, they imparted color, verve, and, of course, vitamins to an otherwise simple diet. Another asset was that tomatoes were relatively easy to keep. Farmers and city dwellers alike preserved *pomodori* as conserve or tomato paste.

By the end of the nineteenth century, a sultry tomato sauce topped Italian street foods, pasta and pizza. Naples was a bastion of these cheap repasts. "All of the streets of the city's popular quarters have one of those taverns that set up their cauldron outside, where macaroni [is] always on the boil, with pots of simmering tomato sauce and mountains of grated cheese," Neapolitan journalist Matilde Serao reported in 1884.

Tomatoey Italian dishes had their most fervent following among Naples's commoners. "Pizza and spaghetti with red sauce soon became symbols of the Neapolitan lively plebeian port culture," historian Donna Gabaccia points out.

Italian farmers perfected tomato varieties that meshed well with the emerging cuisine. Plum tomatoes were ideal for making flavorful sauce. Canned whole plum tomatoes were the basis for *pomodori pelati*, the quintessentially Italian style of peeled tomatoes. The most celebrated sauce tomato was the pear-shaped San Marzano, which flourished in the volcanic soil on the slopes of Mount Vesuvius outside Naples. A network of cultivators, processors, and factories sprang up to take field tomatoes and turn them into canned pastes and sauces.

One large enterprise, the Cirio Company, whose emblem was the San Marzano tomato, turned out such a vast quantity of products that it spurred large-scale tomato cultivation in the nation. Cirio broadened the appeal of the tomato from the south to the whole country.

The cultivation of tomatoes and manufacture of tomato products soared to meet the demand from the Italian diaspora in the United States, Latin America, and Europe. In waves, millions of Italians left their birthplace for new homes between 1870 and 1920. Communities in New York, Toronto, and Buenos Aires had such an insatiable appetite for these items that one Italian agronomist called it "tomato fever." By 1910, in the Parma area, historian David Gentilcore details, thirty-six plants were employing three thousand workers during the fifty-day canning season.

In the developing Italian enclaves, enterprising merchants sold Old Country foods shipped by their compatriots. In the early twentieth century, Giuseppe Uddo, a young immigrant who settled in New Orleans's "Little Palermo" neighborhood (in today's French Quarter area), hauled cans of imported tomato paste in a horse-drawn cart to sell in Italian truck-farming communities outside the Crescent City. From this small venture, Progresso Foods, the large seller of Italian foods, evolved.

Before long, American-based farmers and tomato companies were targeting Italian ethnics with goods once almost exclusively supplied from abroad. Cans of "Italian tomatoes" that were actually homegrown were displayed on grocery shelves. By 1937, twelve Italian companies in California, historian Gentilcore points out, were selling more tomato-based items than were being imported by all their Italian counterparts combined.

In post–World War II America, an expanding market of chain stores and supermarkets was opening up, and purveyors of Italian foods set their sights on it. Hector Boiardi, a chef and restaurant owner, dreamed up the idea of canning pasta and tomato sauce together. His product, which was first shrewdly marketed with packets of dry spaghetti and grated cheese, was enormously popular with American soldiers. Boiardi had contracted with the US Army to supply it with cans of "Chef Boyardee." (Boiardi invented this new spelling because he felt Americans would struggle with the Italian version.) After the war housewives were eager for convenient foods, and they snapped up the popular grocery item.

The hallmark of the Italian food Americans were discovering was the tomato. Southern Italians, especially those from Naples and the surrounding Campania region, dominated the neighborhoods that blossomed from the massive immigration that began in the late nineteenth century. Since the trattorias, groceries, and other food businesses were mostly run by this group, the food that Americans came to think of as Italian was, in fact, regional cooking that revolved around the tomato. Italian food "was, for the most part, the essentially Campanian tomato, garlic and olive oil–based cuisine which reigns in most Italian-American homes and restaurants down to the present," historian Harvey Levenstein observed. (Parmesan cheese was another feature.) Diners only learned about *pasta al pesto* and other northern Italian specialties much later.

"There's only two things that money can't buy—and that's true love and homegrown tomatoes," the country song reminds us. Many Americans and Italians still assume that these succulent beauties came from Italy, a natural misconception. Reared in the Americas, the tomato was reborn in Italy. It came back as a zesty fruit, ready to be fully embraced and enjoyed.

THE SCENT OF VANILLA

Climbing as high as a hundred feet and clinging to tree trunks, the vanilla vine, a member of the vast orchid family, twists upward in the rain forests of the Americas, their native habitat.

Long before the Spanish conquest, the Totonac Indians of Mexico were fascinated by these "green garden hoses," to use anthropologist Sophie Coe's image. Clusters of greenish-yellow flowers grow up once a year on the stem of the vanilla plant. Since they bud early in the morning and drop off by nightfall, unless they are pollinated, the opportunity for fruiting is limited. Self-pollination is impossible because a membrane blocks the male from the female reproductive parts. The small number of flowers lucky enough to be fertilized by orchard bees bear the green vanilla bean, in whose pod are stored thousands of black seeds.

It was the vanilla pod that attracted the Indians, even though the pod has little fragrance on the vine. Only after a period of drying, curing, and fermentation does the fruit, now a black color, give off its tantalizing aroma, a scent produced by the chemical *vanillin*. It was the Totonacs who developed this ingenious process.

Lovers of incense, the Totonacs were transfixed by the aromatic, using it to give their houses a pleasing smell. It was also a prized aphrodisiac. To make themselves alluring, women placed the oiled beans in their hair.

Vanilla's mystique gave rise to fantastic myths. In Totonac legend, the orchid sprang from the blood of a wayward princess who ran off with a young tribesman. Her father sent his agents to capture the couple, who were then decapitated and thrown into a mountain ravine. In that spot, a vanilla bush grew up. The

flower and its fruit, whose fragrance emanated from the princess's soul, were sacred in their culture.

The aristocratic Aztecs, who conquered the Totonacs, demanded part of the vanilla harvest as tribute. Their chiefs wore amulets around their necks that contained vanilla flowers and other fragrances as a lucky charm. They added its ground pods to *cacahuatl*, the royal drink that is the ancestor of modern hot chocolate. The "bitter water" infused with ground cacao beans, maize, chilies, and other pungent flavorings was moderated with the gentler vanilla.

The nobility reveled in the luxurious drink at banquets and other ceremonial occasions. The king himself, Spanish friar Bernardino de Sahagún writes, was served a specially prepared goblet in the comfort of his home. "[H]is chocolate was served: green cacao-pods, honeyed chocolate, flowered chocolate, flavored with green vanilla."

Spanish visitors to the Americas extolled vanilla for its medicinal properties. In the 1570s, Dr. Francisco Hernández recounted some of the bean's benefits: "A decoction of vanilla beans steeped in water causes the urine to flow admirably . . . they warm and strengthen the stomach . . . give strength and vigor to the mind." However, Hernández warned that the spice could be sexually arousing. It stimulated the "venereal appetite."

The Spaniards, who relished chocolate, adopted vanilla as one of the flavorings in their drink. Unlike the Aztecs, they took the beverage hot and sweetened with sugar. By the latter half of the sixteenth century, factories in Spain were manufacturing a chocolate powder flavored with imported vanilla.

The nation's lords embraced the new aromatic. King Philip II swigged a vanilla-laced *chocolatl* before going to bed. Nobles smoked cigars that perfumed the room with the smell of vanilla.

In Europe, the aromatic lost one more link to its aboriginal past. The Spaniards began calling what the Aztecs knew as *tlilxochitl* ("black flower") *vainilla*. *Vainilla*, "little pods," is the diminutive of *vaina*, which means "pod, sheath, or scabbard" in Spanish. *Vaina* itself comes from the Latin, *vagina*.

In England, Hugh Morgan, apothecary to Queen Elizabeth, convinced his patron to become a vanilla enthusiast. The queen, the story goes, insisted that all her food and drink be infused with it.

The French were even more enamored of what they called *vanille*. Louis XIV drank his chocolate scented with vanilla. Perfume makers seized on the scent, which, in later years, would distinguish Chanel No. 5 and Shalimar. Its erotic reputation led the Marquis de Sade, according to some accounts, to offer his dinner guests chocolates spiked with Spanish fly (the aphrodisiac) and vanilla.

Determined to have their own vanilla supply, the French transplanted cuttings from Mexico in the 1820s to their Indian Ocean colony of Réunion, but the plants bore little fruit. Montezuma, it was rumored, had cursed the plant to prevent it from growing elsewhere. In fact, it was the absence of a tiny bee, which pollinated Mexico's orchids, that was the real cause.

To solve this problem, Edmond Albius, an inventive former plantation slave, devised a way to hand-pollinate the flower. In 1841, Albius lifted the flap that separated the male from the female organs with a bamboo splinter. He then transferred pollen from the anther to the surface of the stigma. "Orchid marriage" was the vanilla industry's salvation.

The new technique of pollination made mass cultivation on plantations possible. "Bourbon" vanilla production exploded in Madagascar, Réunion, and France's Indian Ocean colonies, which, by the end of the nineteenth century, exported most of the world's vanilla. An industry of growers, brokers, and processors would organize the vanilla business from plantation to grocery shelf.

Large-scale cultivation of a product once confined to wild forests in Mexico transformed American cooking. Vanilla was an obscure, unusual flavor in American kitchens until after the Civil War. Rose water, for example, was more likely to be used for cakes, puddings, and custards than the now more common aromatic, food historian Charles Perry points out. In the first American cookbook, *American Cookery* (1796), Amelia Simmons called for rose water in gingerbread and apple pie. As vanilla became more readily available, chefs discovered that it was a natural companion to desserts made with cream or chocolate. Vanilla would be required in thirty-two recipes of Chef Hugo Ziemann's *White House Cookbook* (1887).

Vanilla also gained in popularity for medicinal purposes. Customers purchased tincture of vanilla at nineteenth-century drugstores to soothe their stomachs. The *American Pharmacopoeia* recommended tincture of vanilla as a remedy until 1995.

In time, cooks would be relying on vanilla extract for their dishes, and recipe instructions would measure the flavoring in teaspoons. As it has become more ordinary, the once-exotic flavoring is losing some of its fascination. We have tamed the orchid whose perfume once thrilled and terrified its discoverers. The aromatic is now, literally, plain vanilla.

CRACKING THE WALNUT

So ordinary is the walnut to us, yet so extraordinary in many other cultures. "I went down into the garden of nuts to see the fruits of the valley," King Solomon says of walnuts in the Old Testament. The ancient tree, a long-lived, sturdy hardwood that can tower as high as a hundred feet, impressed the Greeks with its majesty. The puny acorn's fruits were fit for men; the walnut's, for the gods.

The Greeks called the walnut *karya*, some think from *kara*, the word for "head." In their minds, the walnut shell resembled the skull, and its kernels, the hemispheres of the brain. Centuries later, European herbalists, who considered the walnut cerebral nourishment, recommended it for head ailments and mental illness. The seventeenth-century English herbalist William Cole recommended that a crushed walnut laid "upon the Crown of the Head . . . comforts the brain and head mightily."

The Romans invested the nut with similar qualities. They called the celestial walnut *Juglans*, or "Jupiter's acorn." The prolific tree also represented fertility and abundance to the Romans. The charmed walnuts became part of their wedding festivities. Guests celebrated by showering bride and groom with them. After the wedding feast, the couple scattered walnuts around their bedroom.

Native to a swath of land that stretched from the Himalayas to the Caucasus, the nut's heartland was Persia. To the Greeks, the walnut was *persikon*. Since it was the Persian king who sent both the Greeks and the Romans this gift, the walnut acquired a royal aura. In Persia, Greece, and Rome, the walnut was reserved for the royalty and aristocracy. The Persians, scholars surmise, domesticated the

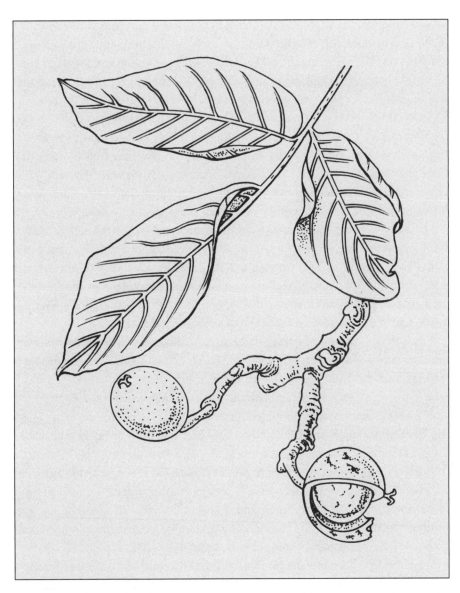

tree that grew widely in the mountainous north of Iran. They picked out trees with the most desirable features and husbanded these varieties. The Persian walnut, as it is still called today, is distinguished by larger, sweeter nuts than those found in the wild. It is also more easily cracked open. (We speak here of the Persian or English walnut, familiar to us in snacks and desserts, rather than the black walnut, a tree native to North America.)

So sacred was the walnut to the Persians that it was considered a "sin" to cut down one of the trees. Parents honored its fecundity by planting a walnut to mark the birth of each new child. Not only was the *gerdu* (Persian for the "round one") revered, but its fruits were also savored. Walnuts were a treat to be shared with guests as well as a street food. Walnuts were hawked by the *gerdu-ee*, or walnut vendor. "In the early to mid-summer months, he would set up his gig on the house-side of the open gutter . . . selling his freshly peeled walnuts by the *fal* (unit of sale equal to six walnuts, if memory serves) from the murky water of a huge glass jar," the Persian writer Guive Mirfendereski recalls. "The salt was a little extra. Sometimes he would set the *fal* up into [a] pyramid structure, which he would scoop with his fingers . . . and place the nuts in a newspaper wrap."

Inventive Persian cooks used walnuts in their dishes. In *fesenjan*, a classic festive stew of duck or pheasant (now chicken) adored by the aristocracy, the bird was braised in a dark brown sauce that married ground walnuts and tart pomegranate syrup. The crunch of sweet walnuts also enhances the flavor of *mâst-o kheeyâr*, a popular yogurt dish of chopped cucumbers fragrant with dill and mint, which can also be made into a refreshing summer soup.

From Persia, the walnut traveled east. The Chinese, who traded with Iran, took advantage of the domesticated "peach of the Westerners." They believed it strengthened the body and possessed other health-giving properties. Migrating west, the walnut reached Britain with the conquering Romans. Initially regarded as a "foreign" nut (or *walh-hnuta* in Old English), the walnut in time was tagged the "English walnut." English ships carried the fruits in their holds and spread them throughout their trading empire.

Europe's gentry supped on the nuts at banquets. Borrowing a technique from Middle Eastern cooking, chefs served stews and soups thickened with ground walnuts at parties. The nut also provided basic sustenance in medieval Europe, feeding the hungry during famines. Walnut milk, made from pounded and ground-up nuts soaked in water, often replaced dairy milk.

America, in whose forests the Eastern (black) walnut already grew, received the Persian walnut from the Spanish Franciscan priests who settled in California during the eighteenth century. The "mission walnuts" they planted were the forebears of the commercially grown walnuts that, years later, were harvested from the state's Central Valley.

It is still in the Middle East and in Central Asia that the virtues of the walnut are most appreciated. The Turks, for example, prepare a thick, garlicky walnut sauce called *tarator* to accompany vegetable and fish dishes. During the Ottoman Empire, this spread gained popularity in Serbia, Macedonia, and other parts of the Balkan realm of the Turks.

Walnuts are also essential to *muhammara*, a Turkish appetizer. The dip, whose name means "brick-colored" in Arabic, is a blend of pureed roasted red peppers, ground walnuts, and bread crumbs. The mixture is fired up with cumin and hot red pepper and infused with the tartness of pomegranate syrup and lemon juice. The oil and crunch of the walnuts enhance the tasty dish.

The most celebrated of walnut dishes is enveloped in myth. Even more than its exotic name, the tales of "Circassian chicken" make it seem seductive. The dish, it is generally agreed, originated in the northwest region of the Caucasus, an area once ruled by the Turks that includes present-day Georgia. A standard of the *mezze* array of small plates, cold chicken suffused in walnut sauce is spiced with paprika in Turkey. Variations of the delicacy are prepared in Armenian, Georgian, and Syrian kitchens.

The dish has become synonymous with the comely women of Circassia, who were brought to Turkey in the sixteenth century after the Ottomans took their homeland. The women were made the brides and concubines of Turkish royalty. Food writer Arto der Haroutunian thinks it likely that the chicken plate was "probably introduced into Turkey by the beautiful Circassian girls who were bought for the whiteness of their skin, their fair hair, and nimble fingers."

Turkish food expert Ghillie Basan offers a different take on its origins. The dish is Circassian, he says, because its "pale colour" resembles the "complexions" of the beautiful women. Or perhaps, as culinary historian Ayla Algar suggests, the silky sensuality of the dish evoked images of those "voluptuous" courtesans. The story of Circassian chicken once more invests the ordinary walnut with an uncommon excitement.

"The natives select them by striking one melon after another with a hatchet, and applying the tongue to the gashes." The Bushmen of the Kalahari Desert in Southern Africa, whom the missionary David Livingstone observed in the 1850s, were choosing *tsamma* melons, the wild ancestors of the watermelon. A source of survival for the African foragers, the wandering gourd would emerge centuries later as a hot-weather refreshment in America. Kin to squash, pumpkins, cucumbers, and other members of the *Cucurbitaceae* family, a group of trailing vines, the watermelon sucks up water through its extensive root system.

The melons, which still grow around desert oases and watering holes, burgeoned after heavy rains. "In years when more than the usual quantity of rain falls, vast tracts of the country are literally covered with these melons," Livingstone remarked. The wild melons, about the size of grapefruit and both sweet and bitter, were saviors in the parched land. The drought-resistant gourds prospered when other vegetables would wilt. The water-saturated melon (90 percent of its weight) quenched the Bushmen's thirst and sustained them on their nomadic treks. An auspicious marker, a melon vine in the desert was usually a sign that water was nearby.

These "botanical canteens," as they have been called, have long served a wide range of needs of the hunter-gatherers. The watermelon itself is easily stored or can be cut into strips, which are hung in trees to dry and saved to feed both tribe members and livestock. Watermelon rinds also made handy drinking and eating cups and other containers.

The seeds were as vital as the flesh. After roasting, they could be nibbled on or ground into flour or processed for cooking oil. The leaves did not go to waste, either; after cooking, they made tasty greens.

North of the Kalahari in the Nile Valley was another seedbed of the watermelon. By 3000 BC, gourds were being plucked from its soil. In their exile, the Israelites yearned for the "cucumbers and melons" they had relished in Egypt. Paintings found in Egyptian tombs honored the revered fruit. Watermelon seeds and leaves uncovered in these chambers were presumably left to provide nourishment in the afterlife.

Years later, the thirteenth-century Arabic writer Zakariya al-Qazwini boasted that the watermelon of Aswan was so huge that a camel could only carry two. Egypt's melon seeds were so prized that they were traded, scholar Andrew Watson notes, to late medieval Europe. The watermelon remains a popular fruit today in Egyptian households. For breakfast, many families enjoy an invigorating plate of watermelon and feta cheese.

By AD 800, the melon had migrated from Africa, probably along the east coast trade routes, to a new home in northwest India. Here the rough fruit was domesticated—"ennobled," to use Andrew Watson's expression. Under the guidance of Indian farmers, the fruit was transformed into a larger gourd with sweeter, more succulent flesh.

Persia, which traded with India, was the next stop on the watermelon's journey. *Hinduwana*, one of its Persian names, meant "melon of India." One of the country's most cherished fruits, it can be a simple repast or the basis of a glorious salad. Watermelon, dates, and pistachios sprinkled with rose water combine to make one such delicacy.

As Persia pushed into Central Asia, the Turkish-speaking peoples of the region, which now includes many of the Soviet Union's former republics, adopted the watermelon. Melons thrived in the area's long, hot summers and withstood the dry, desert climate. Today traders from the former colonies, especially Azerbaijan, travel to Russia during the summer months to market their produce. Along the highway outside Moscow, traders in rows of stands peddle watermelons. Inside Moscow, the streets are thronged with purveyors.

The watermelon business can be perilous. Police harass vendors who are also the victims of (often unfounded) rumors about the safety of their wares. The *Moscow Times* in 1998 reported one striking incident of watermelon hysteria: "A young police sergeant caused panic July 17 when he thought he had been poisoned by silver metal buried in a melon's pink flesh. Emergency teams and police rushed to his apartment and confiscated the watermelon as evidence, while newspapers hurried to call it a terrorist act. But it was a false alarm. Doctors confirmed the next day that the policeman had been poisoned by liquid mercury found on the kitchen table."

Young toughs look for prey among the merchants. "When a group of drunk kids come and demand a melon in the middle of the night, I just tell my workers to hand it over," an Azeri vendor told the *Moscow Times*. In an especially ugly assault in St. Petersburg in 2002, a band of about twenty skinheads, some carrying metal bars, mauled and killed a fifty-three-year-old trader. The ruffians videotaped the attack.

Although derided by some Russians for its Central Asian connection, the watermelon is mostly an object of adulation. When they visit Tashkent or other capitals in the region, Muscovites love to stock up on watermelons. To prevent excess weight on their planes, it is said, Aeroflot carriers leaving Central Asia require passengers to discard watermelons from their overstuffed baggage.

Watermelons, which Russians pickle, make into beer, and snack on with white bread, are considered cleansing. "It gets rid of all the junk that is in your organism—all the junk that accumulates over the months," security guard Vladimir Speransky told *New York Times* reporter Clifford Levy. Some Russian sanatoriums even prescribe a watermelon diet for their patients.

Russian children, Levy points out, are introduced very early to the watermelon. In reading classes, instructors use the word for the fruit—*arbuz*—to teach the first word in the Russian alphabet.

Now the world's largest grower of watermelons, China has only been cultivating them since the twelfth century. A gift from its neighbors in Central Asia, the "Western melon" developed an enthusiastic following. "It is large and round like a gourd, and in color like green jade," the thirteenth-century physician Wu Zui wrote glowingly.

The Chinese have found ingenious uses for the fruit. Cut in half, the gourd has served as a container for steaming food. The rind has been pickled and also stir-fried. More than any other part of the watermelon, the seeds remain the greatest obsession of the Chinese. Some are so eager for them that they save the seeds and throw the gourd away. To satisfy the addiction, varieties were specially bred to have abundant seeds and minimal flesh.

Roasted and salted, the seeds are eagerly nibbled. So all-consuming is this pastime, food writer Amy Goldman says, that many Chinese have hollows in their teeth from years of prying open the seeds.

Watermelon seeds were shared affectionately on social and festive occasions. Hostesses have traditionally offered the seeds as gifts to guests. Customers congregating at teahouses and restaurants savored them. During the New Year's holiday, watermelon seeds were exchanged festively among friends and family.

Chin Tsing Fan, a well-born seventeenth-century lady, recounted one joyful gathering: "Playfully we break and extract the melon-seeds and arrange them into Buddhist symbols; for amusements we impress interlocking circles with the bottoms of our cups."

Abbé Huc, a nineteenth-century missionary who traveled through China, observed the watermelon habit condescendingly: "These watermelon seeds are indeed a treasure of cheap amusement for the three hundred million inhabitants of the Celestial Empire. They are an object of daily consumption . . . and it is amusing to see these extraordinary people munching these seeds before their meals to test the condition of their stomach and appetite. Their long and pointed nails are then extremely useful. The skill and rapidity with which they strip off the hard shell to obtain the tiny kernel must be seen to be appreciated. A troop of squirrels or apes could not manoeuvre more dexterously."

Their reputed medical properties enhanced the appeal of watermelons. One example of its powers impressed Hun Hao, a twelfth-century official: "In P'o-yan there lived a man who for a long time was afflicted with a disease of the eyes. Dried pieces of water-melon were applied to them and caused him relief, for the reason that cold is a property of this fruit."

The incorrigible watermelon enthusiasts kept up their habits in the modern era. During World War II, food writer Greg McNamee recounts, General Chiang Kai-shek demanded that US general Joe Stilwell supply each of his soldiers with a watermelon before they fought.

Several years ago, while exploring Boston's Chinatown, I discovered a surprising item on the menu of the China Pearl restaurant. The eatery's watermelon juice was popular among émigrés from the hot climates of Hong Kong and South China. Nearby, I watched black vendors pulling a cart loaded down with the gourds along the neighborhood's main street.

The watermelon moved west. The Moors, who transplanted spinach, pomegranates, eggplant, and other crops to Spain during their occupation of the country (711–1492), also grew watermelons. The Spanish name, *sandia*, comes from an Arabic word that refers to the Indian origins of the fruit. Already growing in Seville, the gourd caught the eye of Ibn al-Awwam, an Arabic writer in that city. Among the melons he observed were two that resemble the watermelon: "the melon of India . . . includes two varieties; the one has a black seed and the rind of this one is very dark green passing to black; the other has a pure red seed and the green color of its rind passes to yellow."

As the Islamic empire spread, the watermelon was carried to new regions. Candied watermelon and a nutty watermelon pudding, Sicilian delights, are undoubtedly legacies of the Muslim conquest of that island.

The climate of most of Western Europe, however, was not congenial for the fruit. Some Mediterranean households experimented with the import, but it lacked commercial promise. Dazzled by the wide range of black, brown, white, red, and speckled gourds, European botanists viewed the watermelon mostly as a curiosity.

The watermelon gained a foothold in the Americas as a result of early Spanish exploration. By 1576, settlers in Florida were harvesting the fruit. In Mexico and in Spanish territories in the American Southwest, the watermelon was also planted. Native Americans, who more than likely acquired it from Spanish traders and missionaries, were particularly fond of the new arrival. Seeds were passed from tribe to tribe. Less than a century later, the watermelon had reached Indian communities from the Great Lakes to the Mississippi Valley.

Why were the Indians so drawn to the watermelon? The fruit kept well and favored the long, hot summers so prevalent in North America. Most important, it probably reminded them of squash, a mainstay of their gardens, which was cultivated quite similarly.

English settlers soon adopted the plant. By the early 1600s, the fields of the Massachusetts Bay Colony were filled with gourds. A report from 1634 noted that farmers in Maryland were trying out "Musk-mellons, Water-Mellons, and Cow-cumbers." In 1793 Thomas Jefferson planted a "Neapolitan watermelon" in his garden. His watermelons, Jefferson wrote, were superior to those sold in Paris's markets. In France, "there is not enough sun to ripen them and give them flavour."

Americans were also devising new ways to make use of the fruit. Seventeenth-century Swedish geographer Peter Lindstrom found that watermelons along the Delaware River were being pressed to make cider. Other colonists, food historian William Woys Weaver reports, were boiling them to make an "ersatz molasses."

Cooks concocted a tangy condiment, watermelon pickle, made from cooking the white pieces of the rind in a sugar syrup infused with cloves and cinnamon and sharpened with vinegar. Its fans considered it a "sweet meat." The new country's first cookbook, *American Cookery*, written by Amelia Simmons and published in 1796, included a recipe for the pickle. This was the only watermelon dish included in early American cookbooks.

Slaves brought to the South from Africa were already conversant with watermelons. Watermelon seeds were one of a variety of items—sesame seeds, black-eyed peas—carried in the slave ships. Planted in rows in the plantation fields, the fruit was conveniently located for laborers who wanted to slake their thirst.

Because of the great affection blacks had for them, watermelons became a common feature of mocking stereotypes of African Americans. For most people, however, the watermelon was the epitome of unadulterated summer-time enjoyment. The watermelon, Mark Twain wrote in *Pudd'nhead Wilson*, was the loftiest pleasure imaginable. "The true Southern watermelon is a boon apart, and not to be mentioned with commoner things. When one has tasted it, he knows what the angels eat."

The mammoth watermelons of old, big enough to feed a large family or picnic gathering, are fast disappearing, made obsolete by breeders, marketers, and consumers with new preferences. New varieties are displacing the familiar heavy, oblong melons with thick rinds. A changing culture, many merchandisers are convinced, requires a different kind of watermelon. "People don't eat watermelon out of hand like they used to," Robert Schueller, public relations director of California distributor Melissa's Produce, told the *Washington Post*'s Jane Black.

Smaller, "personal" watermelons are more suited to the country's demographics. "Most people, particularly the urban people, would rather have a small one," Terry Kirkpatrick, a watermelon expert at the University of Arkansas, commented in an interview with *New York Times* reporter Kim Severson.

Nostalgic watermelon lovers lament the loss of the fruit's thick rind. For this reason it is harder these days, watermelon historian Ellen Ficklen says, to make watermelon pickle. "The growers want the thinnest possible rind that will protect the melon when it's shipped a long distance."

Seedless watermelons, which constitute more than half of today's market, are increasingly in vogue. Seeds seem to be just one more nuisance for the harried consumer. Robbed of the qualities that endeared it to cultures both old and modern, the watermelon is in danger of losing its vitality.

BIBLIOGRAPHY

Achaya, K. T. *Indian Food: A Historical Companion*. Delhi: Oxford University Press, 1994.

Akkad, Dania. "Thistle Stop: Artichoke Still King in Castroville." *Knight Ridder Tribune Business News*, May 20, 2006, p. 1.

Albala, Ken. *Beans: A History*. New York: Berg, 2007.

———. *Nuts: A Global History*. London: Reaktion Books, 2014.

Algar, Ayla Esen. *The Complete Book of Turkish Cooking*. London; New York: Kegan Paul International, 1995.

Allen, Gary J. *Herbs: A Global History*. London: Reaktion Books, 2012.

Allen, Stewart Lee. *The Devil's Cup: Coffee, the Driving Force in History*. New York: Soho, 1999.

Ames, Oakes. *Economic Annuals and Human Cultures*. Cambridge, MA: Botanical Museum of Harvard University, 1939.

Anderson, Burton. *America's Salad Bowl: An Agricultural History of the Salinas Valley*. Salinas, CA: Monterey County Historical Society, 2000.

———. *Treasures of the Italian Table: Italy's Celebrated Foods and the Artisans Who Make Them*. New York: William Morrow, 1994.

Anderson, E. N. *Food of China*. New Haven, CT: Yale University Press, 1988.

Anderson, Edgar. *Plants, Man, and Life*. Mineola, NY: Dover, 2005.

Andrews, Colman. *Flavors of the Riviera: Discovering Real Mediterranean Cooking*. New York: Bantam Books, 1996.

Andrews, Tamra. *Nectar & Ambrosia: An Encyclopedia of Food in World Mythology*. Santa Barbara, CA: ABC-CLIO, 2000.

Anusasananan, Linda Lau. "Aaahhh—Artichokes." *Sunset* 196, no. 4 (April 1996).

Apple, R. W., Jr. "Following the Pepper Grinder All the Way to Its Source." *New York Times*, October 29, 2003.

"Arak: Liquid Fire." *The Economist*, December 18, 2003. Online at http://www.economist.com/node/2281757. Accessed February 27, 2011.

Aregay, Merid Wolde. "The Early History of Ethiopia's Coffee Trade and the Rise of Shawa." *Journal of African History* 29, no. 1 (1988): 19–25.

Associated Press. "Lebanese to Israel: Hands Off Our Hummus!" *Haaretz*, October 24, 2009.

Atwood, Liz. "Good as Gold." *Baltimore Sun*, October 1, 2003, pp. 1F, 4F.

Ayto, John. *The Glutton's Glossary: A Dictionary of Food and Drink Terms*. London; New York: Routledge, 1990.

Bacon, Josephine. *Exotic Fruits and Vegetables A–Z*. Topsfield, MA: Salem House, 1988.

Baldwin, Brian. "The History of Cabbage." GardenLine, University of Saskatchewan. Available online at http://agbio.usask.ca/community-resources/gardenline/.

Banga, Otto. *Main Types of the Western Carotene Carrot and Their Origin*. Zwolle, The Netherlands: W. E. J. Tjeenk Willink, 1963.

Barboza, David. "You Asked for It, You Got It: The Pint-Size Watermelon." *New York Times*, June 15, 2003.

Barnett, Cynthia. "Cultivating Generations." *FloridaTrend*, September 1, 2006. Available online at http://www.floridatrend.com/article/10678/cultivating-generations. Accessed January 26, 2015.

——. "Keys to Survival." *Florida Trend*, September 1, 2006. Available online at http://www.floridatrend.com/article/10742/keys-to-survival. Accessed November 30, 2014.

Barrow, Mary Reid. "Fruit of August." *The Virginian-Pilot*, August 23, 2000.

Basan, Ghillie. *Classic Turkish Cooking*. London: I. B. Tauris, 2011.

Batmanglij, Najmieh. *A Taste of Persia: An Introduction to Persian Cooking*. Washington, DC: Mage, 2007.

Baumann, Hellmut. *The Greek Plant World in Myth, Art, and Literature*, translated by William T. and Eldwyth Ruth Stearn. Portland, OR: Timber Press, 1993.

Beard, James A. "The Caper Caper." *Los Angeles Times*, April 12, 1973.

Beauman, Fran. *The Pineapple: The King of Fruits*. London: Chatto & Windus, 2005.

Behr, Edward. *The Artful Eater: A Gourmet Investigates the Ingredients of Great Food*. New York: Atlantic Monthly Press, 1992.

Benghiat, Norma. *Traditional Jamaican Cookery*. London: Penguin, 1985.

Bermejo, J. Esteban Hernández, and Expiración García Sánchez. "Economic Botany and Ethnobotany in Al-Andalus (Iberian Peninsula: Tenth–Fifteenth Centuries), and Unknown Heritage of Mankind." *Economic Botany* 52, no. 1 (1998): 15–26.

Bermejo, J. Esteban Hernández, and J. León. *Neglected Crops: 1492 from a Different Perspective*. Rome: Food and Agriculture Organization of the United Nations, 1994.

Bernhardt, Peter. *Natural Affairs: A Botanist Looks at the Attachments between Plants and People*. New York: Villard Books, 1993.

Bhide, Monica. "Queen of Spices: Sweet, Strong, and Invigorating, Cardamom Is One of the World's Most Prized Ingredients." *Saveur* 128 (March 8, 2010).

Bitting, A. W. "The Art of Canning: Its History and Development." *The Trade Pressroom*, San Francisco, CA, 1937.

Bittman, Mark. "A Fruit that's Good to Eat Before It's Sweet." *New York Times*, February 1, 2006, p. D3.

Black, Jane. "Watermelons: What Happened to the Seeds?" *Washington Post*, August 31, 2010.

Bladholm, Linda. *The Asian Grocery Store Demystified*. Los Angeles: Renaissance Books, 1999.

———. *The Indian Grocery Store Demystified*. Los Angeles: Renaissance Books, 2000.

———. *Latin & Caribbean Grocery Stores Demystified*. Los Angeles: Renaissance Media, 2001.

Blake, A. "The Most Travelled Food in the World, the Peanut," in Harlan Walker, ed., *Oxford Symposium on Food & Cookery* (1996: Saint Antony's College). Devon, UK: Oxford University Press, 1997.

Blake, Leonard W. "Early Acceptance of Watermelon by Indians of the United States." *Journal of Ethnobiology* 1, no. 2 (December 1981): 193–99.

Bloch-Dano, Evelyne. *Vegetables: A Biography*. Chicago; London: University of Chicago Press, 2012.

Block, Eric. "The Chemistry of Garlic and Onions." *Scientific American* 252, no. 3 (March 1, 1985): 114–19.

———. *Garlic and Other Alliums: The Lore and the Science*. Cambridge: RSC, 2010.

Blumenthal, Heston. "The Nutty Professor." *The Guardian*, September 6, 2002. Available online at http://www.theguardian.com/lifeandstyle/2002/sep/07/foodanddrink.shopping1. Accessed December 5, 2014.

Boardman, J., Kathleen M. Kenyon, E. J. Moynahan, and J. D. Evans. "The Olive in the Mediterranean: Its Culture and Use." *Philosophical Transactions of the Royal Society B* 275, no. 936 (July 27, 1976): 187–94.

Bober, Phyllis Pray. *Art, Culture, and Cuisine: Ancient and Medieval Gastronomy*. Chicago: University of Chicago Press, 1999.

Borden, Neil Hopper. "D'Arrigo Brothers Company: Advertising of Branded Fresh Vegetables," in *Advertising: Text and Cases*. Chicago: R. D. Irwin, 1950.

Boswell, Victor R. "Our Vegetable Travelers." *National Geographic* 96, no. 2 (1949): 145–217.

Bowen, Dana. "Why We Love Watermelon." *Saveur* 113 (July 17, 2008): 72–86.

Boxer, Arabella. *Mediterranean Cookbook*. London: J. M. Dent, 1981.

Boxer, Charles Ralph. *The Portuguese Seaborne Empire, 1415–1825*. New York: Alfred A. Knopf, 1969.

Brandes, Stanley. "The Perilous Potato and the Terrifying Tomato," in Leonard Plotnicov and Richard Scaglion, eds., *Consequences of Cultivar Diffusion*. Pittsburgh: University of Pittsburgh, 1999.

Brennan, Jennifer. *Cuisines of Asia: Nine Great Oriental Cuisines by Technique*. New York: St. Martin's/Marek, 1984.

Brock, Wendell. "Deep Roots." *Saveur* 86 (August/September 2005): 80–89.

Brooke, Elizabeth Heilman. "Brazil's Cooling Alternative to All That Coffee? Fruit Juice." *New York Times*, February 21, 1990, Section C, p. 4.

Brooks, Andree. "When Household Habits Betrayed the Jews." *New York Times*, February 20, 1997.

Brown, Cora Lovisa, Rose Johnston Brown, and Bob Brown. *The South American Cook Book, Including Central America, Mexico, and the West Indies.* New York: Dover, 1971.

Bruman, Henry J. "The Culture History of Mexican Vanilla." *Hispanic American Historical Review* 28 (August 1948): 360–76.

"Bugle Heralds Artichoke Ban by La Guardia." *Chicago Tribune,* December 22, 1935, p. 15.

Bullen, Claire. "Kick the Cold with Spicy Cardamom." *Columbia Spectator,* November 2008. Available online at http://columbiaspectator.com/2008/02/03/kick-cold-spicy-cardamom. Accessed January 5, 2015.

Burkill, Isaac Henry. *A Dictionary of the Economic Products of the Malay Peninsula.* London: published on behalf of the governments of the Straits settlements and Federated Malay states by the Crown agents for the colonies, 1935.

——. "Habits of Man and the Origins of the Cultivated Plants of the Old World." *Proceedings of the Linnean Society of London Session 1951–1952* 164, no. 1 (March 1953): 12–42.

Burros, Marian. "Eating Well: Another Reason to Eat Cranberries." *New York Times,* November 21, 2001.

Burton, David. *Savouring the East: Feasts and Stories from Istanbul to Bali.* London: Faber & Faber, 1998.

"California Artichoke and Vegetable Growers Corporation: A Short History." Document provided to author by California Artichoke Advisory Board.

Canine, Craig. "Building a Better Banana." *Smithsonian Magazine* 36, no. 7 (October 1, 2005): 97–105.

Capatti, Alberto, and Massimo Montanari. *Italian Cuisine: A Cultural History,* translated by Aine O'Healy. New York: Columbia University Press, 2003.

Carney, Judith Ann. *In the Shadow of Slavery: Africa's Botanical Legacy in the Atlantic World.* Berkeley: University of California Press, 2009.

"Cashew Juice Makes Use of the 'Apple' Part of the Plant." *Montreal Gazette,* June 7, 2008.

Castelli, Artie C., and C. A. Castelli. *The Sensuous Artichoke: Magic of the Artichoke.* Riverdale, NY: A. C. Castelli Associates, 1998.

Castelvetro, Giacomo. *The Fruit, Herbs and Vegetables of Italy: An Offering to Lucy, Countess of Bedford,* translated by Gillian Riley. Totnes, Devon, UK: Prospect Books, 2012.

"Celery Cultivation." Available online at MIGenWeb, http://www.migenweb.org/kalamazoo/celeryflats.htm. Accessed February 3, 2015.

Chang, Kenneth. "Before Kisses and Snickers, It Was the Treat of Royalty." *New York Times,* June 10, 2003, p. D1.

Chang, K. C., ed. *Food in Chinese Culture: Anthropological and Historical Perspectives.* New Haven, CT: Yale University Press, 1977.

Charles, Jeffrey. "Searching for Gold in Guacamole: California Growers Marketing the Avocado 1910–1994," in Warren Belasco and Philip Scranton, eds., *Food Nations: Selling Taste in Consumer Societies,* 131–54. New York: Routledge, 2002.

Christensen, Judy. "Pomegranate, the Fruit of Temptation." *Shelburne News,* December 20, 2001, p. 11.

Ciezadlo, Annia. *Day of Honey: A Memoir of Food, Love, and War.* New York: Free Press, 2011.

Clément-Mullet, J.-J. *Le Livre de l'Agriculture.* Tunis, Tunisia: Les Editions Bouslama, 1977.

Coe, Sophie Dobzhansky. *America's First Cuisines*. Austin: University of Texas Press, 1994.

Coe, Sophie Dobzhansky, and Michael D. Coe. *The True History of Chocolate*. London: Thames & Hudson, 2013.

Cooley, J. S. "The Sweet Potato—Its Origin and Primitive Storage Practices." *Economic Botany* 5, no. 4 (October–December 1951): 378–86.

Corn, Charles. *The Scents of Eden: A Narrative of the Spice Trade*. New York: Kodansha International, 1998.

Correll, Donovan S. "Vanilla—Its Botany, History, Cultivation, and Economic Impact." *Economic Botany* (1953): 291–358.

Cost, Bruce. *Bruce Cost's Asian Ingredients: Buying and Cooking the Staple Foods of China, Japan, and Southeast Asia*. New York: William Morrow, 1988.

Crosby, Alfred W. *The Columbian Exchange: Biological and Cultural Consequences of 1492*. Westport, CT: Praeger, 2003.

———. *Ecological Imperialism: The Biological Expansion of Europe, 900–1900*. Cambridge: Cambridge University Press, 1986.

Culpeper, Nicholas. *Culpeper's Complete Herbal*. London: Milner and Company, 1880.

Dalby, Andrew. "Christopher Columbus, Gonzalo Pizarro, and the Search for Cinnamon." *Gastronomica* 1, no. 2 (Spring 2001).

———. *Dangerous Tastes: The Story of Spices*. Berkeley: University of California Press, 2000.

———. *Food in the Ancient World, from A to Z*. London; New York: Routledge, 2003.

———. *Siren Feasts: A History of Food and Gastronomy in Greece*. London; New York: Routledge, 1997.

Damrosch, Barbara. "Celery Worth the Trouble to Grow." *Washington Post*, March 18, 2004, p. H08.

Darby, William Jefferson, Paul Ghalioungui, and Louis Grivetti. *Food: The Gift of Osiris*. London; New York: Academic Press, 1977.

Darrah, Helen H. "The basils in folklore and biological science." *The Herbarist* 38 (1972): 3–10.

"D'Arrigo Bros. Co. of California Celebrates Diamond Anniversary." Pamphlet, n.d.

Darrow, George M. *The Strawberry: History, Breeding, and Physiology*. New York: Holt, Rinehart & Winston, 1966.

Dasgupta, KumKum. "Will Feni Be the New Tequila?" *Hindustan Times*, December 2, 2007, p. 16.

Daunay, Marie-Christine, and Jules Janick. "History and Iconography of Eggplant." *Chronica Horticulturae* 47, no. 3 (2007): 16–22.

Davenport, Philippa. "Food, Fuel, Medicine and Magic." *Financial Times*, August 14–15, 2004, p. W9.

Davidson, Alan, and Charlotte Knox. *Fruit: A Connoisseur's Guide and Cookbook*. New York: Simon & Schuster, 1991.

Davidson, Alan, and Tom Jaine, ed. *The Oxford Companion to Food*. New York: Oxford University Press, 2014.

De Andrade, Margarette. *Brazilian Cookery, Traditional and Modern*. Rutland, VT: C. E. Tuttle, 1965.

Denker, Joel Sibley. "The Artichoke Wars." October 2013. Available online at http://www .foodpassages.com. Accessed December 23, 2014.

——. *The World on a Plate: A Tour through the History of America's Ethnic Cuisine.* Lincoln, NE: Westview Press, 2003.

der Haroutunian, Arto. *Middle Eastern Cookery.* London: Grub Street, 2010.

Détienne, Marcel. *The Gardens of Adonis: Spices in Greek Mythology*, translated by Janet Lloyd. Princeton, NJ: Princeton University Press, 1994.

de Vilmorin, Roger L. "Pascal Celery and Its Origin." *Journal of the New York Botanical Garden* 51 (1950): 39–41.

"Dhatri Launches Toothpaste." *Hindu Businessline.* October 13, 2008.

Diamond, Jared M. *Guns, Germs, and Steel: The Fates of Human Societies.* New York: Norton, 2005.

——. "Location, Location, Location: The First Farmers." *Science* 278, no. 4 (November 1997): 1243–44.

Dickerman, Sara. "Queen of Hearts." *New York Times Magazine*, May 27, 2007.

Dickie, James. "The Islamic Garden in Spain," in Elisabeth B. MacDougall and Richard Ettinghausen, eds., *The Islamic Garden*, 87–107. Washington, DC: Dumbarton Oaks, Trustees for Harvard University, 1976.

Dicum, Gregory. "Colony in a Cup." *Gastronomica* 3, no. 2 (Spring 2003): 71.

Di Renzo, Anthony. *Bitter Greens: Essays on Food, Politics, and Ethnicity from the Imperial Kitchen.* Albany: Excelsior Editions/State University of New York Press, 2010.

Disney, Anthony R. *Twilight of the Pepper Empire: Portuguese Trade in Southwest India in the Early Seventeenth Century.* Cambridge, MA: Harvard University Press, 1978.

Dondero, Raymond Stevenson. *The Italian Settlement of San Francisco.* San Francisco: R & E Research Associates, 1974.

Donkin, Robin A. *Between East and West: The Moluccas and the Traffic in Spices up to the Arrival of Europeans.* Philadelphia: American Philosophical Society, 2003.

Dunmire, William W. *Gardens of New Spain: How Mediterranean Plants and Foods Changed America.* Austin: University of Texas Press, 2004.

Ecott, Tim. *Vanilla: Travels in Search of the Ice Cream Orchid.* New York: Grove Press, 2004.

Edge, John T. "The Celery Soda Chronicles." Gourmet.com, May 26, 2009. Available online at http://www.gourmet.com/food/2009/05/the-celery-soda-chronicles.html. Accessed January 26, 2015.

——. "Hummus Catches On in America (as Long as It's Flavored)." *New York Times*, June 15, 2010.

Ehret, Christopher. "On the Antiquity of Agriculture in Ethiopia." *Journal of African History* 20, no. 2 (April 1979): 161–77.

Eiselen, Elizabeth. "Celery Growing in the United States." *Journal of Geography* 37, no. 1 (January 1938): 32–36.

Elliott, Stuart. "A Pitch for Hummus Goes Nationwide." *New York Times*, June 6, 2010.

Erlanger, Steven. "Racial Undertones Emerge in Reactions to France's Exit from the World Cup." *New York Times*, June 24, 2010, p. A4.

Estabrook, Barry. "The Other Side of the Valley." *Gastronomica* 11, no. 4 (November 25, 2011).

Fabricant, Florence. "The Capers Caper: Maybe This Bud's for You." *Nation's Restaurant News* 30, no. 39 (October 7, 1996): 45.

Facciola, Stephen. *Cornucopia II: A Sourcebook of Edible Plants.* Vista, CA: Kampong, 1998.

Faust, Joan Lee. "Sing a Song of Spices, Cinnamon for Sure." *New York Times*, December 7, 1995.

Fearnley-Whittingstall, Hugh. "Golden Wonders." *The Guardian*, July 11, 2008.

———. "Hugh Fearnley-Whittingstall's Caper Recipes." *The Guardian*, January 13, 2012.

Feldman, Charles, and Kathleen Bauer. "Flavoring Culture / Le Goût pour la Cannelle." *Anthropology of Food*, December 15, 2008. Available online at http://aof.revues.org/5162. Accessed January 27, 2014.

Fernandez, Rafi. *Malaysian Cookery.* London: Penguin Books, 1997.

Fernández de Oviedo y Valdés, Gonzalo. *Natural History of the West Indies*, translated and edited by Sterling A. Stoudemire. Chapel Hill: University of North Carolina Press, 1959.

Fernández-Armesto, Felipe. *Near a Thousand Tables: A History of Food.* New York: Free Press, 2002.

Ferrary, Jeanette. "Eat Your Heart Out." *VIA* magazine, May 2000, http://viamagazine.com/top_stories/articles/artichokes00.asp. Accessed August 20, 2004.

Ficklen, Ellen. "Making More of Watermelons." *Washington Post*, July 17, 2002.

———. *Watermelon.* Washington, DC: American Folklife Center, The Library of Congress, 1984.

First, Devra. "Red Menace." Boston.com, August 15, 2010. Available online at http://www.boston.com/bostonglobe/ideas/articles/2010/08/15/red_menace/. Accessed December 22, 2014.

Flandrin, Jean-Louis, and Massimo Montanari. *Food: A Culinary History from Antiquity to the Present*, English edition by Albert Sonnenfeld, translated by Clarissa Botsford, Arthur Goldhammer, Charles Lambert, Frances M. López-Morillas, and Sylvia Stevens. New York: Columbia University Press, 1999.

Fletcher, Janet. "Yogurt Salad: Cool and Cultured." *San Francisco Chronicle*, August 2, 2006.

Fletcher, June. "Pushing the Envelope on Vegetables." *Wall Street Journal*, May 16, 2008.

Flint-Hamilton, Kimberly B. "Legumes in Ancient Greece and Rome: Food, Medicine, or Poison." *Hesperia* 68, no. 3 (July–September 1999): 371–85.

Ford, Richard. *Gatherings from Spain.* Paris: A. and W. Galignani and Co., 1849.

Fortini, Amanda. "Pomegranate Princess." *New Yorker* 84, no. 7 (March 31, 2008): 92–99.

Foster, Nelson, and Linda S. Cordell, eds. *Chilies to Chocolate: Food the Americas Gave the World.* Tucson: University of Arizona Press, 1992.

Frank, Robert. "Going for 'The Gold' Turns Pineapple World Upside Down." *Wall Street Journal*, October 7, 2003, pp. A1, A14.

Freedman, Paul, ed. *Food: The History of Taste.* Berkeley: University of California Press, 2007.

———. *Out of the East: Spices and the Medieval Imagination.* New Haven, CT: Yale University Press, 2008.

Freyre, Gilberto. *The Masters and the Slaves (Casa-Grande & Senzala): A Study in the Development of Brazilian Civilization*, translated by Samuel Putnam. New York: Knopf, 1964.

Friedland, Susan R. *Vegetables: Proceedings of the Oxford Symposium on Food and Cookery 2008.* Totnes, Devon, UK: Prospect Books, 2009.

Fusco, Mary Ann Castronovo. "Pineapple Is Every Season's Sweet Showoff." *Star-Ledger*, March 10, 2014.

Fussell, Betty Harper. *I Hear America Cooking: The Cooks and Recipes of American Regional Cuisine*. New York: Penguin Books, 1997.

Gabaccia, Donna R. "Ethnicity in the Business World: Italians in American Food Industries." November 1997, copy of lecture sent to author.

——. "Pizza, Pasta and Red Sauce: Italian or American?" *Migration* 11 (Autumn 2006). Available online at http://www.history.ac.uk/ihr/Focus/Migration/articles/gabaccia.html. Accessed December 22, 2014.

——. *We Are What We Eat: Ethnic Food and the Making of Americans*. Cambridge, MA: Harvard University Press, 1998.

Garfield, Eugene. "From Tonic to Psoriasis: Stalking Celery's Secrets." *Essays of an Information Scientist* 8 (May 6, 1985): 164–73.

Gentilcore, David. *Pomodori!: A History of the Tomato in Italy*. New York: Columbia University Press, 2010.

Gerard, John. *The Herbal: or, General History of Plants*. New York: Dover, 1975.

Gibson, Walter S. "The Strawberries of Hieronymus Bosch." *Cleveland Studies in the History of Art* 8 (2003): 25.

Gitlitz, David M., and Linda Kay Davidson. *A Drizzle of Honey: The Lives and Recipes of Spain's Secret Jews*. New York: St. Martin's Press, 1999.

Goldman, Amy. *Melons for the Passionate Grower*. New York: Artisan, 2002.

Gollner, Adam Leith. "The Glabrous Apricots of Tajikistan." *Hazlitt*, November 19, 2012.

Goodman, Matthew. *Jewish Food: The World at Table*. New York: HarperCollins, 2005.

Goody, Jack. *Cooking, Cuisine, and Class: A Study in Comparative Sociology*. Cambridge; New York: Cambridge University Press, 1982.

Goor, Asaph. "The Place of the Olive in the Holy Land and Its History through the Ages." *Economic Botany* 20, no. 3 (July–September 1966): 223–43.

Goor, Asaph, and Max Nurock. *Fruits of the Holy Land*. Jerusalem: Israel Universities Press, 1968.

Gould, Kevin. "Bands of Gold." Available online at Spudbucket.com, http://spudbucket.blogspot.com/2006/08/bands-of-gold-what-middle-east-and-my.html. Accessed January 30, 2015.

Grafton, Gillian. "Pears and Perry in the UK." The New Real Cider & Perry Page, January 15, 1996. Available online at http://homepage.ntlworld.com/scrumpy/cider/history2.htm. Accessed January 10, 2015.

Gray, Patience. *Honey from a Weed: Fasting and Feasting in Tuscany, Catalonia, the Cyclades, and Apulia*. Devon, UK: Prospect Books, 2002.

Green, Aliza. *Beans: More than 200 Delicious, Wholesome Recipes from around the World*. Philadelphia: Running Press, 2004.

Greenberg, Sheldon, and Elisabeth Lambert Ortiz. *The Spice of Life*. London: Michael Joseph/Rainbird, 1983.

Grewe, Rudolph. "The Arrival of the Tomato in Spain and Italy: Early Recipes." *Journal of Gastronomy* 3, no. 2 (Summer 1987): 67–81.

Grieve, Maud. *A Modern Herbal: The Medicinal, Culinary, Cosmetic, and Economic Properties, Cultivation, and Folklore of Herbs, Grasses, Fungi, Shrubs, and Trees with All Their Modern Scientific Uses*. New York: Hafner Press, 1974.

Griffin, Kawanza L. "Root Work: Carrots' Nutrients Can Be Judged by the Color of Their Skin, Studies Find." *Milwaukee Journal-Sentinel Online*, http://www2.jsonline.com/alive/nutrition/oct01/carrots29102801.asp. Accessed June 18, 2008.

Grigg, David. "Food Consumption in the Mediterranean Region." *Tijdschrift voor economische en sociale geografie* 90, no. 4 (November 1999): 391–409.

Grigson, Jane. *Jane Grigson's Vegetable Book*. Lincoln: University of Nebraska Press, 2007.

Halici, Nevin. *Nevin Halici's Turkish Cookbook*. London: Dorling Kindersley, 1991.

Hall, Trish. "Broccoli, Hated by a President, Is Capturing Popular Votes." *New York Times*, March 25, 1992, p. C1.

Hamilton, Cherie Y. *Cuisines of Portuguese Encounters: Recipes from Portugal, Angola, Brazil, Cape Verde, East Timor, Goa, Guinea-Bissau, Macao, Malacca, Mozambique, São Tomé and Príncipe*. New York: Hippocrene Books, 2008.

Hammond, Norman. "Domestication of the Chickpea Required Summer Irrigation and the Scientific Skills Available at Kharsag." *The Daily Telegraph*, July 3, 2007.

Hanes, Stephanie. "Where Cashew Is King, It Fails to Rule the Economy." *Christian Science Monitor*, July 24, 2008.

Harris, Jessica B. *The Africa Cookbook: Tastes of a Continent*. New York: Simon & Schuster, 1998.

———. *Iron Pots and Wooden Spoons: Africa's Gifts to New World Cooking*. New York: Simon & Schuster, 1999.

———. "You Say Potato, I Say Yam." *New York Times*, November 25, 2009, p. A27.

Harvey, John H. "Gilliflower and Carnation." *Garden History* 6, no. 1 (Spring 1978): 46–57.

Hathaway, Nancy. "Artichoke City: Castroville Is Connected to Its Most Famous Product in the Same Way Detroit Is Connected to the Automobile." *Christian Science Monitor*, September 1, 1987.

Hattox, Ralph S. *Coffee and Coffeehouses: The Origins of a Social Beverage in the Medieval Near East*. Seattle: University of Washington Press, 1988.

Haughton, Claire Shaver. *Green Immigrants: The Plants that Transformed America*. New York: Harcourt Brace, 1978.

Hawkes, J. G. *The Potato: Evolution, Biodiversity & Genetic Resources*. Washington, DC: Smithsonian Institution Press, 1990.

Hawkes, J. G., and J. Francisco-Ortega. "The Potato in Spain during the Late 16th Century." *Economic Botany* 46, no. 1 (1992): 86–97.

Hayes, Jack. "Chai Spices Up Beverage Segment." *Nation's Restaurant News* 37, no. 31 (August 4, 2003): 31.

Hedrick, U. P. *A History of Horticulture in America to 1860*. Portland, OR: Timber Press, 1988.

———. *The Pears of New York*. Albany: J. B. Lyon, 1921.

Hehn, Victor. *Cultivated Plants and Domesticated Animals in Their Migration from Asia to Europe: Historico-Linguistic Studies*. Amsterdam: John Benjamins, 1976.

Heiser, Charles Bixler, Jr. *Nightshades the Paradoxical Plants*. San Francisco: W. H. Freeman, 1969.

——. *Of Plants and People*. Norman: University of Oklahoma Press, 1985.

——. *Seed to Civilization: The Story of Food*. Cambridge, MA: Harvard University Press, 1990.

Helou, Anissa. *Lebanese Cuisine*. London: Grub Street, 2009.

——. *Mediterranean Street Food: Stories, Soups, Snacks, Sandwiches, Barbecues, Sweets, and More, from Europe, North Africa, and the Middle East*. New York: HarperCollins, 2002.

Henderson, Stephen G. "The Queen of Spices: Cardamom Rules in India, Enlivening Dishes from Mangoes to Vindaloo with Clean, Bright Flavor." *Baltimore Sun*, May 3, 2006, p. 4F.

Henry, Diana. *Crazy Water Pickled Lemons: Enchanting Dishes from the Middle East, Mediterranean and North Africa*. London: Mitchell Beazley, 2012.

Herzog, Karen. "A Supercarrot, Purple Carrot, and Other Root Causes: Why the Familiar Orange Article Is a Happy Accident." *Milwaukee Journal Sentinel*, October 29, 1995, Lifestyle and Food, p. 1.

Hesser, Amanda. "En Route: France; Where the Noble White Asparagus Is King." *New York Times*, May 27, 1998.

——. "Follow that Watermelon." *New York Times*, July 18, 2001.

——. "From Out of the Mists: The Artichoke." *New York Times*, March 10, 1999, p. D1.

——. "The Midas Spice: From Flower to Saffron." *New York Times*, October 27, 1999, pp. D1, D6.

——. "The Plantain: Anything You Want It to Be." *New York Times*, July 29, 1998, pp. C1, C4.

Higman, B. W. *Jamaican Food: History, Biology, Culture*. Jamaica: University of the West Indies Press, 2008.

"History of Celery in Kalamazoo." Kalamazoo County, Michigan, United States MIGenWeb page. Online at http://www.migenweb.org/kalamazoo/celery.htm#Celery%20in%20Kalamazoo. Accessed July 13, 2010.

Ho, Ping-ti. "The Introduction of American Food Plants into China." *American Anthropologist* 57, no. 2 (April 1955): 191–201.

Hobhouse, Henry. *Seeds of Change: Five Plants that Transformed Mankind*. New York: Harper & Row, 1986.

Hoexter, Corinne K. "Fare of the Country: On the Cape, Cranberries Everywhere." *New York Times*, December 4, 2008.

Holloway, Joseph E. "African Crops and Slave Cuisines." Available online on the *Slave Rebellion* website, http://slaverebellion.org/index.php?page=crops-slave-cuisines. Accessed October 23, 2014.

Hooker, Richard. *Food and Drink in America: A History*. Indianapolis: Bobbs-Merrill, 1981.

"How Ocean Spray Gave Cranberries Some Sparkle." *New York Times*, November 26, 1992.

Hudak, Andrew F. *Slovaks in Florida*. Winter Park, FL: Agency DaVel, 1991.

"Hugo Tottino: An Artichoke Perennial." *Produce News*, May 1, 2006. Available online at http://www.producenews.com/category-list/10-feature-cat/1232-1115. Accessed December 7, 2014.

Hultman, Tami, ed. *The Africa News Cookbook: African Cooking for Western Kitchens*. New York: Viking, 1986.

Humphries, John. *The Essential Saffron Companion*. Berkeley: Ten Speed Press, 1996.

Hyams, Edward. *Plants in the Service of Man: 10,000 Years of Domestication*. London: J. M. Dent & Sons, 1971.

Jackson, Ian. "Formulae Most Secret: Fragments of the History of the Pear." *Petits Propos Culinaires* 49 (1995): 7–17.

Jaffrey, Madhur. *Climbing the Mango Trees: A Memoir of a Childhood in India*. London: Ebury, 2005.

——. *An Invitation to Indian Cooking*, Hopewell, NJ: Ecco Press, 1999.

——. *A Taste of India*. New York: Atheneum, 1986.

Jakle, John A., and James O. Wheeler. "The Changing Residential Structure of the Dutch Population in Kalamazoo, Michigan." *Annals of the Association of American Geographers* 59, No. 3 (1969): 441–60.

Janick, Jules. "The Pear in History, Literature, Popular Culture, and Art," in L. Corelli-Grapadelli, J. Janick, S. Sansavini, M. Tagliavini, D. Sugar, A. D. Webster (eds.), *Proceedings of the Eighth International Symposium on Pear, Volume 1, Acta Horticulturae 596*. Leuven, Belgium: International Society for Horticultural Science (2002): 41–42.

Janick, Jules, and James N. Moore, eds. *Advances in Fruit Breeding*. West Lafayette, IN: Purdue University Press, 1975.

Jefford, Andrew. "A Toast to Absinthe Friends." *London Evening Standard*, July 7, 1992, p. 36.

Jenkins, J. A. "The Origin of the Cultivated Tomato." *Economic Botany* 2, no. 4 (October–December 1948): 379–92.

Jenkins, Nancy Harmon. *The Essential Mediterranean: How Regional Cooks Transform Key Ingredients into the World's Favorite Cuisines*. New York: HarperCollins, 2003.

Johnson, Dennis Victor. "The Cashew of Northeast Brazil: A Geographical Study of a Tropical Tree Crop." PhD dissertation, Geography. Los Angeles: University of California, 1972.

Johnson, Robert. "Saffron and the Good Life." *Petits Propos Culinaires* 41 (1992): 30–51.

Jolique. "The Origins of Eau de Cologne." Available online at https://archive.is/kg68F. Accessed January 9, 2015.

Jones, Evan. *American Food: The Gastronomic Story*. New York: Vintage Books, 1981.

Kaneva-Johnson, Maria. *The Melting Pot: Balkan Food and Cookery*. Totnes, Devon, UK: Prospect, 1999.

Kantor, Jodi. "A History of the Mideast in the Humble Chickpea." *New York Times*, July 10, 2002, pp. D1, D10.

Karnes, Thomas L. *Tropical Enterprise: The Standard Fruit and Steamship Company in Latin America*. Baton Rouge: Louisiana State University Press, 1978.

Karp, David. "Pomegranates for One and All." *New York Times*, October 30, 2002, p. D1.

——. "The Skin Isn't Great, But the Heart Is Pure Gold." *New York Times*, June 25, 2003, p. 1.

——. "Strawberries and Dreams." *New York Times*, April 13, 2005, p. 12.

——. "Sweet Rewards for Apricot Explorers." *New York Times*, June 18, 2008.

Katz, Solomon H., and William Woys Weaver, eds. *Encyclopedia of Food and Culture*. New York: Scribner, 2003.

Kawash, Samira. "Sex and Candy." *New York Times*, February 14, 2014, p. A25.

Kazin, Alfred. *A Walker in the City*. New York: Grove Press, 1958.

Keay, John. *The Spice Route: A History*. Berkeley: University of California Press, 2006.

Kelsey, Mary Wallace. "Mints: The Stray Cats of Herbs," in Harlan Walker, ed., *Spicing Up the Palate: Proceedings of the Oxford Symposium on Food & Cookery (1992: Saint Antony's College)*, 145. Blackawton, UK: Prospect Books, 1993.

Kennedy, Diana. *The Cuisines of Mexico*. New York: Harper & Row, 1986.

Kinzer, Stephen. "Thoughts on Drinking of Raki." Available online at http://www.turkishcul ture.org/culinary-arts/cuisine/raki/thoughts-on-drinking-309.htm?type=1. Accessed April 23, 2006.

Kiple, Kenneth F., and Kriemhild Coneè Ornelas, eds. *The Cambridge World History of Food*, volume 1 and volume 2. Cambridge; New York: Cambridge University Press, 2000.

Kleiman, Dena. "New York Puts Its Papaya Where Its Hot Dogs Are." *New York Times*, August 21, 1991.

Kleinberg, Ann. *Pomegranates*. Berkeley: Ten Speed Press, 2004.

Koeppel, Dan. *Banana: The Fate of the Fruit that Changed the World*. New York: Plume Books, 2008.

——. "Fruit of the Future: Is the World Headed for a Banana Revolution?" Saveur.com, April 5, 2010. Available online at http://www.saveur.com/article/Kitchen/Fruit-of-the-Future. Accessed January 5, 2015.

Krapovikas, A. "The Origin, Variability, and Spread of the Groundnut (*Arachis hypogaea*)," in Peter J. Ucko and G. W. Dimbleby, eds., *The Domestication and Exploitation of Plants and Animals*. London: Duckworth, 1969.

Krondl, Michael. *The Taste of Conquest: The Rise and Fall of the Three Great Cities of Spice*. New York: Ballantine Books, 2007.

"La Granada—The Pomegranate in New Spain." *Collector's Guide*. Available online at http:// www.collectorsguide.com/fa/fa115.shtml. Accessed December 24, 2014.

Land, Leslie. "Plain Vanilla." *Journal of Gastronomy* 2, no. 4 (1986–1987).

Langer, Richard W. "Dill: The Herb that Time Forgot." *New York Times*, June 7, 2000, p. F5.

Laszlo, Pierre. *Citrus: A History*. Chicago: University of Chicago Press, 2007.

Laudan, Rachel. "Agua Fresca 20. From Apricot Leather (Amardine)," January 26, 2009. Available online at http://www.rachellaudan.com/2009/01/agua-fresca-20-from-apricot-leather-amardine.html. Accessed December 23, 2014.

——. *Cuisine and Empire: Cooking in World History*. Berkeley: University of California Press, 2013.

Laufer, Berthold. "The American Plant Migration." *Scientific Monthly* 28 (March 1929): 239–51.

——. *Sino-Iranica: Chinese Contributions to the History of Civilization in Ancient Iran, with Special Reference to the History of Cultivated Plants and Products*. New York: Kraus Reprint Corp., 1967.

Laurioux, Bruno. "Spices in the Medieval Diet: A New Approach." *Food and Foodways* 1 (1985): 43–75.

Law, Ruth. *The Southeast Asia Cookbook*. New York: D. I. Fine, 1990.

Lawrence, Janet. "Cardomom," in Harlan Walker, ed., *Spicing up the Palate: Proceedings of the Oxford Symposium on Food & Cookery (1992: Saint Antony's College).* Blackawton, UK: Prospect Books, 1993.

Lawrence, Sue. "Pod Casting." *Scotland on Sunday,* November 13, 2005, p. 24.

Lawton, Barbara Perry. *Parsleys, Fennels, and Queen Anne's Lace: Herbs and Ornamentals from the Umbel Family.* Portland, OR: Timber Press, 2007.

Leach, Helen. "Rehabilitating the 'Stinking Herbe': A Case Study of Culinary Prejudice." *Gastronomica* 1, no. 2 (Spring 2001): 10–15.

Lee, Matt, and Ted Lee. "Chocolate, Lemon, Clove: Yes, This Is Basil." *New York Times,* June 28, 2000, p. D1.

Lehner, Ernst and Johanna. *Folklore and Symbolism of Flowers, Plants and Trees.* New York: Tudor, 1960.

———. *Folklore & Odysseys of Food & Medicinal Plants.* New York: Farrar, Straus and Giroux, 1973.

Leonard, Jonathan Norton. *Latin American Cooking.* New York: Time-Life Books, 1968.

Levenstein, Harvey A. "The American Response to Italian Food, 1880–1930." *Food and Foodways* 1, no. 1 (1985): 1–24.

Levenstein, Harvey A., and J. R. Conlin. "The Food Habits of Italian Immigrants to America: An Examination of the Persistence of a Food Culture and the Rise of 'Fast Food' in America," in Ray B. Browne, Marshall W. Fishwick, and Kevin O. Browne, eds., *Dominant Symbols in Popular Culture,* 231–46. Bowling Green, OH: Bowling Green State University Popular Press, 1990.

Levy, Clifford J. "Seeking Purification at Russia's Melon Stands." *New York Times,* September 21, 2009.

Levy, Faye. "Stick with Carrots." *Jerusalem Post,* September 10, 2009.

Lin, Judith. "Kalamazoo, MI: Celery Days." *Chicago Reader,* September 6, 1990. Available online at http://www.chicagoreader.com/chicago/kalamazoo-mi-celery-days/Content?oid=876254. Accessed November 30, 2014.

Lovelock, Yann. *The Vegetable Book: An Unnatural History.* New York: St. Martin's Press, 1972.

Luard, Elisabeth. *The Latin American Kitchen: A Book of Essential Ingredients with More than 200 Authentic Recipes.* San Diego, CA: Laurel Glen, 2002.

———. *The Old World Kitchen: The Rich Tradition of European Peasant Cooking.* Brooklyn: Melville House, 2013.

Lubinsky, Pesach, Séverine Bory, Juan Hernández-Hernández, Seung-Chul Kim, and Arturo Gómez-Pompa. "Origins and Dispersal of Cultivated Vanilla (Vanilla Planifolia Jacks. [Orchidaceae])." *Economic Botany* 62, no. 2 (2008): 127–38.

Lucier, Gary, and Biing-Hwan Lin. "Stalking Celery." *Agricultural Outlook,* Economic Research Service, USDA (November 2000): 4–7.

Lunde, Paul. "New World Foods, Old World Diet." *Saudi Aramco World* 43, no. 3 (May/June 1992): 47–55.

Luxner, Larry. "The Cardamom Connection." *Saudi Aramco World* 48, no. 2 (March/April 1997): 28–31.

MacFarquhar, Neil. "Lebanon's Stills, Chilled by War, Are Rekindling the Old Fire." *New York Times*, January 19, 2005, Section F, p. 3.

MacKie, Cristine. *Life and Food in the Caribbean*. New York: New Amsterdam Books, 1992.

"Making a Killing in the Artichoke Market." December 21, 1935, Foggy Gardens. Available online at http://siftingsoil.blogspot.com/2010/06/aristocratic-thistle-artichoke-half.html. Accessed December 24, 2014.

Manniche, Lise. *An Ancient Egyptian Herbal*. Austin: University of Texas Press, 1989.

Margolick, David. "The Seeds of a Summer Revolt." *New York Times*, August 15, 2003.

Marks, Copeland. *The Exotic Kitchens of Peru: The Land of the Inca*. Lanham, MD: M. Evans, 1999.

Marks, Copeland, and Mintari Soeharjo. *The Indonesian Kitchen*. New York: Atheneum, 1981.

Mason, Laura. *Sugar-Plums and Sherbet: The Prehistory of Sweets*. Totnes, Devon, UK: Prospect Books, 2004.

Mattingly, D. J. "First Fruit? The Olive in the Roman World," in G. Shipley and J. Salmon, eds., *Human Landscapes in Classical Antiquity: Environment and Culture*, 213–53. London: Routledge, 1996.

——. "Oil for Export? A Comparison of Libyan, Spanish and Tunisian Olive Oil Production in the Roman Empire." *Journal of Roman Archaeology* 1 (1988): 33–56.

May, Allan. "Tales of the Artichoke King." *Crime Magazine*. Available online at http://cm.vndevgroup.com/tales-artichoke-king. Accessed December 7, 2014.

Maynard, Donald N., Xingping Zhang, and Jules Janick. "Watermelons: New Choices, New Trends." *Chronica Horticulturae* 47, no. 4 (2007): 26–29.

Mazda, Maideh. *In a Persian Kitchen: Favorite Recipes from the Near East*. Rutland, VT: C. Tuttle, 1960.

McCann, James C. *Stirring the Pot: A History of African Cuisine*. Athens: Ohio University Press, 2009.

McDermott, Maura. "The Mysterious Pear: The Secrets of This Underappreciated Fruit Are Worth Discovering." *Field Notes*, Kerr Center for Sustainable Agriculture, Spring 2011.

McDonald, Lucile Saunders. *Garden Sass: The Story of Vegetables*. New York: T. Nelson, 1971.

McGee, Harold. "Cilantro Haters, It's Not Your Fault." *New York Times*, April 13, 2010.

——. *On Food and Cooking: The Science and Lore of the Kitchen*. New York: Scribner, 2004.

——. "Understanding the Smelly Ones that Make Us Cry." *New York Times*, June 9, 2010, p. D5.

McLaughlin, Katy. "Cranky's Pineapple Acid Test." *Wall Street Journal*, October 28, 2003, p. D2.

McNamee, Gregory. *Moveable Feasts: The History, Science, and Lore of Food*. Lincoln: University of Nebraska Press, 2008.

McNeill, John Robert. "Biological Exchange and Biological Invasion in World History." Draft paper prepared for prepared for the 19th International Congress of the Historical Sciences, Oslo, August 6–13, 2000. Available online at http://www.oslo2000.uio.no/program/papers/m1b/m1b-mcneill.pdf. Accessed February 2, 2015.

McNeill, John Robert, and William Hardy McNeill. *The Human Web: A Bird's-Eye View of Human History*. New York: W. W. Norton, 2003.

McNeill, William Hardy. "How the Potato Changed the World's History." *Social Research* 66, no. 1 (1999): 67–83.

———. "The Introduction of the Potato into Ireland." *Journal of Modern History* 21, no. 3 (September 1949): 218–22.

———. *The Rise of the West: A History of the Human Community.* Chicago: University of Chicago Press, 1991.

———. *The Shape of European History.* New York: Oxford University Press, 1974.

McPhee, John. *Oranges.* New York: Farrar, Straus and Giroux, 1967.

"Meet a Grower." Document provided to author by California Artichoke Advisory Board.

"Melons and Cucumbers." Colonial Williamsburg Mobile. Available online at http://174.143.19.147/history/cwland/resrch6.cfm?showSite=mobile. Accessed February 3, 2015.

Meneley, Anne. "Like an Extra Virgin." *American Anthropologist* 109, no. 4 (December 2007): 678–87.

Mesfin, Daniel J. *Exotic Ethiopian Cooking: Society, Culture, Hospitality & Traditions: 178 Tested Recipes with Food Composition Tables.* Falls Church, VA: Ethiopian Cookbook Enterprises, 1990.

Meyer, Frederick G. "Notes on Wild Coffea Arabica from Southwestern Ethiopia, with Some Historical Considerations." *Economic Botany* 19, no. 2 (April–June 1965): 136–51.

Midgley, John. *A Sprig of Mint: Twenty-Five Classic Recipes.* Boston: Little, Brown, 1994.

Miller, James Innes. *The Spice Trade of the Roman Empire, 29 BC to AD 641.* Oxford: Clarendon Press, 1969.

Miller, Ron. "The Artichoke King: Castroville Man Devotes 60 Years—and Counting—to the Tasty Thistle." *AgAlert*, March 8, 2006. Available online at http://www.agalert.com/story/?id=549. Accessed December 20, 2014.

Millman, Joel. "Mexico's Newest Export: Your Meal." *Wall Street Journal*, January 19, 2000, p. B1.

Milton, Giles. *Nathaniel's Nutmeg, or, The True and Incredible Adventures of the Spice Trader Who Changed the Course of History.* New York: Farrar, Straus and Giroux, 1999.

Mintz, Sidney Wilfred. *Caribbean Transformations.* New Brunswick, NJ: Aldine Transaction, 2007.

———. "Devouring Objects of Study: Food and Fieldwork." Text of lecture delivered April 30, 2003, David Skomp Distinguished Lectures in Anthropology, Indiana University.

———. "Pleasures of the Table, The Old and New World Exchange." *Nutrition Today* 33, no. 3 (May/June 1998): 1–5.

———. *Sweetness and Power: The Place of Sugar in Modern History.* New York: Viking, 1985.

———. *Tasting Food, Tasting Freedom: Excursions into Eating, Culture, and the Past.* Boston: Beacon Press, 1996.

Mintz, Sidney Wilfred, and Christine M. Du Bois. "The Anthropology of Food and Eating." *Annual Review of Anthropology* 31 (October 2002): 99–119.

Mirfendereski, Guive. "Gerdu: An Iranian Love Affair." Iranian.com, December 24, 2005. Available online at http://iranian.com/GuiveMirfendereski/2005/December/Gerdu/index.html. Accessed January 9, 2015.

Moldenke, Harold M. and Alma L. *Plants of the Bible.* New York: Dover, 1986.

Montanari, Massimo. *Cheese, Pears, & History in a Proverb*, translated by Beth Archer Brombert. New York: Columbia University Press, 2010.

———. *The Culture of Food*, translated by Carl Ipsen. Oxford; Cambridge, MA: Blackwell, 1994.

———. *Food Is Culture*, translated by Albert Sonnenfeld. New York: Columbia University Press, 2006.

———. *Let the Meatballs Rest, and Other Stories about Food and Culture*, translated by Beth Archer Brombert. New York: Columbia University Press, 2012.

Morales, Mario, and Jules Janick. "Arugula: A Promising Specialty Leaf Vegetable," in Jules Janick and Anna Whipkey, eds., *Trends in New Crops and New Uses: Proceedings of the Fifth National Symposium New Crops and New Uses: Strength in Diversity*. Alexandria, VA: ASHS Press, 2002.

Morton, Julia F. "The Cashew's Brighter Future." *Economic Botany* 15, no. 1 (January–March 1961): 57–78.

Musgrave, Sarah. "Arak Delivers Anise Flavor with Fire and Ice." *The Gazette (Montreal)*, November 25, 2006, p. K4.

Mydans, Seth. ". . . But a Good Cigarette Is a Fantasy of Flavor." *New York Times*, September 3, 2001, p. A4.

Nadelson, Regina. "The Sweet Taste of Decadence." *Metropolitan Home* XVI, no. 11 (November 1982): 62–67.

Narayan, Shoba. *Monsoon Diary: A Memoir with Recipes*. New York: Villard, 2003.

Nathan, Joan. *Jewish Cooking in America*. New York: Alfred A. Knopf, 1998.

———. "Small Fry Artichokes Charm Chefs." *New York Times*, May 15, 2002, p. D5.

———. "Tsimmes Worth the Big Fuss." *Milwaukee Journal Sentinel*, September 24, 2000, ENTREE, p. 01N.

Nevar, Pam. "Pigment Power in Carrot Color." College of Agricultural and Life Sciences, University of Wisconsin-Madison. Available online at http://www.uwex.edu/ces/news/cenews .cfm?ID=1012. Accessed May 7, 2008.

Newman, L. F. "Some Notes on Nutmeg Graters in Folk Medicine." *Folklore* 54, no. 3 (1943): 334–37.

Nguyen, Andrea. "Like Butter." *Saveur* 104 (September 2007): 76–87.

Nichols, Rick. "On the Side: The Amazing, Sustaining Sweet Potato Pie." *Philadelphia Inquirer*, December 3, 2009, p. F33.

Norman, Jill. *Herbs and Spices*. New York: DK Publishing, 2002.

O'Brien, Patricia J. "The Sweet Potato: Its Origin and Dispersal." *American Anthropologist* 74, no. 3 (June 1972): 342–65.

Okihiro, Gary K. *Pineapple Culture: A History of the Tropical and Temperate Zones*. Berkeley: University of California Press, 2009.

The Old Foodie. "Capers, Real and Not," November 18, 2010. Available online at http://www .theoldfoodie.com/2010/11/capers-real-and-not.html. Accessed November 30, 2014.

———. "Shakespearian Strawberries," June 13, 2007. Available online at http://www.theold foodie.com/2007/06/shakespearian-strawberries.html. Accessed November 3, 2014.

Ondaatje, Michael. *The Cinnamon Peeler: Selected Poems*. New York: Vintage International, 1997.

O'Neill, Molly. "Best Herb; This Bulb's Life." *New York Times Magazine*, April 18, 1999.

———. "Bringing Up Basil." *New York Times Magazine*, August 11, 1996.

———. "Food: Crunch Time." *New York Times Magazine*, June 7, 1998, p. 107.

———. "Food: A Regular Sweet Heart." *New York Times*, September 19, 1993, p. 83.

———. "Food: Sweet on Yams." *New York Times*, February 23, 1992.

———. "Spicy Conditions." *New York Times*, January 21, 1996.

Orta, Garcia de. *Colloquies on the Simples & Drugs of India*, edited by Conde de Ficalho, translated by Sir Clements Markham. Delhi: Periodical Agency Book Agency, 1979.

Ortiz, Elisabeth Lambert. *The Book of Latin American Cooking*. New York: Vintage Books, 1980.

———. *The Complete Book of Caribbean Cooking*. New York: M. Evans, 1973.

Osborne, Troy David. "A Taste of Paradise: Cinnamon," essay for Bell Library's Expansion of Europe seminar, University of Minnesota, no date. Available online at https://www.lib.umn.edu/bell/tradeproducts/cinnamon. Accessed January 26, 2015.

Oseland, James. *Cradle of Flavor: Home Cooking from the Spice Islands of Indonesia, Malaysia, and Singapore*. New York: Norton, 2006.

Owen, Sri. *Indonesian Food and Cookery*. London: Prospect Books, 1980.

Palmer, Hans Christian. "Italian Immigration and the Development of California Agriculture." PhD dissertation. Berkeley: University of California, 1965.

Palter, Robert. *The Duchess of Malfi's Apricots, and Other Literary Fruits*. Columbia: University of South Carolina Press, 2002.

Pankhurst, Rita. "The Coffee Ceremony and the History of Coffee Consumption in Ethiopia." *PICES* 13, no. 2 (1997): 515–39.

Parry, John Horace. *The Age of Reconnaissance*. Berkeley: University of California Press, 1981.

Parsons, Russ. "Artichokes: Spanning the Globe—How a Thistle from Sunny Spain Came to Thrive in Foggy Castroville." *Los Angeles Times*, March 9, 1995.

———. "Downright Voluptuous." *Los Angeles Times*, September 17, 2003, pp. D8–D11.

———. "A Short History of a Quiet Fruit." *Los Angeles Times*, October 28, 1992.

Pauly, Philip J. *Fruits and Plains: The Horticultural Transformation of America*. Cambridge, MA: Harvard University Press, 2007.

Peabody, Erin. "Carrots with Character." *Agricultural Research*, November 1, 2004.

Pearson, M. N., ed. *Spices in the Indian Ocean World*. Aldershot, Hampshire, UK; Brookfield, VT: Variorum, 1996.

Pellegrini, Angelo M. *The Food-Lover's Garden*. New York: Lyons & Burford, 1989.

Pendergrast, Mark. *For God, Country and Coca-Cola: The Definitive History of the Great American Soft Drink and the Company that Makes It*. New York: Basic Books, 2013.

———. *Uncommon Grounds: The History of Coffee and How It Transformed Our World*. New York: Basic Books, 2010.

"Peppery Arugula Can Help Spice Up a Salad." *Fresno Bee*, January 13, 2007, p. C1.

Perry, Charles. "The Carrot Question." Available on *Zester Daily* website, http://zesterdaily.com/cooking/the-carrot-question/. Accessed January 30, 2015.

———. "Cloves, Nails and Carnations." *Los Angeles Times*, December 30, 1998.

———. "Cooking with the Caliphs." *Saudi Aramco World* 57, no. 4 (July/August 2006): 14–23.

———. "Eggplant: The Fried and the Prejudice." *Los Angeles Times*, October 10, 1996.

——. "The Fine Madness of Eggplant." *Saveur* (January 23, 2007).

——. "Garbanzos: The Big Lentil." *Los Angeles Times*, June 16, 1994.

——. "Humble Peanut a Favorite around World." In *Daily Gazette*, Schenectady, NY, April 13, 1994. Available online at http://news.google.com/newspapers?nid=1957&dat=19940413&id=Q3xGAAAAIBAJ&sjid=GOkMAAAAIBAJ&pg=5432,3174775. Accessed October 23, 2014.

——. "It's Raining Potatoes." *Los Angeles Times*, March 1, 2000, p. H2.

——. "Orange Drops." *Los Angeles Times*, May 31, 2000, p. H2.

——. "Our Daily Spread: E Pluribus Chunky: American History: The Spread Made from 'Goober Peas' Was No Overnight Sensation. It Took an Ex-Slave Scientist and Inventor to Develop Peanut Butter's Potential." *Los Angeles Times*, March 10, 1994, p. 10.

——. "Peanut Butter and Tahini: Separated at Birth?" Available on *Zester Daily* website, http://zesterdaily.com/cooking/peanut-butter-and-tahini-separated-at-birth/. Accessed October 23, 2014.

——. "The Pomegranate Mess." *Los Angeles Times*, May 24, 2000.

——. "Purple Fruit, Green Nut." *Los Angeles Times*, September 30, 1998.

——. "When Rosewater Ruled the Pantry." *Los Angeles Times*, March 26, 2003.

Perry, Charles, and Valli Herman-Cohen. "How the Watermelon Got Its Slurp." *Los Angeles Times*, June 25, 2003, p. F-1.

Peterson, Cass. "Cuttings: Now You Don't See It, Now You Do: Asparagus." *New York Times*, February 25, 1996.

Peterson, T. Sarah. *Acquired Taste: The French Origins of Modern Cooking*. Ithaca, NY: Cornell University Press, 1994.

Pliny the Elder. *Natural History, a Selection*, translated by John F. Healy. London; New York: Penguin Books, 1991.

Plotnikoff, David. "Tender at Heart." *Saveur* 118 (March 2009): 62–77.

Polyglot Vegetarian. "Pineapple," January 30, 2010. Available online at http://polyglotveg .blogspot.com/2010/01/pineapple.html. Accessed January 5, 2015.

——. "Watermelon," October 1, 2008. Available online at http://polyglotveg.blogspot .com/2008/10/watermelon.html. Accessed December 7, 2014.

Popenoe, Wilson. *Manual of Tropical and Subtropical Fruits, Excluding the Banana, Coconut, Pineapple, Citrus Fruits, Olive, and Fig*. New York: Macmillan, 1920.

——. "Origin of the Cultivated Races of Avocado." *California Avocado Association 1935 Yearbook* 20: 184–94.

Popik, Barry. "Papaya & Hot Dogs ('Tastier than Filet Mignon')." The Big Apple, April 11, 2005. Available online at http://www.barrypopik.com/index.php/new_york_city/entry/papaya_hot_dogs_tastier_than_filet_mignon. Accessed February 3, 2015.

"Potato World." *Saveur* 79 (November 2004): 46–69.

Prance, Ghillean. *The Cultural History of Plants*, edited by Mark Nesbitt. New York: Routledge, 2005.

Presilla, Maricel E. *Gran Cocina Latina: The Food of Latin America*. New York: Norton, 2012.

Raichlen, Steven. "Rich Reward: Avocados, Great in Guacamole, Offer Other Treasures Too." *Chicago Tribune*, March 15, 2000.

Rain, Patricia. *The Artichoke Cookbook*. Berkeley: Celestial Arts, 1985.

Ramon-Laca, L. "The Introduction of Cultivated Citrus to Europe via Northern Africa and the Iberian Peninsula." *Economic Botany* 57, no. 4 (2003): 502–14.

Ravindran, P. N., K. Nirmal Babu, and M. Shylaja. *Cinnamon and Cassia: The Genus Cinnamomum*. Boca Raton: CRC Press, 2004.

Raviv, Yael. "Falafel: A National Icon." *Gastronomica* 3, no. 3 (2003): 20–25.

"References to Artichoke, Asparagus and Celery in 18th Century Virginia Records." Stems and Buds, Colonial Williamsburg Mobile. Available online at http://174.143.19.147/history/cwland/resrch13.cfm?showSite=mobile#section2c. Accessed February 3, 2015.

Rentschler, Kay. "A Flag for Spring: Green, White, and Purple." *New York Times*, May 7, 2003.

Riccardi, Victoria Abbott. "A Cook's Turkish Delight." *Boston Globe*, October 6, 1999, pp. C1–C2.

Rice, Robert A., and Russell S. Greenberg. "The Chocolate Tree." *Natural History Magazine* 112, no. 6 (July/August 2003): 36–43.

Richardson, Tim. *Sweets: A History of Candy*. New York: MJF Books / Fine Communications, 2005.

Riley, Gillian. *The Oxford Companion to Italian Food*. Oxford; New York: Oxford University Press, 2007.

Rivera, Diego, Cristina Inocencio, Concepion Obon, and Francisco Alcaraz. "Review of Food and Medicinal Uses of Capparis L, Subgenus Capparis (Capparidaceae)." *Economic Botany* 57, no. 4 (Winter 2003): 515–34.

Robbins, Paula I. *The Travels of Peter Kalm, Finnish-Swedish Naturalist, through Colonial North America, 1748–1751*. Fleischmanns, NY: Purple Mountain Press, 2007.

Roberts, Jonathan. *The Origins of Fruit and Vegetables*. New York: Universe Publishing, 2001.

Robison, Jim. "Central Europeans Were Dirt Poor But Toiled for a Better Life in Slavia." *Orlando Sentinel*, July 4, 1993.

———. "Family Farm Empire Took Root in Tiny Community of Slavia." *Orlando Sentinel*, June 27, 1993.

Roden, Claudia. *Arabesque: A Taste of Morocco, Turkey, and Lebanon*. New York: Knopf, 2006.

———. *The Book of Jewish Food: An Odyssey from Samarkand to New York*. New York: Knopf, 1996.

———. *Coffee: A Connoisseur's Companion*. New York: Random House, 1994.

———. *Mediterranean Cookery*. New York: Knopf, 1987.

———. *The New Book of Middle Eastern Food*. New York: Knopf, 2000.

———. "The Spread of Kebabs and Coffee: Two Islamic Movements," in Alan Davidson, ed., *Food in Motion: The Migration of Foodstuffs and Cookery Techniques: Proceedings: Oxford Symposium 1983*. Stanningley, Leeds, UK: Prospect Books, 1983.

Rodinson, Maxime, A. J. Arberry, and Charles Perry. *Medieval Arab Cookery*. Devon, UK: Prospect Books, 2006.

Rolfe, R. A. "Vanillas of Commerce." *Bulletin of Miscellaneous Information, Royal Botanic Gardens, Kew* 104 (August 1895): 169–78.

Root, Waverley Lewis. *Food: An Authoritative and Visual History and Dictionary of the Foods of the World*. New York: Smithmark, 1996.

———. *The Food of Italy*. New York: Vintage Books, 1992.

Root, Waverley Lewis, and Richard de Rochemont. *Eating in America: A History*. New York: Ecco Press, 1981.

Rosenblum, Mort. *Chocolate: A Bittersweet Saga of Dark and Light*. New York: North Point Press, 2005.

Rosengarten, Frederic. *The Book of Edible Nuts*. Mineola, NY: Dover, 2004.

———. *The Book of Spices*. Wynnewood, PA: Livingston, 1969.

Ross, Lawrence J. "The Meaning of Strawberries in Shakespeare." *Studies in the Renaissance* 7 (1960): 225–40.

Roueche, Berton. "The Humblest Fruit." *The New Yorker*, October 1, 1973, pp. 43–50.

Rozin, Elisabeth. *Blue Corn and Chocolate*. New York: Knopf, 1992.

———. *Crossroads Cooking: The Meeting and Mating of Ethnic Cuisines—From Burma to Texas in 200 Recipes*. New York: Viking, 1999.

———. *Ethnic Cuisine: The Flavor-Principle Cook-Book*. Lexington, MA: S. Greene Press, 1983.

———. *The Universal Kitchen*. New York: Viking, 1996.

Rubatzky, V. E., C. F. Quiros, and P. W. Simon. *Carrots and Related Umbelliferae*. Wallingford, UK: CABI, 1999.

Rubenstein, Sarah. "Across the Land, People Are Fuming Over an Herb (No, Not That One): Cilantro Haters Boo 'Fetid Barb of Green'; A Prominent Critic Recants." *Wall Street Journal*, February 13, 2009.

Rumphius, Georgius Evberhardus. *The Ambonese Herbal: Being a Description of the Most Noteworthy Trees, Shrubs, Herbs, Land- and Water-Plants which Are Found in Amboina and the Surrounding Islands According to Their Shape, Various Names, Cultivation, and Use: Together with Several Insects and Animals*, translated by E. M. Beekman. New Haven, CT: Yale University Press & National Tropical Botanical Garden, 2011.

Rupp, Rebecca. *How Carrots Won the Trojan War: Curious (But True) Stories of Common Vegetables*. North Adams, MA: Storey Publishing, 2011.

Russell, Mark. "Heart of the Matter: Stalking the Roots of Celery's History." *Wall Street Journal*, September 20, 1984.

Russell-Wood, A. J. R. *The Portuguese Empire, 1415–1808: A World on the Move*. Baltimore: Johns Hopkins University Press, 1998.

Saberi, Helen. *Afghan Food and Cookery*. New York: Hippocrene Books, 2000.

Sahni, Julie. *Classic Indian Cooking*. New York: William Morrow, 1980.

———. *Classic Indian Vegetarian and Grain Cooking*. New York: William Morrow, 1985.

Salaman, Redcliffe Nathan. *The History and Social Influence of the Potato*. Cambridge: Cambridge University Press, 1949.

Salaman, Rena. *Greek Food: An Affectionate Celebration of Traditional Recipes*. New York: HarperCollins, 1994.

Sanders, Edmund. "Zanzibar Loses Some of Its Spice." *Los Angeles Times*, November 24, 2005.

Sass, Lorna. "The Preferences for Sweets, Spices and Almond Milk in Late Medieval English Cuisine," in Alexander Fenton and Trefor M. Owen, eds., *Food in Perspective: Proceedings of the Third International Conference on Ethnological Food Research, Cardiff, Wales, 1977*. Edinburgh: John Donald, 1981.

Sauer, Carl Ortwin. *Agricultural Origins and Dispersals: The Domestication of Animals and Foodstuffs*. Cambridge, MA: MIT Press, 1969.

———. "Cultivated Plants of South and Central America," in Julian H. Steward, ed., *Handbook of American Indians*, vol. 6. Washington, DC: US Government Printing Office, 1950.

———. *The Early Spanish Main*. Berkeley: University of California Press, 1992.

Sauer, Jonathan D. *Historical Geography of Crop Plants: A Select Roster*. Boca Raton: CRC Press, 1993.

Saul, Kathleen Triesch. "An Enviable Green—Fresh Arugula Adds Rocket Power to Almost Anything on the Menu." *Seattle Times*, May 30, 1999.

Sawaya, Linda Dalal. *Alice's Kitchen: My Grandmother Dalal & Mother Alice's Traditional Lebanese Cooking*. Portland, OR: Linda Sawaya Design, 2005.

Schafer, Edward H. *The Golden Peaches of Samarkand: A Study of T'ang Exotics*. Berkeley: University of California Press, 1963.

Schier, Volker. "Probing the Mystery of the Use of Saffron in Medieval Nunneries." *The Senses and Society* 5, no. 1 (March 2010): 57–92.

Schivelbusch, Wolfgang. *Tastes of Paradise: A Social History of Spices, Stimulants, and Intoxicants*, translated by David Jacobson. New York: Vintage Books, 1993.

Schneider, Elizabeth. "Artichoke Artistry." *Food Arts*, March 1997.

———. *Vegetables from Amaranth to Zucchini: The Essential Reference: 500 Recipes and 275 Photographs*. New York: William Morrow, 2001.

———. *Uncommon Fruits & Vegetables: A Commonsense Guide*. New York: William Morrow, 1998.

Schrambling, Regina. "The Dazzling Crunch." *Los Angeles Times*, February 25, 2004.

———. "The Lentil Moves Uptown." *Los Angeles Times*, January 26, 2005, p. E11.

Schroeder, C. A. "The Origin, Spread, and Improvement of the Avocado, Sapodilla, and Papaya." *The Indian Journal of Horticulture Special Symposium Number 15*, Nos. 3 & 4 (1958).

Seabrook, John. "Renaissance Pears." *The New Yorker*, September 5, 2005, pp. 102–7.

Secord, Anne. "Hotbeds and Cool Fruits: The Unnatural Cultivation of the Eighteenth-Century Cucumber," in Roberta Bivins and John Pickstone, eds, *Medicine, Madness and Social History: Essays in Honour of Roy Porter*. Basingstoke, UK: Palgrave Macmillan, 2007.

Sedgwick, Stephanie Witt. "Cabbage, Right under Your Nose." *Washington Post*, March 7, 2007, pp. F1, F5.

Sen, Colleen Taylor. *Food Culture in India*. Westport, CT: Greenwood Press, 2004.

Severson, Kim. "Sweet Potatoes Step Out from under the Marshmallows." *New York Times*, November 25, 2010, p. A1.

———. "Watermelons Get Small." *New York Times*, August 17, 2010.

Shaer, Matthew. "Conflicts Spread: The Politics of Hummus." *New York* magazine, March 25, 2012.

Shaida, Margaret. *The Legendary Cuisine of Persia*. Brooklyn: Interlink Books, 2002.

Shapiro, Stephanie. "Olives, Olives Everywhere." *Baltimore Sun*, February 15, 2006, pp. F3, F5.

Shaw, Steven A. *Asian Dining Rules: Essential Strategies for Eating Out at Japanese, Chinese, Southeast Asian, Korean, and Indian Restaurants*. New York: William Morrow Cookbooks, 2008.

Shenton, James P. *American Cooking: The Melting Pot.* New York: Time-Life Books, 1971.

Shepard, Richard F. "The Panache of Pistachios." *New York Times Magazine,* October 21, 1979, p. 32.

Shephard, Sue. *Pickled, Potted, and Canned: How the Art and Science of Food Preserving Changed the World.* New York: Simon & Schuster, 2006.

Sheraton, Mimi. "The Caper Chase." *New York Times,* August 26, 1990.

Sheriff, Abdul. *Slaves, Spices, & Ivory in Zanzibar: Integration of an East African Commercial Empire into the World Economy, 1770–1873.* Athens: Ohio University Press, 1987.

Simarski, Lynn Teo. "A Harvest of Legume Research." *Saudi Aramco World* 39, no. 3, May/June 1988.

Simeti, Mary Taylor. *Pomp and Sustenance: Twenty-Five Centuries of Sicilian Food.* Hopewell, NJ: Ecco Press, 1998.

Simmonds, Norman Willison, ed. *Evolution of Crop Plants.* London; New York: Longman, 1976.

———. *Bananas.* London: Longman, 1959.

Simon, Philipp W. "Carrot Facts." US Department of Agriculture, Agricultural Research Service, Vegetable Crops Unit. Available online at http://www.ars.usda.gov/Research/docs.htm?docid=5231. Accessed May 27, 2008.

———. "Domestication, Historical Development, and Modern Breeding of Carrot." *Planting and Breeding Reviews* 19, edited by Jules Janick, 157–90. New York: John Wiley, 2000.

Simoons, Frederick J. *Food in China: A Cultural Historical Inquiry.* Boca Raton, FL: CRC Press, 1991.

———. *Plants of Life, Plants of Death.* Madison: University of Wisconsin Press, 1998.

Skinner, Charles Montgomery. *Myths and Legends of Flowers, Trees, Fruits, and Plants in All Ages and in All Climes.* Philadelphia; London: J. B. Lippincott, 1911.

Slater, Nigel. "Nigel Slater's Classic Tartare Sauce Recipe." *The Guardian,* March 6, 2010.

Smith, Andrew F., ed. *The Oxford Companion to American Food and Drink.* Oxford; New York: Oxford University Press, 2007.

———. *Peanuts: The Illustrious History of the Goober Pea.* Urbana: University of Illinois Press, 2002.

———. *The Tomato in America: Early History, Culture, and Cookery.* Columbia: University of South Carolina Press, 1994.

Smith, Nigel J. H. *Tropical Forests and Their Crops.* Ithaca, NY: Comstock Publishing Associates, 1992.

Smitter, Wessel. "The Mysterious Avocado." *Saturday Evening Post* 221, no. 35 (February 26, 1949): 30–31, 113–15.

Sokolov, Raymond A. "Cabbage Fit for Kings." *Saturday Evening Post* 249, no. 4 (May/June 1977): 100, 102.

———. *A Canon of Vegetables: 101 Classic Recipes.* New York: William Morrow, 2007.

———. *The Cook's Canon: 101 Classic Recipes Everyone Should Know.* New York: HarperCollins, 2003.

———. "The Peripatetic Potato." *Natural History* 99, no. 3 (1990): 86–91.

———. "A Serious Candy." *Natural History* 101, no. 8 (August 1992): 66.

———. "The Sweet Potato Perplex." *Natural History* 95, no. 3 (March 1986): 96, 98.

———. "The Well-Traveled Tomato." *Nutrition Today* 29, no. 4 (July/August 1994): 21–23.

———. *Why We Eat What We Eat: How the Encounter between the New World and the Old Changed the Way Everyone on the Planet Eats*. New York: Summit Books, 1991.

Sonnante, Gabriella, Domenico Pignone, and Karl Hammer. "The Domestication of Artichoke and Cardoon: From Roman Times to the Genomic Age." *Annals of Botany* 100, no. 5 (2007): 1095–1100.

Spencer, Colin. *The Vegetable Book*. New York: Rizzoli, 1995.

Springer, Rita G. *Caribbean Cookbook*. London: Evans Bros., 1968.

Standage, Tom. *A History of the World in 6 Glasses*. New York: Walker, 2005.

Sterngold, James. "Deep in the Heart of Artichoke City." *New York Times*, July 27, 1986.

Stewart, Jude. "Feast Your Eyes: Brilliantly Colored, Everyday Vegetables Hit the Middle-Market." STEP Inside Design, 2006, http://judestewart.com/writing/stepvegetables.htm. Accessed June 10, 2008.

Stobart, Tom. *Herbs, Spices, and Flavorings*. Woodstock, NY: Overlook Press, 1982.

Stuckey, Maggie. *The Complete Spice Book*. New York: St. Martin's, 1997.

Sturtevant, Edward Lewis. "History of Celery." *The American Naturalist* 20, no. 7 (July 1886): 599–606.

———. *Notes on Edible Plants*, edited by U. P. Hedrick. Albany: J. B. Lyon Co., 1919.

———. *Sturtevant's Edible Plants of the World*, edited by U. P. Hedrick. New York: Dover, 1972.

Sugarman, Carole. "Holy Guacamole!" *Washington Post*, January 21, 1998, p. E-1.

Sumner, Judith. *American Household Botany: A History of Useful Plants, 1620–1900*. Portland, OR: Timber Press, 2004.

Tannahill, Reay. *Food in History*. London: Review, 2002.

Thick, Malcolm. "The Contrasting Histories of Florence Fennel, Spanish Cardoons, Broccoli and Celeriac in England from the Early Eighteenth Century until the 1970s," in Harlan Walker, ed., *Disappearing Foods: Proceedings of the Oxford Symposium on Food & Cookery, 1994*, 204–14. Totnes, Devon, UK: Prospect Books, 1995.

Thornton, Tamara Plakins. *Cultivating Gentlemen: The Meaning of Country Life among the Boston Elite, 1785–1860*. New Haven, CT: Yale University Press, 1989.

———. "The Moral Dimensions of Horticulture in Antebellum America." *New England Quarterly* 57, no. 1 (March 1984): 3–24.

Tidbury, G. E. *The Clove Tree*. London: C. Lockwood, 1949.

Tolkowsky, Samuel. *Hesperides: A History of the Culture and Use of Citrus Fruits*. London: J. Bale, Sons & Curnow, 1938.

Tomsho, Robert. "The Sweet Potato Is Everybody's Friend But a Fleeting One." *Wall Street Journal*, November 21, 2007, p. A1.

Toussaint-Samat, Maguelonne. *History of Food*. Malden, MA: Blackwell, 1998.

Trager, James. *The Food Chronology: A Food Lover's Compendium of Events and Anecdotes from Prehistory to the Present*. New York: Henry Holt, 1995.

Tuchscherer, Michel. "Coffee in the Red Sea Area from the Sixteenth to the Nineteenth Century," in William Gervase Clarence-Smith and Steven Topik, eds., *The Global Coffee*

Economy in Africa, Asia and Latin America, 1500–1989, 50–66. Cambridge; New York: Cambridge University Press, 2003.

Turan, Kenneth. "Cel-Ray Is on the Way: Ethnic Tonic, or a Way of Life?" *Washington Post,* December 28, 1977.

"Turkish National Drink, Raki." Online at http://www.raki.com/raki.asp. Accessed November 6, 2014.

Turner, Jack. *Spice: The History of a Temptation.* New York: Knopf, 2004.

Turner, Steve. "One from the Heart." *Image,* September 14, 1986, pp. 27–33.

Uvezian, Sonia. *Recipes and Remembrances from an Eastern Mediterranean Kitchen: A Culinary Journey through Syria, Lebanon, and Jordan.* Northbrook, IL: Siamanto Press, 2001.

"Vanillas of Commerce." Bulletin of Miscellaneous Information, Royal Gardens, Kew, Vol. 1895, No. 104 (1895): 169–78.

van Linschoten, Jan Huygen. *The Voyage of John Huyghen van Linschoten to the East Indies:* from the old English translation of 1598. New Delhi: Asian Educational Services, 1988.

Vavilov, Nikolaï Ivanovich. *The Origin, Variation, Immunity and Breeding of Cultivated Plants: Selected Writings,* translated from the Russian by K. Starr Chester. Waltham, MA: Chronica Botanica, 1951.

Vegetarians in Paradise. "The Sex Life of the Pistachio." Available online at http://www.veg paradise.com/highestperch35.html. Accessed December 5, 2014.

Viola, Herman J., and Carolyn Margolis, eds. *Seeds of Change: A Quincentennial Commemoration.* Washington, DC: Smithsonian Institution Press, 1991.

Visser, Margaret. "Moretum: Ancient Roman Pesto," in Harlan Walker, ed., *Spicing Up the Palate: Proceedings of the Oxford Symposium on Food & Cookery (1992: Saint Antony's College),* 263. Blackawton, UK: Prospect Books, 1993.

——. *Much Depends on Dinner: The Extraordinary History and Mythology, Allure and Obsessions, Perils and Taboos, of an Ordinary Meal.* New York: Grove Press, 1987.

Wade, Lizzie. "Clues to Prehistoric Human Exploration Found in Sweet Potato Genome." *Science,* January 21, 2013. Available online at http://news.sciencemag.org/biology/2013/01/clues-prehistoric-human-exploration-found-sweet-potato-genome. Accessed December 22, 2014.

Waines, David. *In a Caliph's Kitchen: Mediaeval Arabic Cooking for the Modern Gourmet.* Beirut: Riad El-Rayyes Booksellers, 1989.

Walker, Harlan, ed. *Spicing Up the Palate: Proceedings of the Oxford Symposium on Food & Cookery (1992: Saint Antony's College).* Blackawton, UK: Prospect Books, 1993.

Walker, Rob. "A Fruit's Stand." *New York Times Magazine,* April 2, 2006, p. 22.

Watson, Andrew M. *Agricultural Innovation in the Early Islamic World: The Diffusion of Crops and Farming Techniques, 700–1100.* Cambridge; New York: Cambridge University Press, 1983.

Weaver, William Woys. *100 Vegetables and Where They Came From.* Chapel Hill: Algonquin Books, 2000.

Webber, Herbert John, and Leon Dexter Batchelor, eds. *The Citrus Industry.* Berkeley and Los Angeles: University of California Press, 1943.

Wehr, Paul. *Like a Mustard Seed: The Slavia Settlement.* Chuluota, FL: Mickler House, 1982.

Weil, Andrew T. "Nutmeg as a Narcotic." *Economic Botany* 19, no. 3 (July–September 1965): 194–217.

Weise, Elizabeth. "Digging the Baby Carrot." *USA Today*, August 11, 2004, Lifestyle.

Weiss, E. A. *Oilseed Crops*. Oxford; Malden, MA: Blackwell Science, 2000.

Wells, Diana. *Lives of the Trees: An Uncommon History*. Chapel Hill: Algonquin Books, 2010.

Westrip, Joyce P. *Moghul Cooking: India's Courtly Cuisine*. London: Serif, 2005.

Wheaton, Barbara Ketcham. *Savoring the Past: The French Kitchen and Table from 1300 to 1789*. Philadelphia: University of Pennsylvania Press, 1983.

Whitaker, Thomas W., and G. W. Bohn. "The Taxonomy, Genetics, Production, and Uses of the Cultivated Species of Cucurbita." *Economic Botany* 4 (1950): 52–81.

White, Joyce. "Sweet Spuds: Satisfying and Healthy." *Chicago Times*, January 31, 2007.

Whiteaker, Stafford. *The Compleat Strawberry*. New York: Crown, 1985.

Wibisono, Djoko, and David Wong. *Food of Singapore: Authentic Recipes from the Manhattan of the East*. Boston: Periplus Editions, 2001.

Wild, Antony. *Coffee: A Dark History*. New York: W. W. Norton, 2005.

Wilhelm, Stephen. "The Garden Strawberry: A Study of Its Origin." *American Scientist* 62 (1974): 264–71.

Wilhelm, Stephen, and James E. Sagen. *A History of the Strawberry, from Ancient Gardens to Modern Markets*. Berkeley: University of California, Division of Agricultural Sciences, 1974.

Willan, Anne. "In Mint Condition." *Washington Post*, May 2, 2001, pp. F1, F4.

———. "Saffron by the Pinch." *Washington Post*, March 12, 2003, pp. F1, F2.

Willinger, Faith Heller. *Red, White & Greens: The Italian Way with Vegetables*. New York: HarperCollins, 1996.

Wilson, C. Anne. *Food and Drink in Britain: From the Stone Age to the 19th Century*. Chicago: Academy Chicago Publishers, 1991.

———. "The Saracen Connection: Arab Cuisine and the Medieval West." *Petits Propos Culinaires* 7 (1981): 13–22; 8 (1981): 19–28.

Wilson, David Scofield, and Angus Kress Gillespie, eds. *Rooted in America: Foodlore of Popular Fruits and Vegetables*. Knoxville: University of Tennessee Press, 1999.

Wolfe, Linda. *The Cooking of the Caribbean Islands*. New York: Time-Life Books, 1970.

Wolfert, Paula. *The Cooking of the Eastern Mediterranean: 215 Healthy, Vibrant, and Inspired Recipes*. New York: HarperCollins, 1994.

———. *Couscous and Other Good Food from Morocco*. New York: Harper & Row, 1973.

———. *Mediterranean Cooking*. New York: Harper Perennial, 1994.

Woodward, Sarah. *Tastes of North Africa: Mouthwatering Recipes from Morocco and the Mediterranean*. London: Kyle Cathie, 2005.

World Carrot Museum. "History of Carrots: A Brief Summary & Timeline." Available online at http://www.carrotmuseum.co.uk/history.html. Accessed November 10, 2007.

———. "History of the Carrot, Part Two: Origins and Development, Neolithic to AD 200." Available online at http://www.carrotmuseum.co.uk/history1.html. Accessed November 10, 2007.

———. "History of the Carrot, Part Three: From Medicine to Food AD 200 to 1500." Available online at http://www.carrotmuseum.co.uk/history2.html. Accessed November 10, 2007.

"The World on a String: Celery." *Art Culinaire* 80, Spring 2006.

Wright, Clifford A. "Did the Ancients Know the Artichoke?" *Gastronomica* 9, no. 4 (2009): 21–28.

———. *A Mediterranean Feast: The Story of the Birth of the Celebrated Cuisines of the Mediterranean, from the Merchants of Venice to the Barbary Corsairs.* New York: William Morrow, 1999.

———. *Mediterranean Vegetables: A Cook's ABC of Vegetables and Their Preparation in Spain, France, Italy, Greece, Turkey, the Middle East, and North Africa with More than 200 Authentic Recipes for the Home Cook.* Boston: Harvard Common Press, 2001.

Wrigley, Gordon. *Coffee.* New York: Wiley, 1988.

Yariv, Amit. "Making Anise Impression." *Jerusalem Post*, November 12, 2009.

Yoon, Howard. "Don't Forget the Fennel." NPR, January 3, 2007. Available online at http://www.npr.org/templates/story/story.php?storyId=6710330. Accessed January 26, 2015.

Zaouali, Lilia. *Medieval Cuisine of the Islamic World: A Concise History with 174 Recipes.* Berkeley: University of California Press, 2007.

Zohary, Daniel, Maria Hopf, and Ehud Weiss. *Domestication of Plants in the Old World: The Origin and Spread of Cultivated Plants in Southwest Asia, Europe, and the Mediterranean Basin.* New York: Oxford University Press, 2000.

Zubaida, Sami, and Richard Tapper, eds. *Culinary Cultures of the Middle East.* London; New York: I. B. Taurus, 1996.

Zuckerman, Larry. *The Potato: How the Humble Spud Rescued the Western World.* Boston: Faber and Faber, 1998.

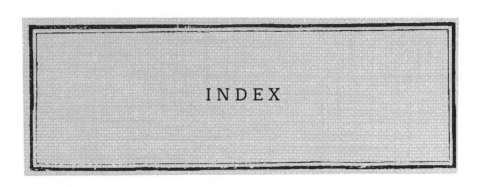

INDEX

ABOUT THE AUTHOR

Joel S. Denker, a Washington-based food historian, is the author, among other books, of *The World on a Plate: A Tour through the History of America's Ethnic Cuisine* (2003) and *Capital Flavors: Exploring Washington's Ethnic Restaurants* (1989). He has written for the *Boston Globe*, the *Washington Post*, and other publications. He was also a longtime food columnist for *The InTowner*, a Washington, D.C., monthly newspaper. A graduate of Yale University and a holder of a doctorate from Harvard, he has taught American history and a wide range of other subjects at George Washington University, Rutgers University, SUNY/ College at Old Westbury, the University of the District of Columbia, and other institutions. His rich background in educational innovation includes developing an early alternative high school in Washington, D.C.; teaching refugees in Tanzania; and organizing a labor studies degree at Washington's city university.

ARCTURUS

IQ

POCKET PUZZLES

ARCTURUS

This edition published in 2011 by Arcturus Publishing Limited
26/27 Bickels Yard, 151–153 Bermondsey Street,
London SE1 3HA

Copyright © 2011 Arcturus Publishing Limited
Puzzles copyright © 2011 Puzzle Press Ltd

ISBN: 978-1-84858-102-9
AD001984EN

Printed in China